"Tosouni unravels many issues that affect troubled young girls, especially those held in detention facilities. When treatment is advocated and applied, the trouble begins. By failing to interview the child in an in-depth fashion, parents and practitioners often miss the source of the problem. Tosouni has gathered evidence that taps into the 'voices' of such girls which will help to formulate and direct interventions. This issue must involve the individuals concerned. Watching, talking and listening to them is essential to understanding them, all of which are strengths of Tosouni's approach."

J. Diego Vigil, *Professor Emeritus, Criminology, Law & Society, School of Social Ecology, University of California, Irvine, USA*

"Grounded in feminist research, *Gendered Injustice* gives marginalized girls hidden in the recesses of juvenile detention a voice. It recounts stories of victimhood and abandonment but also stories of survival and hope. This meticulously crafted study reveals how penal culture disempowers girls in detention through regimes that demand unquestioned subservience and reinforces gender normative ideas about womanhood. This book should appeal to a wide readership of students, policy makers, activists and scholars from social science, youth studies, social work, law, psychology, criminology, and gender studies."

Kerry Carrington, *Professor and Head of the School of Justice, Queensland University of Technology, Australia*

Gendered Injustice

Without strong proof, policy advocates along with some scholars have causally linked declines in juvenile offending and incarceration with evidence-based and rehabilitation-oriented policy reform. Such studies have called for a shift back to rehabilitative ideals augmented by innovative strategies that emphasize cultures of care, and in the cases of system-involved girls, 'gender-responsive' programs, anchored in feminist literature. These programs have also caught the attention of feminist scholars who cast doubt on both their design and implementation. *Gendered Injustice* offers a unique contribution to the latter line of scholarship, and critically examines claims of innovation, empowerment, and gender-responsivity in youth correction that currently dominate the field.

Drawing on rich ethnographic data, this book uncovers the reality of, and gives voice to, the experiences and continued mistreatment of marginalized girls housed in locked institutions in the US State of California. By providing detailed insight into the detention experiences and the pathways of several young women, this book draws stark comparisons between the lived experience of young women in detention with the official rhetoric of empowerment that dominates public discourse. This book reveals the ways in which institutional policies and practices are designed to neglect and, in many instances, re-victimize inmates.

This is essential reading for those engaged in corrections, juvenile justice, gender and crime, and feminist criminology.

Anastasia Tosouni is an Assistant Professor in the Department of Criminology and Criminal Justice Studies at Sonoma State University. Dr. Tosouni earned her Ph.D. in Criminology, Law and Society at the University of California at Irvine, and a Law Degree (LLB) from the University of Athens, Greece. She has experience counseling and advocating for victims of family violence. Her areas of academic specialization include law and inequality; race and gender; juvenile delinquency; restorative justice and social justice.

Routledge Critical Studies in Crime, Diversity and Criminal Justice

Edited by Sharon Hayes
Macquarie University, Australia
and Patricia Faraldo Cabana
University of A Coruña, Spain

The works in this series strive to generate new conceptual and theoretical frameworks to address the legal, organizational and normative responses to the challenges that diversity and intersectionality present to criminal justice systems. This series aims to present cutting edge empirically informed theoretical works from both new and established scholars around the world.

Drawing upon a range of disciplines including sociology, law, history, economics, and social work, the series encourages different approaches to questions of mobility and exclusion with a cross-section of theorists, empiricists, and critical policy researchers. It will be key reading for scholars who are working in criminal justice, criminology, criminal law and human rights, as well as those in the fields of gender and LGBTI studies, migration studies, anthropology, refugee studies and post-colonial studies.

Gender Responsive Justice
A Critical Appraisal
Karen Evans

The Political Economy of Punishment Today
Visions, Debates and Challenges
Edited by Dario Melossi, Máximo Sozzo and José A. Brandariz-García

Transgender Cops
The Intersection of Gender and Sexuality Expectations in Police Cultures
Heather Panter

Race, Crime and Restorative Justice
William R Wood and Juan Tauri

Gendered Injustice
Uncovering the Lived Experience of Detained Girls
Anastasia Tosouni

For more information about this series, please visit: www.routledge.com/criminology/series/CDCJ

Gendered Injustice

Uncovering the Lived Experience of Detained Girls

Anastasia Tosouni

Routledge
Taylor & Francis Group
LONDON AND NEW YORK

First published 2019
by Routledge
2 Park Square, Milton Park, Abingdon, Oxon OX14 4RN

and by Routledge
52 Vanderbilt Avenue, New York, NY 10017

Routledge is an imprint of the Taylor & Francis Group, an informa business

British Library Cataloguing-in-Publication Data
A catalogue record for this book is available from the British Library

Library of Congress Cataloging-in-Publication Data
A catalog record has been requested for this book

ISBN: 978-0-8153-8151-8 (hbk)
ISBN: 978-1-351-21028-7 (ebk)

Typeset in Times New Roman
by Wearset Ltd, Boldon, Tyne and Wear

Contents

Foreword

I am delighted to be able to introduce this important monograph on the lived experiences of incarcerated young women. In an age when neoliberal ideals such as individualism, self-reliance and personal responsibility rank high on the national and international agendas of the West, this group of women ranks among the very lowest. It is no coincidence that they comprise young women of color, many of them born to immigrant parents from neighborhoods steeped in economic depression. Their incarceration is the result of immense power imbalances, grounded in the intersection of race, class, ethnicity, immigration status and sexual orientation that form the basis of their systemic oppression both as a group and as individuals.

In a painstakingly rigorous examination of the current scholarship on prison reform for women and female youth, Tosouni reveals that there is a deep chasm between the rhetoric of empowerment evident in contemporary gender-specific reintegration programs, and the real lives of those who participate. While the former claims to move beyond "correcting" the individual with the goal of achieving normalcy and acceptance, these programs more often than not simply mirror the patterns of power and domination they are seeking to eradicate. Thus, instead of empowering these young women in ways that transcend gendered ideals and challenge sexist stereotypes, they in fact do the opposite.

This book is timely for two reasons: it challenges the largely white, male middle-class agenda that has not-so-insidiously infiltrated the governing of the United States in recent times; but it also challenges the largely quantitative, malestream criminological agenda currently dominating academic work in the area of prison governance and reform. Such scholarship and the programming that arises from it, relies almost exclusively on "evidence-based" research that is purely quantitative, and for that reason fails to give voice to those who are subject to it. As Tosouni notes in Chapter 1, "while claiming to empower young women, they narrowly focus on raising confidence and self-esteem, individualizing girls' problems and decontextualizing attitudes shaped by systemic violations." I couldn't have said it better myself. Historically, when the oppressors become the ones charged with fixing the oppression, it typically leads to more entrenched and complex oppressions, something that Tosouni's interviews with young female inmates of a Southern Californian juvenile hall make incredibly and very sadly apparent.

This equally fascinating and sobering exploration of the lived experiences of these young women in juvenile hall should be read by every person who works within the justice system, as well as those purporting to provide the evidence base for such programs, and those implementing them. This research demonstrates a clear power imbalance that works to reinforce conditions of confinement that are anathema to young women, and which in fact mirror the gendered abuse and neglect that most of them have experienced their entire lives. It results in them seeing themselves as the problem, as deserving of punishment and deprivation; indeed, as "fallen women."

As there is very little in the way of qualitative, particularly narrative scholarship on the experiences of incarcerated peoples – male, female, youth or otherwise – in the West, but particularly in the United States, this book provides a much needed shock to both the criminological project and the more practical task of rehabilitating and reintegrating marginalized girls within the prison system. I share Dr Tosouni's hope that it will also provide an impetus for much needed further qualitative research on this and related issues.

Sharon Hayes, Griffith University, Brisbane, Australia

Acknowledgments

I am very grateful to the many friends and colleagues who have contributed directly and indirectly to the effort required to write this monograph and get it published.

First and foremost, I owe an enormous thank you to my professor, advisor, and friend Elliott Currie, who has believed in and supported me in various, innumerable ways throughout my academic career, of which this study is a major part, and who is just an all-around cool person to talk to and hang out with.

Thank you to my Routledge team, Tom Sutton, Sharon Heyes, Hannah Cattheral, and Jake Rainbow for their enthusiastic support for this project and for assisting me in getting it done.

Thank you to all UCI faculty, especially Henry Pontell and Diego Vigil for their invaluable advice throughout the early stages of this research. Thank you to my Clayton State family, Rafik Mohamed, Jason Davis, and Lisa Holland-Davis (AKA the A-Team) for always having my back; my UMD friends, Laure Weber-Brooks, Justine Madoo, Christine White, and Kyle Dorsey; and my new home, the CCJS department at Sonoma State, especially Pat Jackson, Eric Williams, Diana Grant, Nap Reyes, Cindy Stearns, and Emily Asencio for their collegial warmth and camaraderie.

Love and respect go out to a few folks who are or have become family, for contributing instrumental and emotional support in different stages of this project, and for shaping *my* life-story: my parents Epameinondas and Victoria Tosouni; my colleague, best man, and BFF Ryan Fischer; my friend and confidant Rachel Dioso-Villa; and my cousin and "soul mate" Mary Christianakis. I am grateful for my girlfriends Anna Souridi, Sandy Malaxianaki, Foula Lazarou, Eldi Dritsoula, Evi Patargia, Poly Soumailakaki, and Elena Mandyla, all of whom I've known for most of my life.

Speaking of family, I dedicate this work to the center of my world, my girl, Victoria Elizabeth (*Vella*) Mischel; I am grateful for her and for her dad, my husband, David Mischel for inspiring me and giving me reason to smile every day.

Last, I am indebted to all young women who trusted me with their life-stories and allowed me to share them with the world. I remember each and every one of you, and wherever it is that you ended up, I hope it is somewhere safe.

Chapter 1

Prologue

Juvenile justice – promises made

Yolanda, 18 – A Poem

My self-esteem is broken,
My hope is Shattered
I never felt as if,
I really mattered
My Mama calls me retarded
Because I have ADD,
My teachers think I'm stupid
Cause I can't even get a "B"
I'm always filled w/stress because my brother's better
And I have no success
"I'm not capible" is what they say.
Will they always feel that way?
Mama says, I'm evil
Just like my Dad
Having someone believe in me is something I never had
Treated like I'm worthless like I can obtain no goal.
But their thoughts and feelings
I cannot control

Philadelphia, PA 1838

Mary Crouse had just about had enough with her juvenile daughter's "vicious conduct." Controlling Mary Ann at home had become impossible, and was beyond her power anymore. Someone with higher authority needed to step in and play parent, instead – the state, perhaps. To that end, Mary Crouse filed a complaint, substantiated on evidence of her daughter's "incorrigibility." This convinced a county court judge that detention into a juvenile correctional institution was necessary for the sake of Mary Ann's "moral and future welfare." Justice Morton McMichael ordered her placement in one of the country's first juvenile offender jails, the Philadelphia House of Refuge (*Ex Parte Crouse*, 1838).

Whereas the wishes of the child's mother were satisfied, the decision did not sit well with the father, who following his daughter's incarceration filed a writ of *habeas corpus*, challenging the constitutionality of the confinement. Mary Ann had committed and had been convicted of no crime, she had not even received a trial before being thrown in prison; her Sixth Amendment rights had been violated, he claimed. The Supreme Court begged to differ: the father had grossly misunderstood children rights, parental rights, and most importantly, the function and purposes of the institution inside which his daughter was held. First, government had the right to intervene in families where child welfare was at stake. Some parents are not capable of being good parents and keeping their children safe and well adjusted. Like a good father, the state had the moral and legal authority to take responsibility for rearing these very children. If the state had evidence suggesting that parents were doing a poor job parenting, which Mary Ann Crouse's vicious behavior suggested, then government officials were allowed to step in and take charge. Second, the father's complaint was ill-informed: his daughter was not sent to a prison, but to a House of Refuge – a school. She was sent there, not to be punished, but to be helped, educated, and reformed. If it had been punishment that Justice McMichael and the House of Refuge managers were aiming to administer, then the father would have been right. But, it was not punishment at all. Everything that was done to Mary Ann was done with her best interest in mind. From the looks of it, the young woman was heading down the wrong path, a path that without doubt would end in self-destruction. The parents could not protect her, so the state had to. It was for her own good.

Her own good. Was penal control an effective way to advance a child's best interest? Was this self-contradictory concept of coercive welfare a good idea? And most importantly, was it a feasible one? In other words, benevolent intentions notwithstanding, was the idea truly implemented on the ground, or was it all just make-believe? These all-time classic questions with which Juvenile Justice scholars and field experts have grappled since the early 1800s, are of particular significance to the current study, especially with respect to system-involved girls, like Mary Ann Crouse. As history has shown, theory and practice did not always overlap inside juvenile corrections. As Bernard and Kurlychek, for example, characteristically (2010) note while reviewing the House of Refuge history:

> The comparison between good intentions and actual performance is the one that will be made several times in the legal history of the juvenile justice system.
>
> (p. 58)

The current study's qualitative data focus on actual performance, exposing the lived reality inside a juvenile jail for female offenders, for those contemporary Mary Anns. The findings are discussed in light of a rhetoric that shields this reality from the public eye, deflects attention from criminogenic structural conditions that include a stigmatizing justice system, and draws it to the moral deficiencies of "fallen girls." This rhetoric differs very little from the one the Supreme Court uncritically parroted in its 1838 decision about Mary Ann Crouse: What happens inside juvenile detention has girls' best interest in mind. These are our children, and when our children are out of control, we put them back on track. We do what parents would do, if they could, or knew how to. Almost 200 years later, these ideological roots have lost little integrity. In fact, thanks to professional literature, legislative developments, and experience, the goals of state intervention into minor children's lives have been both expanded and specified: these goals now involve rehabilitative punishment; de-institutionalization of status offenders; restorative/reintegrative justice; and lately, responsivity (in our case, gender-responsivity), and empowerment. With few exceptions (Feld, 1997), the conceptualization of juvenile justice as a system within which all these goals *could* be effectively met is not problematized. Most doubts have been cast toward the *implementation* of these goals on the ground, and whether practice reflects intentions. When it is shown that no, we are not actually doing what we say we are doing, then top-down reform, change in the law or change in management is the proposed remedy. The systemic framework is kept in place. New methods about how the original idea ought to be realized in practice arise, are theorized, adopted, and celebrated.

One of these new ideas that has gained significant popularity and garnered enthusiastic legal and academic support in the US, Canada, the UK and elsewhere is that system-involved women's welfare is best served through gendered justice – a kind of justice that employs and effects empowerment. Gender empowerment inside a carceral context, and one that was put in place primarily to define, control, and shape poor and immigrant girls' attitudes and behaviors in the first place is clearly a contradiction. But, this is nothing new; contradiction has encapsulated the Juvenile Justice system since its inception: benevolence and contempt; welfare and coercion; court yet little due process; civil procedure and criminal punishment; the child's environment is the problem, but let's fix the child only; *parens patriae* and otherizing offenders; rhetoric and practice; promise and delivery. All these are contradictions in which juvenile justice perpetually traffics.

This chapter will briefly examine these inherent contradictions of the Juvenile Justice foundation by discussing what its promises are, how they are articulated in speech, and how well they have been implemented in practice. Special emphasis will be placed on the promises that pertain to young women who find themselves caught up in the system by way of either victimhood or delinquency, but usually both. We will talk about a newfound interest in the plight of system-involved girls, one that is grounded in feminist research, and has been translated into well-funded programming. I will summarize what research says we *should* do about female delinquency, what justice officials and program administrators say we *are* doing to female delinquents, and will explain how the current study will contrast theory and rhetoric with the lived experiences of detained girls. This, I hope, will set the stage for the concluding discussion which will challenge not only whether juvenile justice philosophy is reflected in current practices, but whether the philosophy in and of itself is deficient and thus, unrealizable in the existing system. But first, how did this philosophy emerge, how was it institutionalized, which treatment goals reflect it, and how do girls fit in it? Let's go back to Mary Ann Crouse.

Parens Patriae

Ex Parte Crouse (1838), the Supreme Court case whose facts are related above, established *Parens Patriae* as the philosophical doctrine on which state governance of minor children is grounded in the US. *Parens Patriae* derived from English Common Law. The King, Patriarch of his country, was to care for the life and property of children whose parents were absent or otherwise incapacitated. Such cases were processed in medieval England's Chancery Courts (Rendleman, 1971). In the US, the King's patriarchal authority is embodied in government officials. Until 1838, however, the cases of incorrigible children were dealt by criminal courts. Whereas Mary Ann Crouse had received neither a trial, nor a conviction, her case was reviewed by a judge who sent her to secure confinement, presumably without her will.

The confinement institution where Mary Ann was sent, the House of Refuge, first established by the Refuge Act in 1825, housed vagrant and delinquent children who were previously at risk of being thrown in adult prisons. Before Houses of Refuge opened, most minor juvenile offenders received either severe punishment by being sentenced to adult prison, or no punishment at all when juries felt prison would be inappropriate for them (Fox, 1970). The House of Refuge, guised as a charitable rather than carceral institution, fixed the problem by expanding state control over bothersome, that is, poor and immigrant, yet not seriously criminal children (Rendleman, 1971). Headed by religious leaders of the time, Houses of Refuge offered parental discipline, labor, religious instruction, education, and apprenticeships. In 1836, 60+ years before the formation of first Juvenile Court, state Assembly amended the Refuge Act, to legally permit in the House of Refuge the confinement of children who were not even criminal. The law expanded coercive confinement of other people's kids to non-delinquent minors who nevertheless exhibited troublesome behavior that parents were "incapable or unwilling" to effectively discipline (Packel, 1976). Mary Ann's behavior warranted state intervention, not because *it* was criminal, but because *she* was a minor. Justice McMichael saw in Mary Anne Crouse the type of child for whom the 1835 amendment to the Refuge Act was written, and consequently had her committed.

The *parens patriae* doctrine justified the criminal punishment of individuals who would have received either none, or very little, had they been adults. The *parens patriae* philosophy allowed judges to argue that Houses of Refuge were not in the business of retribution, because that is not what parents do. As it turned out, subsequent to *Crouse*, the majority of minors detained in them had not violated the law; they were, in other words, status offenders (Fox, 1970). The Supreme Court was fine with that, because it believed the rhetoric advanced by the institution's managers. Several years after Mary Ann Crouse's detention, however, the Supreme Court became more realistic about conditions of confinement in Houses of Refuge.

By 1870, the Court had been aware of these so-called reform schools' performance in dealing with children. Several testimonies of abusive treatment and violence inside them had been brought to light. It turned out that there was a gap between speech and practice here. Justices' views were no longer swayed by rhetoric but by reality: the House of Refuge punished its detainees and could no longer claim that it acted like a good father (Pisciotta, 1982). If it was not acting like a father, then the *parens patriae* doctrine did not apply. In *People v. Turner* (1870), the Supreme Court found that the confinement of juveniles who had committed no criminal offenses was violative of the constitution and effectively put an end to the practice of incarcerating children without crime or conviction.

The State was no longer legally allowed to control "undesirable" children by removing them from their homes or from the streets. Yet many believed that this was exactly what ought to happen in order for these children to be "saved": saved from their own moral deficiencies, their parents' inadequacies, social disorganization, and a future fraught with poverty, victimization, corruption, and violence. Among these believers was a group of well-educated, well-connected, wealthy, and "progressive" women who took the saving upon themselves. They would eventually be known as the Child Savers, the movement that successfully lobbied for a new, separate, perfectly legal justice system to deal with street kids. Neglected, abused, unruly, or criminal: to them there was no difference. Children's crime is a result of child neglect, anyway, they asserted; one reinforces the other. Both needed to be dealt with by the justice system, by a court that is not criminal (because remember, only adults can be criminal), but nevertheless possesses coercive power over citizens. That court would be organized in a similar way to the Chancery court, the court that was founded on and practiced *parens patriae*. That court was the Juvenile Court, with the establishment of which *parens patriae* re-emerged as the legal and philosophical foundation of a justice system for persons under the age of 18: the Juvenile Justice System.

Rehabilitation: the goal

The Child Savers' efforts culminated in the establishment of the first juvenile court in 1899. The juvenile court centralized a network of separate child-saving practices and institutions that delivered a welfare-based response to youth offending (Platt, 1969). Whereas Platt is rightfully critical of the Child Savers' motivations as self-serving, and the material effects of their efforts as ultimately oppressive to poor urban children, the persons running the court, juvenile judges, showed sincere empathy and willingness to supervise the children's care. In 1909, Julian Mack, who presided in the first juvenile court in Cook County, Illinois outlined the objectives of the juvenile court as both "palliative" and "curative" (p. 122); focused on the root causes of delinquency and the particular needs of each child. The court's aim would be to involve community, probation officers, and parents in assisting the child's reintegration. Judge Mack placed emphasis on the Juvenile Court Judge's personality, as much as on his/her legal training and reasoning abilities. He envisioned the Juvenile Court Judge as a cross between a judicial authority and a benevolent social worker:

> He must be a student of and deeply interested in the problems of philanthropy and child life, as well as a lover of children. He must be able to understand the boys' point of view and ideas of justice; he must be willing and patient enough to search out the underlying causes of the trouble, and to formulate the plan by which, through cooperation, oftentimes, of many agencies, the cure maybe effected.
>
> (p. 119)

Clearly, the juvenile justice system in the beginning of the twentieth century was focused on reforming both the individual as well as the criminogenic context in which the troublesome behavior was developed, and on doing so in collaboration with other helping social institutions. Reform anchored in an understanding of youth crime as a social disease that has contaminated the individual was then the guiding philosophy of a justice system that rationalized its legal authority through the *parens patriae* doctrine.

The problem with this approach was that eventually, the practice of saving children shifted away from reforming society to an exclusive focus on reforming the individual (Bernard & Kurlychek, 2010). Ultimately, social reform was replaced by the goal of rehabilitation, a goal which is both welfare-esque and punitive. Rehabilitation as a theory/goal of punishment is based on the assumption that crime, deviance, and delinquency are behavioral symptoms of a weakness within the individual, such as for example, addiction, trauma, or criminal thinking patterns. To fix the offending behavior, one must fix that which is wrong with the person. It is not that the rehabilitation perspective rejects the impact of social conditions on crime rates; it is that it assumes that personal strength and integrity, both of which may be instilled in a person, given appropriate treatment, may transcend societal disadvantage. In assuming that, it also places a lot of faith on an individual's potential to be transformed, which is of particular significance in the cases of youthful offenders. There is little doubt that the US justice system's over-reliance on prison and jail as a response to adult crime reflects a shift away from such faith. The idea that children and adolescents can change, however, and must be given a second and third chance to do so without acquiring a criminal stigma in the process, still drives much of juvenile justice philosophy today. Yes, this philosophy has been eroded from time to time allowing for practices that shift away from the original goal. And yes, existing crime control responses such as adult court waivers, life sentences, and sex offender registries for minors, are antithetical to principles of rehabilitation and *parens patriae*, but similarly punitive responses always existed in tandem with rehabilitative efforts. Moreover, recent developments, such as the outlawing by the Supreme Court of the death penalty in 2005 and of mandatory life without parole for minors in 2012, suggest that today more than ever, a commitment to the welfare model of justice is becoming stronger. Both these decisions, as well as renewed commitments to diverting troubled youth out of carceral settings (Annie E. Casey Foundation, 2013; Mendel, 2010) indicate that, notwithstanding notable crime control erosions, the primary purposes of juvenile justice processing and treatment have historically been and still are rehabilitation, labeling prevention, trauma healing, and reintegration (Howell et al., 2013). At least, that is the theory.

What about the girls?

You might have noticed the gendered language Judge Mack used to describe the purpose and functions of the juvenile court in the previous section. The ideal judge was a "he" and the quintessential troubled child before the court was a "boy." That is to be expected in a document written in the early 1900s. Women judges or lawyers hardly existed back then, and as for juvenile offenders, the majority were boys. Whereas women participate in courtroom justice today, judges and law violators alike remain disproportionately male. About two thirds of all state judges are men (George & Yoon, n.d.). With respect to juveniles processed in court in 2013, seven out of ten were boys (Hockenberry & Puzzanchera, 2015),[1] despite notable increases in female delinquency in the past 20 years or so. Ironically, given the male-focus of the juvenile justice system, girls' troubles were very much in mind, when Child Savers embarked on their mission to reform courts and confinement institutions. It was precisely the non-criminal, yet "inappropriate" behavior of young women that the new juvenile court was most useful in controlling.

As mentioned earlier, *Turner* put an end to the practice of detaining youths like Mary-Anne Crouse. However, it was "out of control" *girls* that offended the Child Savers' protestant ethic the most. Young women uninterested in domestic duties, going and staying out late, disregarding parental discipline, engaging in pre-marital sex, all these immoral acts were viewed as gateways to criminal ones, especially for girls. The Child Savers aimed at stopping this trajectory, and as such, revolved their campaign around the moralization of young immigrant women. This moralization focused on problematizing and oppressing female sexuality, which they conflated with female deviance (Odem & Schlossman, 1991). Whereas the Child Savers' reform efforts benefited juvenile offenders by removing them from adult prisons and connecting them with welfare-informed institutions, the reform resulted in casualties: the girls (Shelden, 1998). The new

Juvenile Court, with its legitimate paternal authority to intervene in young people's lives, regulated working families' daughters' lives through extreme intervention. Not only were girls more likely than boys to be processed for status offenses, they were also more likely to be punished with detention for them (Odem & Schlossman, 1991; Shelden, 1998). While in detention, rehabilitation was fixated on turning female offenders into "ladies," because girls' troubles with the law were considered a manifestation of their nonconformity to the narrow gender norms of middle-class culture (Pisciotta, 1982). Purity, domesticity, dependence, and nurturance were the patriarchal ideals that structured rehabilitative interventions in youth corrections for girls. She was forced to be or remain celibate, find a good husband to obey and serve, have children of her own to raise, learn how to cook, and clean, and take care of the household. So really, *parens patriae* and rehabilitation in the past (and as we shall see, in the present), were qualitatively different for girls than boys, and reflected the gendered paternalism that sought to restrict women's choices, whether criminal or not.

Goal, reloaded

Aggressive statutory law enforcement was challenged in the 1970s, because juvenile delinquency scholars and practitioners acknowledged its adverse effects on youth crime, a phenomenon that had been subject of growing public concern since the mid 1960s (Raley, 1995). The juvenile justice system as a whole faced heavy criticism for being "intransigent, bureaucratic, and punitive" (Holden & Kapler, 1995, p. 3). In response to these criticisms, Congress enacted the Juvenile Justice and Delinquency Prevention Act of 1974, federal legislation that pressured state juvenile systems to stop placing status offenders in secure confinement and to divert these youth to community-based alternatives. Whereas the reviews of the Act's actual effects have been mixed, ranging from transformative (Holden & Kapler, 1995) to pointless (Logan & Rausch, 1985), the understanding of its intents is uniform: this law marked a re-investment in the juvenile justice system's original goals of prevention and rehabilitation without stigma, and a commitment to gender and race equity. This commitment and the funding to those state institutions that share it has been secured and fortified with each subsequent reauthorization and amendment.

A review of the JJDPA's effectiveness is beyond the scope of the study, although it is worth mentioning that despite legislative efforts at the federal, state, and local levels, neither gender, nor race equity was realized. To the contrary, gender and race disparities especially in the adjudicative phase (court processing) still exist, with girls, especially black girls receiving harsh responses for minor violations (Peck, Leiber, & Brubaker, 2014). What is of particular relevance to this study, however, is the JJDPA's role in shaping the goals and content of delinquency prevention programs for girls.

Gendered justice: the promise

In 1992, the JJDPA turned its attention to system-involved girls and women by acknowledging they were becoming a growing problem we knew little about and did even less to prevent. At the time, female delinquency and crime were on the rise and would continue to grow for the next 10–15 years, even when male offending was decreasing (Acoca, 1998; Poe-Yamagata & Butts, 1996). Due to malestream scholarship and policy's longstanding disinterest in female offending, the juvenile justice system found itself unprepared to effectively deal with the influx of young women in its institutions. Perhaps inspired by feminist research that pointed to contextual and situational differences between men and women's deviance, the 1992 amendment to the JJDPA sought to address the gender gap in prevention and treatment programming by giving funds to state agencies that would employ empirical evidence to achieve exactly that.

Federally funded research projects focusing on what works with female offenders resulted in training protocols (OJJDP, 1998) that informed practices adopted across the nation by institutions that served at-risk and delinquent girls. The proliferation of feminist theory-anchored studies examining the crucial role of gender in offending generated a consensus that preventive and treatment programming for girls must be responsive to their particular circumstances, needs, and strengths – all three of which differed from those of boys in meaningful ways. A call was made for justice that is "gendered," that is equitable, yet not identical (Bloom, 2003). Increased funding became available for those institutions that would answer that call by offering "gender-specific" or "gender-responsive" programming (GSP/GRP) to their female clients.

A new era emerged in youth corrections, in which GSP was established as the new dominant paradigm for interventions with girls in North America (Sharpe, 2016; Totten, 2002), and slowly but surely has now gained popularity in penal systems across the globe, with the United Nations including "gender-sensitivity" language and principles in its protocols (Hannah-Moffat, 2010). GSP principles derive from and reflect the implications of three theoretical approaches:

1 Pathways Theory
2 Relational Theory
3 Empowerment

These three approaches offer the theoretical framework on which specific guidelines are allegedly adopted by institutions and non-profit organizations serving at-risk and system-involved girls and women.

Pathways

Girls and boys enter the justice system through different pathways that generate specific needs. In theorizing women's offending, Kathleen Daly (1992) argued that women find their way into the criminal justice system through a pathway that begins in early childhood abuse, continues on the streets, matures in abusive relationships, and is perpetually shaped by alternating or overlapping experiences of both victimization and victimizing. These "experiences reflect a process of reproducing physical and emotional harm" (p. 47). This feminist pathways approach to female offending acknowledges girls and women's intersecting identities as both victims and offenders, and offenders and victims (Belknap, 2001; Belknap & Holsinger, 2006; Chesney-Lind, 1998; Owen & Bloom, 1997; Schaffner, 2006) and connects them to women's disadvantaged societal status.

Therefore, the most significant and distinct factor shaping girls' delinquent pathways is victimization: it is both more prevalent and more harmful to female victims. Whereas many delinquent boys have also experienced abuse or neglect as children, such experiences are far more typical and begin at younger ages for girls who end up in the system (Herrera & McCloskey, 2003; Siegel & Williams, 2003). The impact of abuse, especially sexual abuse on criminal behavior is also more *salient* among girls. For example, Conrad et al. (2014) found that even when controlling for other factors, sexual abuse predicts recidivism among girls, but not for boys.

Most importantly, and commonly among the adolescent female population in juvenile corrections, experiences with childhood abuse, and the trauma in which they result, are closely linked to both mental health and substance abuse issues (Dixon, Howie, & Starling, 2004; Ouimette et al., 2000; Teplin et al., 2002; Tripodi & Pettus-Davis, 2013). Girls suffering PTSD, depression, and anxiety often self-medicate with alcohol and drugs, inadvertently worsening their well-being and their legal troubles by adding addiction into the mix of their problems. So, victimization trauma, mental health disorders, and substance addiction are interrelated and revolving issues that are particularly prevalent and consequential in system-involved girls' delinquent pathways.

Victimization at home, however, also shapes the context of involvement with the law differentially for the two genders. Female delinquents are more likely to run away to flee their abusive situations and subsequently immerse themselves with "street" culture and individuals who introduce them to dangerous and often unlawful life-styles (Daly, 1992; Gavazzi, Yarcheck, & Chesney-Lind, 2006). In attempting to protect themselves, girls are commonly charged with crimes related to their family environment, such as incorrigibility and more recently, domestic violence (Gavazzi et al., 2006).[2] However, juvenile justice system processes and agents disregard the contexts of girls' offending and end up penalizing their survival attempts rather than protecting them from future harm (Chesney-Lind & Shelden, 1998).

Girls' victimization, then, must organize policy responses to girls' problems, so that the responses avoid re-victimization, first, and second, heal the devastating trauma it has caused. Gendered justice requires rehabilitative interventions that are *trauma-informed*. Such interventions are designed to recognize the presence and significance of trauma in young women's lives, and employ a targeted, strengths-based restorative approach toward healing (Harris & Fallot, 2001;

Randall & Haskell, 2013). But these interventions also ought to take the healing one step further. Feminist scholarship has placed female victimization and offending in its larger, gendered context. Gender disparities in the onset, prevalence, impact, repetition, and reactions to violent victimization are a manifestation of women's secondary, inferior social status. Programming for girls, especially girls who have been subjected to childhood abuse must focus on therapeutic treatment that is both individualized, but also contextualized. Such treatment will help young women connect their individual tragedies with a parochial, patriarchal system of oppression that enables, rationalizes, and tolerates women's victimizations, while at the same time defining and demonizing victims' responses.

Connections and disconnections (relational theory)

Appropriate interventions with girls which take under consideration the role of gender in shaping female pathways to crime should not be informed only by their histories of abuse, but also by their unique *developmental* pathways. Psychological and sociological literature on child and adolescent developmental processes uphold feminist arguments regarding the differential construction of gender (Belknap, 2001; Chesney-Lind, 1989). Indeed, girls and boys are trained in a variety of differential gender norms, but the most relevant one here relates to how central human connections are to the development of girls as compared to boys. Girls thrive through healthy connections with others.

First, contrary to boys, girls are socialized to be emotional and passive, to listen rather than to talk and to feel rather than act (Loeber & Hay, 1997). This affects how the two genders respond but also are *expected* to respond to conflicts. Rather than in overt aggression and physical cruelty for example, girls are said to engage in *relational* aggression, that is social sabotage, name-calling, gossip and defamation (Crick & Grotpeter, 1995; Underwood, 2003). Girls use physical aggression as well, but they are more likely to do that in a more secretive way (Craig & Pepler, 1998), perhaps having learned that would be unacceptable, unbecoming behavior that receives harsh responses. This literature has contributed to gender essentialism (the understanding that there is one universal female experience divorced from cultural, structural, and race factors) on which juvenile justice professionals draw their attitudes about girls' deviance. What is expected from and accepted by girls as normative behavior, thus, perpetuates the misunderstanding and misplaced judgments regarding conflict expressions that adult caretakers often are entrapped in (Brown, 2010; Hipwell & Loeber, 2006). In other words, juvenile justice professionals, especially correctional counselors have trouble understanding the importance of connections in young women's wellbeing, often viewing them as problematic, dangerous, or even indulging; but they also have trouble "placing" and thus appropriately responding to girls' physical aggression, which is met with exceeding disapproval and harsh punishment.

Second, gender differences in socialization are exacerbated and place girls at increased risk of trouble during adolescence. Adolescence is a particularly brutal developmental phase for girls, frequently permeated by self-esteem, self-worth, sexual objectification, and victimization problems (Gilligan, 1982; Taylor, Gilligan, & Sullivan, 1995). Persistent and contradictory messages about gender roles and feminine identity contribute to girls' fear of asserting themselves as the persons they really feel or want to become. In fact, there is evidence that during adolescence, girls start to doubt and dislike themselves, feel inadequate or incompetent, and resign from trying to excel or distinguish themselves in fear of being rejected by others (Beyer, 1999).

"Others" are extremely significant in adolescent women's lives. Girls are particularly vulnerable to the damaging consequences of abusive relationships with others, while on the other hand, experience growth through attachments and mutually supportive relationships (MS Foundation for Women, 1993). Boys, on the other hand, are said to experience growth through asserting independence and autonomy, both highly valued goals in American and Western European "stand on your own two feet" cultures[3] Relational traits, which young women are trained into developing, are not revered or appreciated as much. To the contrary, they are undervalued in strongly individualistic patriarchal societies, where independence and autonomy are viewed as ideal norms. As is true with most "feminine" attributes, being relational is often seen as a handicap. The "relational" self has also been problematized because of the huge pressure it places on girls to strive for third party acceptance, often by sacrificing their own needs.

It should not be so, however, if Jean Baker Miller (1976) and Carol Gilligan (1982; Gilligan, Lyons, & Hanmer, 1990) have anything to say about it. Both scholars reject this hegemonic and masculinity-informed understanding of humanity. They stress the crucial role relationship participation plays in fostering human growth, for both men and women, as long as this participation is not one-sided, as it has historically been for women. Miller (1976; 1986; 1990) argues that building connections with others, a task societies assign exclusively to women, can be problematic and usually results in negative consequences because the connections that women are expected to enter are *not* mutual: "women have been fostering other people's growth" because that is how society has constructed gender. If the relational suits of women can be employed to foster growth for them as well as others, however, then these must be encouraged rather than squashed.

With this relational theory in mind, Stephanie Covington (2007) urges correctional institutions that house a disproportionate number of women facing trauma, addiction, and mental health problems, to inform their practices on relational theory. Correctional officers working with female populations must develop an understanding of what this means in order to a) avoid replicating "relationships of disconnection and violation on a systemic level" (p. 12), and b) adjust their communication styles and programming goals to foster healthy relationships with significant others and the community. Covington (2007) stresses that not all relationships are equally as empowering and to the same degree for all women. Each woman's personal history and cultural background must be first taken into account, her own voice and opinions must be heard, and the reality of her life must guide programming that seeks to repair broken relationships and to nurture new ones. Growth fostering and empowering connections are based on relationships that are mutual and emphatic. It is these types of connections gender-specific programs are designed to promote.

Empowerment

The overarching goal of girls' programming is gender empowerment. Empowerment as a concept is frequently discussed in human services disciplines such as psychology, social work, and victimology, in international movements concerned with the advancement of women's position in society, and in the Restorative Justice field. Recently, primarily because of its use in framing gender-specific programming for female offenders, it has accumulated significant impetus in the field of criminology as well. Empowerment is of great relevance to this study, first because it is a key element in its theoretical framework, and second, because it is a central goal of gender-specific interventions in general, and of the so-called gender-specific program that is implemented in the juvenile institution where this research was conducted, in particular.

Defining the concept of empowerment is as challenging as understanding and turning it into practice. As Young (1994) characteristically stated, when it comes to empowerment, just like democracy "everyone is for it, but rarely do people mean the same thing by it" (p. 48). Chamberlin (1997) argued that because the word is employed in conservative political rhetoric seeking to undermine rather than promote social welfare programming for underprivileged persons, the concept is in danger of becoming meaningless. The same author operationalized empowerment as the process by which a person acquires a range of choices, informed decision-making power, assertiveness, critical thinking, group mentality, hopefulness, positive self-image, skills, and an interest in effecting personal and collective change. Empowerment within therapeutic contexts is like a journey toward taking control of one's life, with rehabilitation counselors providing the map rather than steering the wheel (Chamberlin).

Simmons and Parsons (1983) defined it as the process of achieving personally meaningful goals through the acquisition of skills, knowledge, emotions, and material resources that will enable individuals to become active agents in their own lives. The authors identified two components of empowerment: an internal, which refers to the belief that one has control over outcomes in their life, and an external, which refers to problem solving capacity. The former, thus, refers to attitudes, feelings and perceptions, such as confidence and self-esteem. This internal component is similar to Zimmerman's (1995) psychological empowerment concept, concerned primarily with individual traits, which may interact with contextual factors to effect change in one's circumstances, and to Bandura's

(1982) *self-efficacy*, the belief in one's ability to act and reach desired goals. The latter, external component of empowerment takes a more tangible form, as it revolves around actual knowledge, practical skills, and access to available community resources through which internal talents and motivations may be channeled, and intermediate, informal social institutions such as families may be served (Rappaport, 1987). Empowerment processes in that sense underscore a strengths- rather than a deficits-based approach to treatment where clients become participatory agents rather than passive recipients of care (Damen et al., 2017).

A dual view of empowerment that moves beyond the individual is conducive to circumventing the tendency of traditional therapeutic (rehabilitative) programs to aim at "correcting" individuals so they can fit a model of normalcy and acceptability, which arguably reflects domination and power over rather than with others. Parsons (1989) suggests that particular groups in society, such as working women of color are disempowered not necessarily due to lack of internal, perceived strength, but due to lack of material resources, stigmatization and marginalization, which reflect the external component of (dis)empowerment. Historically, correctional programs for youth, especially minority youth, and more so minority female youth, failed because they subjected their clients to the ideal standards of white, male-dominated, middle-class groups, which most of the time were responsible for their suffering and subsequent delinquency in the first place. Rather than dominion (Braithwaite & Pettit, 1994), that is freedom from abusive authority, this encouraged domination, which is material and ideological power over others. Moreover, these regulations reinforced women's subordination to sometimes-abusive patriarchal authority. Consequently, the purpose of gender-specific programming for young girls is to transcend, if not subvert these dated, ineffective, and oppressive methods of correcting juvenile offenders and instead, to encourage self-expression, self-governance, and pride in racial, ethnic, and gender identity.

Pollack (2000), however, questions whether actual empowerment paradigms in correctional treatment settings can depart their commonly narrow and one-sided origins. Although she acknowledges that a treatment model of "parental care" encourages individuals to develop a sense of self that takes under consideration their social situation, she warns that it still does not escape an individualistic approach that communicates to its clients a "you need to stand on your own feet" ideology (Young, 1994). In other words, it overemphasizes the role of agency as a *subjective* condition, a psychological trait that is conducive to self-determination, and is positively correlated with self-esteem. This emphasis on subjectivity glosses over the fact that agency, or the ability to make constructive decisions about one's life, is heavily dependent upon objective, contextual and situational conditions surrounding system-involved women (Pollack).

Iris Marion Young (1994) argues that true empowerment is the organizing principle of treatment practices offered to marginalized women within a *feminist ethic of care*. This type of care which draws heavily on Jean Baker Miller and

Carol Gilligan's theories of women's development, grounds therapeutic work on a culture of empathy and on an understanding of personal troubles as manifestations of social troubles. Consequently, she expands the empowerment definition to include processes that employ dialogue to politicize the individual, and develop a sense of collective resistance against systems of oppression.

Both Young (1994) and Pollack (2000) then, advocate for the adoption of an additional, broader definition of empowerment that is less individualistic and more political and collective. Young's empowerment is "a process in which individual, relatively powerless persons engage in dialogue with each other and thereby come to understand the social sources of their powerlessness and see the possibility of acting collectively to change their social environment" (p. 55), whereas Pollack prefers the term "relational autonomy," which "theorizes the impact of oppression in women's choices, identities, and actions" (p. 85). This conceptualization of empowerment draws on Brazilian pedagogue and activist Paolo Freire's (1973; 2000) *critical consciousness* construct. Freire (2000) defined critical consciousness raising as "learning to perceive social, political, and economic contradictions, and to take action against the oppressive elements of reality" (p. 35), blending thus, cognitive development, critical thinking, social justice, and activism in one pedagogical method. Critical consciousness reflects awareness of how personal and familial dysfunctions are linked, or even caused by larger structural societal dysfunctions such as inequality, racism, and sexism. It is that awareness that motivates people to challenge these dysfunctions, and transforms the objects of social injustice to agentic subjects of social change. As Watts, Diemer, & Voight (2011) put it, critical consciousness is the "antidote" of oppression, which is why it is incorporated into curricula of programs serving marginalized groups (Hernández, Almeida, & Dolan-Del Vecchio, 2005; Diemer et al., 2006; Watts et al., 2011).

Along with the critical consciousness/political component, both Young (1994) and Pollack's (2000) approaches incorporate the psychological/internal, and pragmatic/external notions of empowerment as well, and imply that gender-specific programs must work to develop all three (arguably interconnected) components in order to be true to their rhetoric, honest in their intentions, and effective in their desired outcomes.

Consequently, the current study aims to include all three empowerment interpretations, internal/psychological, external, and political/critical consciousness in evaluating the treatment of adolescent girls detained in juvenile hall. In particular, a central point of inquiry in this study is whether and how a gender-specific reintegration program offered to incarcerated girls in my sample manages to deliver its promise of "empowerment," in a way that transcends gendered language and ideals, challenges sexist and racist stereotypes, and is based on notions of participatory democracy, dominion, and autonomy.

GSP guidelines

GSP is where pathways scholarship, relational theory, and the empowerment construct meet in practice. Policy and advocacy organizations such as the National Institute of Corrections (Zavlek & Maniglia, 2007), the OJJDP (1998), and the Valentine Foundation (1990), part inspired by this feminist/critical scholarship and part motivated by federal funding (Juvenile Justice and Delinquency Prevention Appropriations Authorization, 1992) have translated abstract concepts into specific practices by which field employees structure their treatment responses. I have summarized the most prominent literature's suggestions regarding effective programming for female delinquents (Bloom, Owen, & Covington, 2003; Chesney-Lind & Paramore, 2001; Covington & Bloom, 2006; Matthews & Hubbard, 2008; Zavlek & Maniglia, 2007) in the following guidelines:

1 Create normative environments for girls to live and be treated in.
2 Create a safe space for girls by avoiding re-victimization and trauma triggers, encouraging self-expression, and allowing some control over one's body and space.
3 Use gender- and culturally-responsive cognitive behavioral therapy to heal abuse-related trauma and its corollaries, mental health and addiction problems.
4 Avoid replicating disconnections, and offer relationship support and restoration of healthy, mutually empowering connections with others.
5 Follow a strength-based assessment protocol that acknowledges and respects differences among girls.
6 Promote an understanding of gender, race, sexual orientation, socio-economic class, religion, and other social categories and individual life experiences as all interconnecting to shape self-identity, and experiences with victimization, offending, and juvenile justice processing.
7 Encourage advocacy concerning all forms of oppression.
8 Provide comprehensive, collaborative, and meaningful aftercare and reintegration services.
9 Show and promote empathy, authenticity, and mutuality; encourage dialogue; listen to girls' voices; and embrace dominion.

The ideal GSP would follow all nine guidelines without sacrificing either security or bureaucracy. Even as I write this, however, the multiple contradictions these guidelines represent within a penal context are jumping out with force. Whether this ideal is achieved is an empirical question (more on this in a minute). Whether it is even *achievable* is a question that requires both empirical evidence and critical reflection in order to be answered. To begin with, juvenile corrections, similar to adult prisons and other non-voluntary commitment institutions are hardly places where these ideals are usually promoted, or even accepted. In fact, the correctional setting is by definition and design disempowering and opposing to all principles on which GSP guidelines are based.

The recent "rush" for gender-responsive programs that followed the reauthorization of the Juvenile Justice and Prevention Act, and the funding possibilities it created for state and local agencies may have resulted in an unintended consequence: the development of interventions that adopt the *letter*, but not the *spirit* of the gender-responsivity mandate. That could be both unfortunate and dangerous. As Hannah-Moffat (2010) stresses, such alleged reforms must be met with a critical and reflexive attitude, as their rhetoric may "disguise and minimize systemic and interpersonal power relations" (p. 208). I would add that this rhetoric may also disarm feminist critiques of juvenile corrections as places inappropriate for system-involved girls, because girls are "being helped" in ways that feminist scholarship has long advocated. This argument seems to be going full circle back to 1838, when objections against incarcerating youth were met with a similar response ("but we're helping, not punishing") only to be validated several decades later, in face of evidence that "helping" was in practice nothing less than "hurting" under the pretext of rehabilitation and parental care. Similarly, today:

> Evoking terms such as "empowerment" ... "healing" and "responsive" contributes to the overshadowing of the coercive qualities of penal power.
>
> (Hannah-Moffat, 2010, p. 208)

With the growing interest in and popularity of gender-specific correctional programs, the possibility of yet another reincarnation of the problem of good intentions getting lost in the reality of juvenile correctional practice, this time with the blessings of feminist and women rights groups, warrants careful exploration. Several correctional facilities housing women or girls have, in theory, adopted programs that seem to run by gender-specific principles. This is also the case for the particular correctional institution where the current study was conducted. However, whether the language in these facilities' mission statements, or/and in their managers' rhetoric, truly reflects the reality of the experiences of system-involved females, is doubtful. It is also an empirical question that very few studies have explored thus far, at least not by examining how GSP works on the ground and how it is experienced by the inmates. An over-reliance on "evidence-based" research which habitually uses quantitative methods to evaluate program effects, hardly gives voice to the most appropriate evaluators of these services: the female offenders who are enrolled in them and who are able to provide valuable insights about their own experiences.

Unfortunately, evidence based on scarce qualitative research (Gaarder & Hesselton, 2012; Goodkind & Miller, 2006;) seems to validate this assumption: it points out the failure or inability of the correctional system to realize the goals of gender-specific programming as outlined in previously referenced guidelines. To the contrary, GSP as practiced within youth correctional institutions often reinforces stereotypical gender norms that reflect a regressive sexist philosophy that has been dominant in shaping juvenile justice programs for girls since its inception (Goodkind & Miller, 2006). While claiming to empower young women, they narrowly focus on raising confidence and self-esteem (Gaarder & Hesselton, 2012; Goodkind, 2009), individualizing girls' problems and decontextualizing attitudes largely shaped by systemic violations. This decontextualization is particularly harmful to young women who typically find themselves trapped in the revolving doors of the US juvenile justice system: young women of color, born to immigrant parents, and raised in economically depressed neighborhoods face the unique oppressions that occur in the intersection of gender, race, class, ethnicity, immigration status, and sexual orientation, that disempower and marginalize them as a group and as individuals.

The current study

The purpose of this study is to contextualize both female delinquency and punishment in a contemporary Western system of youth corrections. This system claims to treat system-involved girls like a good, caring parent would; to focus on rehabilitation, restoration, and reintegration; and to empower young women through gender-responsive interventions. For once again in the history of juvenile justice institutions, these claims have been evaluated on the basis of intent rather than actual performance. In fact, recent declines in both juvenile offending and incarceration (Eurostat, 2016; Puzzanchera, 2013; Richards, 2011) in Western jurisdictions have been interpreted on the basis of those claims: juvenile offending has gone down, we must be doing things right (Annie E. Casey Foundation, 2013; De Leon & Teji, 2012 Junger-Tas & Decker, 2006; Mendel, 2010). Although this decline has been accompanied by a relative increase in the numbers of system-involved girls, and the overrepresentation of female status offenders inside secure detention facilities stubbornly persists today (Puzzanchera & Ehrmann, 2018), there is optimism that a new era is emerging in youth corrections. The claim is that there has been a shift back to rehabilitative ideals augmented by innovative strategies that emphasize cultures of care (Stohr, Jonson, & Cullen, 2014). The lived realities of young persons, especially less visible groups such as young women, are conveniently hidden behind these (arguably promising) numbers, and by declarations of progressive reforms. My study takes these hidden figures out of the shadows and places them in the spotlight and the center of its inquiry. What do *they* have to say about how things work on the ground?

Using a feminist framework and qualitative methodology, this study juxtaposes claims of progressive reform, therapeutic care, and gender-responsivity with the reality of life inside a juvenile detention facility (juvenile hall) for girls though the perspectives of the inmates themselves. In doing so, this study aims to contribute to a line of scholarship (Goodkind, 2005, 2009; Hannah-Moffat, 2010; Pollack, 2000; Sharpe, 2016) that seeks to critically examine dominant claims of innovation, trauma-informed therapy, empowerment, and gender-responsivity in youth corrections. I believe that leaving these claims unchallenged removes youth corrections' accountability and silences young women's protests. So, I challenged them.

Like all juvenile institutions, especially those operating in "progressive" California, the detention center in which my study was conducted also claims to be a rehabilitative place that wants girls to be successful, empowered, and confident. With both skepticism of such proclamations as well as hope that they reflect reality, I sought to explore what really happens to, for, and with girls detained in this southern California juvenile hall. Yes, juvenile detention rates have dropped, yet there is still a large number of youths processed in the system, the vast majority of whom are members of disadvantaged communities of color. Some of them are young women who have committed no serious offenses and have been victimized at home and on the street. It is important to know how they are treated and which services they are offered when they are placed under correctional supervision. There is no good way of knowing what it really means to be detained, whether reform commitments are materialized or whether GR interventions are truly empowering without listening to the voices of those who are detained. My research does exactly that: it goes inside the institution; it reaches beyond the reform rhetoric shield; it sheds a light in the lived experiences of detained delinquent girls, and attempts to place them in the context of marginalization and intertwined societal oppressions. And by doing so, it gives this marginalized, vulnerable, and neglected population something that they are often denied: a voice.

Research questions

I analyze observational, interview, and content data in order to explore:

a The life circumstances (life-stories) surrounding girls' deviant – sometimes delinquent – behaviors.
b Girls' lived experience inside detention, especially with regard to therapeutic and gender-responsive principles the institution's management advertises.

Findings and book organization

My findings suggest that there is discrepancy between rhetoric and practice: in fact, not only is the counter-rehabilitation climate of the institution incompatible with, it is *directly antithetical* to each and every GSP guideline feminist literature and scholarship have proposed for effective girls' programming (as outlined in this chapter). More disturbingly, conditions of confinement in this juvenile hall mirror the gendered abuse and neglect experiences that drench detained girls' life-stories, reinforcing and normalizing the traumas these experiences have resulted in. This has a tremendous impact on the self-concept and the self-efficacy of detained girls who have come to see themselves as the problem, sometimes excusing their victimization, and have constructed the identity of a "fallen" woman who deserves to be punished and deprived of everything good. Rather than ameliorating this negative impact, therapeutic interventions, either traditional or "gender-specific" adjust their goals and methods to fit the disempowering culture of penal control and individualize girls' troubles, contribute to self-blame, communicate paternalistic norms, and discourage challenges against gendered and raced systems of oppression. The following chapters illustrate these points through the voices of detained girls.

Discussion is organized around two themes: Deprivation as Intervention (Part I), examines the specific ways through which the institution undermines GSP guidelines and, instead, deprives young women of basic human rights, emotional support, and personal safety. My objective is to illustrate how this deprivation unfolds, to highlight its devastating consequences, and to help explain *why* it is (still) the dominant and systematic intervention offered to female detainees. More specifically, Chapter 3, *Disconnection as Intervention*, focuses on examples of isolation, lack of programming and recreation, and the deliberate undermining of relationships, in opposition to relational theory's implications. I examine the reasoning behind these approaches and their consequences for girls' lives, and I contrast girls' accounts of relationship interruption and loneliness prior to detention with the deprivation they are subjected to once they make it inside the institution. Chapter 4, *Suppression as Intervention*, focuses on the daily routine inside the facility and the myriad of nonsensical or/and authoritarian rules that dictate it. Contrary to policy suggestions for creating normative environments for incarcerated girls, I show how the institution goes out of its way to create the least comfortable living space and to suppress girls' self-expression, dignity, and self-respect. The chapter is embellished throughout with examples of attacks on self-respect, control, and dignity girls have experienced prior to incarceration, and how the experience of incarceration represents a continuation of what they had lived through before. Chapter 5, *Abuse as Intervention*, examines how this facility failed to qualify as a safe space, where physical, emotional, and cultural safety are guaranteed. Throughout the chapter, the stories that the girls relate highlight their past traumatic experiences, which staff's verbal, emotional, and psychological abuse often trigger.

Programming as If Girls Do Not Matter (Part II), examines how therapeutic programs that claim to heal traumas and respond to delinquent girls' unique needs and strengths, disempower young women by silencing them, demanding docility, and perpetuating domination, in reverence of ideals that have prevailed in the juvenile justice paradigm since the early 1800s. I argue that the reason why this happens is because such programming, too "small" to survive inside a carceral institution, bends to the demands of and is consequently subsumed by a hegemonic penal culture, primarily concerned with the punishment and regulation of "undesired" and "undeserving" youth, especially female youth of color.

Chapter 6, *We're All Hurting: The Paucity of Targeted Trauma Treatment*, highlights both the need for and the absence of systematic, comprehensive, therapeutic treatments that are tailored to each girl's needs and strengths, are informed by girls' violence-saturated life-stories, and are uninterrupted by girls' return to the community or transfer to camp. Chapter 7, *She tells us who we are: Empowerment, Juvenile Hall-style* discusses "Operation Empower" a so-called "gender-specific" empowerment and reintegration program that was implemented inside the institution, and reveals how its narrow conceptualization of empowerment contradicts its mission and purpose. Rather than empowering girls who participate in it, the program further oppresses them by silencing their voices, quashing their dissent, individualizing the context of their delinquency, and reinforcing antiquated gender normative ideas about what it means to be a woman. The hegemonic tone as well as content of the program increases feelings of inadequacy, self-blame, and helplessness.

Chapters 3–7 are each introduced by a young woman's life-story narrative. Chapter 8, the *Epilogue*, summarizes the analysis presented in the previous chapters and assesses the findings in light of past research and legislation. It juxtaposes the juvenile justice system's rhetoric and legislative commitments to juvenile justice agents' and institutions' actions and attempts to relate those to their causes and their consequences. In other words, this chapter details and provides arguments in support of the book's thesis and proposals for real reform toward a system that is truly helpful, nurturing, and 'responsive' to girls' needs. A list of all my respondents (names are pseudonyms), their age, and their race/ethnicity is found in Appendix A. My own self-reflections as a woman ethnographer are found in Appendix B. A sample letter from a detained girl to her *OE* counselor is found in Appendix C.

But before all that, an overview of my methodology, including the story of how I gained access to this institution, my sampling, data collection, and methodological framework. You will find all this in Chapter 2.

Notes

1 This is a US figure but the disproportionately male involvement in offending is universal. For example, male offenders represented 8 out of 10 court disposals in England and Wales (Youth Justice Board/Ministry of Justice, 2012–2013).

2 In several states, domestic violence is widely defined as violence among persons sharing the same household – not necessarily romantic partners. Therefore, fights between parents and children are classified as domestic violence and often result in mandatory arrests in those states.

3 Having grown up in a "collectivist" and traditional Mediterranean society, I am having trouble reconciling my cultural experience with this literature about gender differences in autonomy seeking. In my culture, men and women alike are strongly and voluntarily interdependent with their families, especially their parents. And although I believe that this emphasis on American men's independence craving, especially with respect to emotional attachment is largely manufactured, my evidence is anecdotal, and so I will concede that this must be the case, if the literature says so, but note that the literature is predominately North-Americanocentric.

References

Acoca, L. (1998). Outside/inside: The violation of American girls at home, on the streets, and in the juvenile justice system. *Crime and Delinquency*, *44*, 561–589.

Annie E. Casey Foundation. (2013). Reducing Youth Incarceration in the United States. Retrieved from www.aecf.org/m/resourcedoc/AECF-DataSnapshotYouthIncarceration-2013.pdf

Bandura, A. (1982). Self-efficacy mechanism in human agency. *American Psychologist, 37*(2): 122–147. doi:10.1037/0003-066X.37.2.122.

Belknap, J. (2001). *The invisible woman: Gender, crime and justice*. 2nd ed. Belmont, CA: Wadsworth.

Belknap, J., & Holsinger, K. (2006). The gendered nature of risk factors for delinquency. *Feminist Criminology*, *1*: 48–71.

Bernard, T., & Kurlychek, M. (2010). The cycle of juvenile justice (2nd ed.). New York, N.Y.: Oxford University Press.

Beyer, M. (1999). Recognizing the Child in the Delinquent. *Kentucky Children's Rights Journal.*

Bloom, B. (2003). *Gendered justice: Addressing female offenders*. Durham, N.C.: Carolina Academic Press.

Bloom, B., Owen, B., & Covington, S. (2003). *Gender Responsive Strategies: Research, Practice and Guiding Principles for Women Offenders*, National Institute of Corrections, US Department of Justice, Washington DC.

Braithwaite, J., & Pettit, P. (1994). Republican criminology and victim advocacy. *Law and Society Review, 28*(4), 765–776.

Brown, M. (2010). Negotiations of the living space: Life in the group home for girls who use violence. In Chesney-Lind, M., and Jones, N., (Eds.), *Fighting for girls: New perspectives on gender and violence*, 175–199. Albany, NY: SUNY Press.

Chamberlin, J. (1997). A Working Definition of Empowerment. *Psychiatric Rehabilitation Journal, 20*(4), 43–46.

Chesney-Lind, M. (1989). Girls' crime and woman's place: Toward a feminist model of female delinquency. *Crime and Delinquency, 35*(1), 5–29.

Chesney-Lind, M., & Paramore, V. (2001). Are girls getting more violent?: Exploring juvenile robbery trends. *Journal of Contemporary Criminal Justice, 17*(2), 142–166.

Chesney-Lind M., & Shelden, R. (1998). *Girls, delinquency, and juvenile justice* (2nd ed.). Belmont, CA: Wadsworth.

Conrad, S. M., Tolou-Shams, M., Rizzo, C. J., Placella, N., & Brown, L. K. (2014). Gender differences in recidivism rates for juvenile justice youth: The impact of sexual abuse. *Law and Human Behavior, 38*(4), 305–314.

Covington, S. (2007). The relational theory of women's psychological development: Implications for the Criminal Justice System. From R. Zaplin (Ed.) *Female Offenders: Critical Perspectives and Effective Interventions* – See NCJ-225923.

Covington, S., & Bloom, B. (2006). Gender-responsive treatment and services in correctional settings. In E. Leeder (Ed.) *Women and Therapy Journal, 29*(3), pp. 9–33.

Craig, W., & Pepler, D. (1998). Observations of Bullying and Victimization in the School Yard. *Canadian Journal of School Psychology, 13*(2), 41–59.

Crick, N. R., & Grotpeter, J. K. (1995). Relational aggression, gender, and social-psychological adjustment. *Child Development, 66*, 710–722.

Daly, K. (1992). Women's pathways to felony court: Feminist theories of lawbreaking and problems of representation. Southern California Review of Law and Women's Studies, *2*(1), 11–52.

Damen, H., Veerman, J., Vermulst, W., Nieuwhoff, A., De Meyer, A., & Scholte, R. (2017). Parental empowerment: Construct validity and reliability of a Dutch Empowerment Questionnaire (EMPO). *Journal of Child and Family Studies*, *26*(2), 424–436.

De Leon, B. H., & Teji, S. (2012). *Juvenile justice realignment in 2012* (Center on Juvenile and Criminal Justice policy brief). Retrieved from www.cjcj.org/uploads/cjcj/documents/Juvenile_Justice_Realignment_2012.pdf

Diemer, M. A., Kauffman, A., Koenig, N., Trahan, E., & Hsieh, C.-A. (2006). Challenging racism, sexism, and social injustice: Support for urban adolescents' critical consciousness development. *Cultural Diversity and Ethnic Minority Psychology, 12*(3), 444–460. http://dx.doi.org/10.1037/1099-9809.12.3.444

Dixon, A., Howie, P., & Starling, J. (2004). Psychopathology in female juvenile offenders. *Journal of Child Psychology and Psychiatry*, *45*(6), 1150–1158.

Eurostat (2016, May). Crime and Criminal Justice Statistics. Retrieved February 14, 2017 from http://ec.europa.eu/eurostat/statistics-explained/index.php/Crime_and_criminal_justice_statistics

Ex parte Crouse. 4 Whart. 9, Pa. (1838).

Feld, Barry C. (1997). Abolish the juvenile court: Youthfulness, criminal responsibility, and sentencing policy. (Symposium on the Future of the Juvenile Court). *Journal of Criminal Law and Criminology*, *88*(1), 68–136.

Fox, S. (1970). Juvenile Justice Reform: An Historical Perspective. *Stanford Law Review, 22*(6), 1187–1239. doi:10.2307/1227960.

Freire, P. (1973). *Education for critical consciousness.* New York, NY: Seabury

Freire, P. (2000). *Pedagogy of the oppressed* (30th anniversary ed.). (M. Bergman Ramos, Trans). NewYork: Continuum.

Gaarder, E., & Hesselton, D. (2012). Connecting restorative justice with gender-responsive programming. *Contemporary Justice Review*, *15*(3), 239–264.

Gavazzi, S. M., Yarcheck, C. M., & Chesney-Lind, M. (2006). Global risk indicators and the role of gender in a juvenile detention sample. *Criminal Justice and Behavior, 33*(5), 597–612.

George, T. E., & Yoon, A. H. *The gavel gap: Who sits in judgment on state courts? American Constitution Society for Law and Policy*. Available at: http://gavelgap.org/pdf/gavel-gap-report.pdf

Gilligan, C. (1982). *In a different voice*. Cambridge, MA: Harvard University Press.

Gilligan, C., Lyons, N. P., & Hanmer, T. J. (Eds.) (1990). *Making connections*. Cambridge, MA: Harvard University Press.

Goodkind, S. (2005). Gender-specific services in the juvenile justice system: A critical examination. *Affilia 20*(1): 52–70.

Goodkind, S., & Miller, D. L. (2006). A widening of the net of social control? 'Gender-specific' treatment for young women in the US juvenile justice system." *Journal of Progressive Human Services, 17*(1), 45–70.

Goodkind, S. (2009). You can be anything you want, but you have to believe it: Commercialized feminism in gender-specific programs for girls, *Signs, 34*(2), 397–422.

Hannah-Moffat, K. (2010). Sacrosanct or flawed: Risk, accountability and gender-responsive penal politics. *Current Issues in Criminal Justice, 22*(2), 193–215.

Harris, M., & Fallot, R. (2001). *Using trauma theory to design service systems*. San Francisco, CA: Jossey-Bass.

Hernández, P., Almeida, R., & Dolan-Del Vecchio, K. (2005). Critical Consciousness, Accountability, and Empowerment: Key Processes for Helping Families Heal. *Family Process, 44*(1), 105–119.

Herrera, V. M., & McCloskey, L. A. (2003). Sexual abuse, family violence, and female delinquency: Findings from a longitudinal study. *Violence Victimization, 18*(3), 319–334.

Hipwell, A. E., & Loeber, R. (2006). Do we know which interventions are effective for delinquent and disruptive girls? *Clinical Child and Family Psychology Review, 9*(3/4), 221–255.

Howell, J. C., Feld, B. C., Mears D. P., Farrington, D. P., Loeber, R., & Petechuk, D. (2013). *Bulletin 5: Young offenders and an effective response in the juvenile and adult justice systems: What Happens, what should happen, and what we need to know* (Study group on the transitions between juvenile delinquency and adult crime). Report presented to US Department of Justice. Retrieved from https://ncjrs.gov/pdffiles1/nij/grants/242935.pdf

Junger-Tas, J., & Decker, S. H. (Eds.) (2006). *International Handbook of Juvenile Justice*. Dordrecht: Springer. Google Scholar.

Juvenile Justice and Delinquency Prevention Appropriations Authorization (1992), Pub. L. 102–586, § 1, 106 Stat. 4982.

Loeber, R., & Hay, D. (1997). Key issues in the development of aggression and violence from childhood to early adulthood. *Annual Review of Psychology, 48*, 371–410.

Logan, C., & Rausch, S. (1985). Why deinstitutionalizing status offenders is pointless. *Crime and Delinquency, 31*, 501–517.

Mack, J. W. (1909). The juvenile court. *Harvard Law Review, 23*, 104–122.

Matthews, B., & Hubbard, D. J. (2008). Moving ahead: Five essential elements for working effectively with girls. *Journal of Criminal Justice, 36*, 494–502.

Mendel, R. A. (2010). *The Missouri model: Reinventing the practice of rehabilitating youthful offenders*. Report presented to the Annie E. Casey Foundation. Retrieved from www.aecf.org/m/resourcedoc/aecf-MissouriModelFullreport-2010.pdf

Miller, J. B. (1976). *Toward a new psychology of women*. Boston: Beacon Press.

Miller, J. B. (1986). *What do we mean by relationships?* Work in Progress No. 22. Wellesley, MA: Stone Center, Working Paper Series.

Miller, J. B. (1990). *Connections, disconnections, and violations*. Work in Progress No. 33. Wellesley, MA: Stone Center, Working Paper Series.

MS Foundation for Women National Girls Initiative. (1993). *Programmed Neglect, Not Seen, Not Heard: Report on Girls Programming in the United States*. New York, NY: MS Foundation for Women.

Odem, M., & Schlossman, S. (1991). Guardians of Virtue: The Juvenile Court and Female Delinquency in Early 20th-Century Los Angeles. *Crime & Delinquency, 37*(2), 186–203.

OJJDP, Office of Juvenile Justice and Delinquency Prevention (1998). *Guiding Principles for Promising Female Programming*. Washington, DC: US Department of Justice.

Ouimette, P., Kimerling, R., Shaw, J., & Moos, R. (2000). Physical and sexual abuse among women and men with substance use disorders. *Alcoholism Treatment Quarterly, 18*, pp. 7–17.

Owen, B., & Bloom, B. (1997). *Profiling the needs of young female offenders*. Paper presented at the meeting of the American Society of Criminology, San Diego, CA.

Packel, L. (1976). The History of Pennsylvania's juvenile justice institutions: A sesquicentennial review. *Villanova Law Review, 22*(1) Available at: https://digitalcommons.law.villanova.edu/vlr/vol. 22/iss1/4

Parsons, R. J. (1989). Empowerment for role alternatives for low income minority girls; A group work approach. In J. A. B. Lee (Ed.), *Group work with the poor and oppressed* (pp. 27–46). New York: The Howarth Press.

Peck, J., Leiber, M., & Brubaker, S. (2014). Gender, Race, and Juvenile Court Outcomes. *Youth Violence and Juvenile Justice, 12*(3), 250–267.

People v. Turner. (1870). 55 Ill. 280.

Pisciotta, A. W. (1982). Saving the children: The promise and practice of parens patriae, 1838–1898. *Crime & Delinquency, 28*, 410–425.

Platt, A. (1969). The Child Savers. Chicago: University of Chicago Press.

Poe-Yamagata, E., & Butts, J. A. (1996). Female offenders in the juvenile justice system: Statistic summary. Pittsburgh, PA: National Center for Juvenile Justice.

Pollack, S. (2000). Reconceptualizing Women's agency and empowerment: Challenges to self-esteem discourse and women's lawbreaking. *Women & Criminal Justice, 12*(1), 75.

Puzzanchera, C. (2013). *Juvenile Arrests, 2011*. Retrieved from www.ojjdp.gov/pubs/244476.pdf

Puzzanchera, C., & Ehrmann, S. (2018). *Spotlight on Girls in the Juvenile Justice System*. Washington, DC: US Department of Justice, Office of Juvenile Justice and Delinquency Prevention, National Center for Juvenile Justice. Retrieved from: www.ncjj.org/pdf/Data%20snapshots%202016/DataSnapshot_Girls2015.pdf

Rappaport, J. (1987). Terms of empowerment/exemplars of prevention: Toward a theory for community psychology. *American Journal of Community Psychology, 15*(2), 121–145.

Raley, G. A. (1995). *The JJDP Act: A second look*. Washington, DC: US Department of Justice, Office of Juvenile Justice and Delinquency Prevention.

Randall, M., & Haskell, L. (2013). Trauma-informed approaches to law: Why restorative justice must understand trauma and psychological coping. *The Dalhousie Law Journal, 36*, 501–533.

Rendleman, D. (1971). Parens Patriae: From Chancery to the Juvenile Court. *South Carolina Law Review, 23*, 205. Available at: https://scholarlycommons.law.wlu.edu/cgi/viewcontent.cgi?article=1390&context=wlufc

Richards, K. (2011, March). Trends in juvenile detention in Australia. Retrieved February 14, 2017, from www.aic.gov.au/publications/current%20series/tandi/401-420/tandi416.html

Schaffner, L. (2006). *Girls in trouble with the law*. Piscataway, NJ: Rutgers University Press.

Sharpe, G. (2016). Re-imagining justice for girls: A new agenda for research. *Youth Justice, 16(*1), 3–17.

Shelden, Randall G. (1998). Gender bias in the juvenile justice system. *Juvenile & Family Court Journal, 49*(1), 11–25.

Siegel, J., & Williams, L. (2003). The relationship between child sexual abuse and female delinquency and crime: A prospective study. *Journal of Research in Crime and Delinquency, 40*(1), 71–94.

Simmons, C., H., & Parsons, R. J. (1983). Developing internality and perceived competence: The empowerment of adolescent girls. *Adolescence, 18*(72), 917–922.

Stohr, M., Jonson, C. L., & Cullen, F. T. (2014). Lessons learned. In F. T. Cullen, C. L. Jonson, & M. Stohr (Eds.), *The American prison: Imagining a different future*. Los Angeles, CA: Sage Publications.

Taylor, J. M., Gilligan, C., & Sullivan, A. M. (1995). *Between voice and silence: Women and girls, race and relationship*. Cambridge, MA: Harvard University Press.

Teplin, L., Abram, K., McClelland, G., Dulcan, M., & Mericle, A. (2002). Psychiatric disorders in youth in juvenile detention. *Archives of General Psychiatry, 59*, 1133–1143.

Totten, M. (2002). *The special needs of females in Canada's Youth Justice System: An account of some young women's views*. Ottawa: Department of Justice Canada

Tripodi, S. J., & Pettus-Davis, C. (2013). Histories of childhood victimization and subsequent mental health problems, substance use, and sexual victimization for a sample of incarcerated women in the US. *International Journal of Law and Psychiatry, 36*, 30–40.

Underwood, M. K. (2003). *Social aggression among girls*. Guilford Press, New York.

Valentine Foundation and Women's Way (1990). *A Conversation about Girls*. Philadelphia, PA: Valentine Foundation and Women's Way.

Watts, R. J., Diemer, M. A., & Voight, A. M. (2011). Critical consciousness: Current status and future directions. In C. A. Flanagan & B. D. Christens (Eds.), Youth civic development: Work at the cutting edge. *New Directions for Child and Adolescent Development, 134*, 43–57.

Young, I. M. (1994). Punishment, treatment, empowerment: Three approaches to policy for pregnant addicts. *Feminist Studies, 20*(1), 32.

Youth Justice Board/Ministry of Justice. Youth justice statistics bulletin 2012–2013. Available at https://assets.publishing.service.gov.uk/government/uploads/system/uploads/attachment_data/file/278549/youth-justice-stats-2013.pdf

Zavlek, S., & Maniglia, R. (2007). Developing correctional facilities for female juvenile offenders: Design and programmatic considerations. *Corrections Today, 69*(4), 58–63.

Zimmerman, M. A. (1995). Psychological empowerment: Issues and illustrations. *American Journal of Psychology, 23*, 581–599.

Chapter 2

This study

No-one is outside society, the question is where he stands within it.
(Sociologist C. Wright Mills, 1959)

In this study I attempted to adopt a "feminist qualitative framework," which was informed in part by the critiques of Stanley and Wise (1983), Kimberlé Crenshaw's (1989) intersectionality theory, and the work of Gaarder and Belknap (2002), and Belknap, Holsinger, and Dunn (1997) with respect to the design, the data collection, analysis, and discussion. I collected information from casual conversations with, and observations of juvenile hall staff and visitors inside and outside the girls' unit, to gain a holistic understanding of the culture in my research site. The most important goal of my approach, however, was to give voice to the girls detained in it, highlight their experiential accounts, and shed a light to life as they live it. This goal was realized through a qualitative design that included semi-focused interviews, observations, and content analysis of sent letters. All names, including location and programming titles have been changed to protect the participants' anonymity.

Before I discuss my methods in more detail, I would like to situate my data within the setting in which they were collected by describing the research site. Following that, a brief introduction to this study's interview respondents and how they came to participate in this project. But, first, I feel it is necessary to offer some background information with respect to this study's starting point, its evolution, and its final form. This account is aimed at providing readers with "access to details of the contextually-located reasoning processes" (Stanley, 1990, p. 209) that shaped both my research questions as well as my analytical approach.

Study background

The journey to this project started semi-accidentally during volunteer week at the University where I completed my doctoral program. On my way to class, I walked through the several tables on both sides of the path, representing local and national non-profit organizations seeking to appeal to college students' volunteerism. Not too eager to get myself to the classroom on that sunny day, I wandered around looking at informational pamphlets instead. At the time, I was teaching undergraduate courses at a nearby state college, and so, I was interested in having guest speakers who worked on fields not traditionally associated with Criminology show my students that there are careers other than law enforcement and corrections they could pursue after graduation. I stopped by the booth of a local chapter of a national organization focusing on advancing girls' wellbeing and potential. I liked that organization a lot (I still do) because they advance a positive "girl power" message recognizing that this power depends not only on personal attributes but also cultural and socio-economic forces. One would arguably say that the message is grounded on a feminist understanding of social organization, and is reflected in research and practice in which this NGO engages. I invited the Volunteer Coordinator to my classroom and asked her to emphasize the NGO's involvement in primary and secondary prevention of girls' offending and victimization, and she enthusiastically accepted.

Fast forward to the day of her guest talk, the speaker discussed the importance of gender empowerment (as manifested in girls' speaking up, bending repressive sexist norms, joining forces with other similarly situated girls to fight against discrimination of any kind, etc.) in preventing delinquency. She then proceeded to say that her organization was currently collaborating with the Department of Education and the Department of Probation to design and implement a gender-responsive reintegration program that sought to empower girls inside the juvenile hall. I looked up from my notes and doodles with sparked interest: "You are going *inside* juvenile hall to teach all that?" I asked in disbelief. "Yes," she said. They had never done anything like that before; they had worked with "at risk" girls outside corrections, but never with system-involved girls, and never inside the jail. It was an innovative program that they felt very excited about. After class, I approached her and once the conventional "thank-yous" and "that-was-greats" were said and done, I repeated my question. I said something like, how are they going to encourage girls to stand up, be brave, use their words, employ power, in a controlled environment designed to suppress all forms of self-expression? "That is a good question," she conceded. My question was not "good," it was an *empirical* one, I thought. I told her I might be interested in looking at that NGO's program in juvenile hall, perhaps to conduct a research evaluation to see how effective it was. My guest speaker said she would talk to the program's Director (who worked for the Department of Education) and see if he would be OK with that.

He was. That "researchers from the University of California," as my faculty advisor and I were presented in the corresponding email, were interested in a program he had pioneered seemed appealing to him. He formally invited me to a fundraising dinner for the program, which had a name: "*Operation Empower*"[1] (herein after *OE*). I wouldn't have to pay for the dinner, he promised and I sighed with relief. From what I could gather, the price tag was out of my budget.

"Just come and listen to what the speakers and all the people involved have to say, and we'll go from there," he said in the email. *OE's* funding was expected to expire within a year or so and they were seeking the stamp of approval of my prestigious research institution to ground their funding renewal request. Funds for programming were getting shorter and shorter, even as the federal government encouraged states to adopt gender-specific interventions and research; the country was entering an economic recession of great proportion, a recession that had hit California hard. Nevertheless, the dinner was lavish. As I ordered the salmon, I felt guilty and imposturous. This was all happening too fast, and too easy. Then, a couple of charismatic speakers took the podium in the middle of the room and using PowerPoint they presented on the rationale of the program, its purpose, and its significance. "As the number of girls behind detention rises, we need more programs that are responsive to the uniqueness of women's experience as offenders, victims, or both" was the take home message. *OE* would respond to delinquent girls' needs especially with respect to traumas, addiction, poverty, and educational neglect by starting inside juvenile hall and continuing outside of it, offering reintegration assistance. Personal stories of delinquent girls were intertwined with empirical evidence on female pathways to crime in a presentation that was heartfelt and effective. Wealthy patrons around me teared up and wrote checks. I left a tip for the waiters, set up an email appointment with Joe, the program Director, and left content. This program was founded on the pathways literature. They wanted me to look at it, evaluate it, and publish on it. I had found my dissertation project.

My project was going to be great. First, I had bought into the program's philosophy. I was working on something I was passionate about. Second, my methodology would rock. I could imagine tons of publications in my future: it would be a mixed methods design. Random assignment in two groups, pre- and post-surveys, observations, and interviews. Third, my faculty advisor was on board too. In fact, when I talked to him about all this, he said that he had seen an article about that very program in the local paper, and had thought about me. What a coincidence! Or maybe karma! All was going to be well.

Of course, all did not end up being good, or at least not "fast," nor "easy" as I had initially thought. My advisor remained on my side until the study was completed. However, my study's "sponsor," and *OE* Director, Joe did not. Also, it turned out that a rigorous evaluation of the program was impossible, partially because there was no concrete program to work with. Participants in the counseling sessions that *OE* was exhausted in were arbitrarily selected, so random assignment was way off the table. I did try to talk to the Director about a semi-experimental design but he seemed uninterested in helping me to do that. Also, because detention for most girls lasted only a few weeks at a time, many of them received the "treatment" either sporadically (each time they would be readmitted) or for a short time, complicating the measurement of program effects. I was then going to administer entry and exit surveys to all detainees, but the logistics of this were also very complicated for reasons too tedious to mention here.

Although my research design was approved with the survey instrument included, I ended up never using it.

But the most important change in the direction and scope of this project came as a result of the program Director's dissatisfaction with me personally. Once he introduced me to the probation managers with whom I was to sign a contract, his role in the project became significantly smaller, something with which he seemed unhappy. Here is a condensed timeline of what followed and how it led to my fallout with Joe. After probation managers agreed to give me access to the unit, my research project underwent rigorous examination from two Human Subjects Review Boards: my University's, and Probation's (Probation has a research office too). By the time all documentation was reviewed, revised, resubmitted, and approved and the Probation Department finally signed off the contract between my institution and their institution to allow me to do what my research protocol said I was going to do, my University's IRB expired (it had been a year). I filed for an extension, which was swiftly approved. After all this, the research contract required review and approval by the County Board of Supervisors. It is still a mystery to me who these supervisors are and with what qualifications or rationale they evaluate research proposals, but I was told not to worry. It took three more months, until I finally got the Board's approval. While I was awaiting the Board of Supervisors' decision, I did two things: first, I become a volunteer in probation (VIP), as my contract required me to do. I signed up for the one-day training, underwent a background check, and finally got my VIP badge. Second, I visited the girls' unit in juvenile hall to make my acquaintance with the supervisors and frontline staff. The supervisor at the time asked me, since I was now a volunteer, to actually volunteer. They needed help with programming, "any programming I don't care," she said, because they had nothing. Although that surprised me, given that probation management had previously told me that they "were doing great things" with the girls in juvenile hall, I did not hesitate to say yes. So I did volunteer, a couple of times. One of these times, a detained girl asked me for a music CD which I did bring in my next volunteer visit. I showed the CD to the frontline staff and they said that I could not give it to her, and I complied, apologizing to the girl later. Then, once the Board's decision came through, I went back to the unit for a recruitment session (see below). I had been instructed to call each time before I went in, which I always did. Having waited that long, I started interviewing 18-year-olds who had agreed to participate in my study immediately (I had to wait for parental consent from the minors).

Unbeknown to me, Joe became furious. Why had I started interviewing without asking him first? Why was I interviewing girls that he had not suggested I interviewed? Why was I doing programming? That was unprofessional and would compromise my researcher credibility! Why was I bringing gifts to inmates? Did I not know that was not allowed? Who did I think I was? If it was not for him, I would have not been there. I had better not get on his bad side, because and I quote: "If *I* don't want you in there, you are not going in there!"

All this was yelled at me over a phone call. Truth to be told, I might have done some yelling too. Nowhere in my contract or any other documentation I had signed over the past year and a half did it say that I was required to give notice to Joe about starting data collection. I was very firm with him about the boundaries he was crossing. I explained, however, why I was "doing programming" and that I saw nothing wrong with helping in any which way I could. If anything, my prior familiarity with girls in the unit could create rapport with my potential respondents. Immaturely, I pointed out that since I had both training and experience in research while Joe did not, he was not in a position to critique my researcher-hood. That infuriated him. Although I apologized for the CD incident, which had reached him through the grapevine, he continued to reprimand me. Needless to say, I decided to cut all ties with him, which I made very clear. I was fearful that he would derail a project I had been working toward for months, but thankfully, nothing terrible happened after that phone call. *OE* counselors avoided talking to me because of him, but that is just about all the obstruction Joe caused to my project, which after a couple of interviews took a complete turn anyway.

It was not going to be about *OE* after all, and not because or just because Joe had not wanted it to be, but because my preliminary interview and observational data steered the direction of my research inquiry to a different direction. I saw in my respondents' narratives something much bigger and more important than merely evaluating a program: I saw life through their eyes, and thought that their life-stories should be *the* story. *OE* would be evaluated as a peripheral, though theoretically significant part of that story, but the study would center on detained girls' lived realities first and foremost.

Setting

The research site for this study is a secure custody juvenile institution in Southern California. My interview data were collected inside the (only) female unit of this institution.[2] The institution is run by the county's Probation Department, which also runs four more secure and non-secure facilities, only one of which accepts (a limited number of) girls. In other words, the research site is the only secure detention facility for incarcerated girls in this county. It is used both to detain arrestees awaiting Juvenile Court hearings, as well as those who have been adjudicated and are awaiting placement in in-patient drug treatment, or in some sort of community-based alternative, such as intensive probation, house arrest, etc. A large proportion of the residents in this unit, however, and most of my participants, were there to serve a confinement sentence, a consequence of having violated probation, especially by running away from treatment placement or from home.

Ironically, the institution is located in a central, busy, and popular among youth location, across from a large shopping center with retail stores, restaurants, and movie theaters. The vast majority of the youthful inmates residing inside juvenile hall are familiar with the neighborhood; most have lived all their lives in this or adjacent communities, and frequent the shopping mall when not detained on the other side. On that other side of the boulevard, is our justice complex with courts, the jail, an institution for parentless children (orphanage), and of course, the juvenile detention center (hall). The juvenile hall blends in well, just another sand-colored government building in Southern California, a large parking lot in its front, an even larger highway in its back, and some palm trees scattered around it. Once you enter the tall double doors, the atmosphere turns grimmer. An ID check point, lockers to place restricted items like cell phones, a couple of guards ready to be done with their shift, and a sitting area for you to wait for a guard to come and escort you inside the institution. Parents, grandparents, siblings, public defenders, psychiatrists, they all have to go through the same process, although some get called back faster than visitors. A few times, I was let in through the "privileged" side, the one on the left that the employees coming in to start their shift use. There was no difference really. Most times, though, I sat on the plastic chairs across from parents or other caretakers who were visiting their children. I would smile cordially to them in the beginning, but they were not having it. As my data collection progressed, I would not smile either. Once my escort walked me through a sequence of doors that led to the "central monitoring room" as I called it, there was another wait. This time the "centrals" would call a staff member from the corresponding unit each visitor cared to enter. Staff members in the girls' unit often took their time, and, frustrated, one of the "centrals" would magnanimously volunteer to escort me herself instead. The winding path one takes to reach the Unit "G" goes through grassy patches and tiny, wire-fenced courts with basketball hoops. I rarely saw them in use, though when I did, it was always boys who played, two at most, a guard watching close by. Sometimes on my way to the Unit I would cross paths with a group of juvenile detainees walking on lockstep, hands behind their back, in between two staff members, but more often than that it was just single detainees plus staff duos I would see.

Unit "G" a two story courtyard-style building with the staff station, a large, U-shaped desk with computers, security monitor screens, folders, telephones, and a microphone for announcements, located near the entrance, allowing visual access to all room doors. White and grey colors decorated the walls, floors, and furniture. Inmates wore baggy orange-colored shirts and blue pants, and were required to put their hair up. Some were working in the kitchen area, others cleaning up, a few sat on tables across from suited adults, but most were in their rooms.

The unit is designed to house a maximum of 40 girls, but at least in the 18 months it took for the data collection to conclude, this number was rarely reached. When this study began, this institution was faced with a vast increase in the number of female detainees, which averaged about 30–35 per day. However, the trend eventually changed directions. Due to a shift of emphasis toward home-based rather than incarcerative post-adjudication options, by the end of the study the detainee population had dropped. According to correctional staff in the research site, this change was a mere consequence of the budget crisis in California rather than a result of a conscious policy decision based on principles of de-institutionalization or rehabilitation. To quote one of the frontline staff in the unit, "it's not because these girls don't deserve to be locked, up, it's because the county has no money, *that's* why they send them to house arrest."

This study took place during the implementation of *OE*, the gender-specific reintegration program I discussed previously. As mentioned, at that point in time, *OE* was the first one of its kind in Southern California. Among other things, *OE* promised to guide girls toward successful reintegration by helping them in a non-stigmatizing but rather respectful and inclusive manner to develop values and skills they need to become "confident, productive, and responsible." The program's goal was to enable girls to "develop a re-entry plan, connect with their parents and their community, improve their communication skills, achieve self-expression, manage negative feelings, and generally plan a healthier lifestyle."[3]

Gathering from the county's probation website, it is not surprising that such a program was endorsed in one of its youth facilities. The department's stated mission is to use "efficient, innovative, and evidence based practices to promote lawful and productive lifestyles," while its employees are "committed to delivering services with integrity and in a manner which respects the rights and dignity of individuals." *OE* seemed compatible with both empirical evidence on "what works" with juvenile women, and commitments to humanitarian ideals, it was therefore compatible with the mission juvenile hall claimed to promote.

Sampling

Between October 2008 and May 2010, I conducted interviews with 28 young women confined in juvenile hall's Unit G. Because of the low numbers of girls in this institution, as well as the high frequency of the same girls returning into it, all detainees in this unit were eligible for participation. The only group exempt from eligibility were "wards of the state," whom the juvenile court judge (acting as their legal guardian) did not allow me to interview. County Probation made selecting participants a taxing endeavor by insisting that I obtained *written* rather than verbal consent from parents of minors. Parents or other legal guardians who would without hesitation consent over the phone to their daughter's participation in my study, rarely followed through by mailing the signed consent form back. This, and the frontline staff's demand that I interviewed respondents only in two, small time-windows in the weekends, delayed the research tremendously. Given the high turnover rate in the unit, it was not unusual that by the time I was able to go into the site with a signed consent form at hand, my respondent had either been released to house arrest, or transferred to a camp or a drug treatment facility.

I recruited respondents through announcing to groups of 10 to 15 (depending on how busy the unit was) the purpose and method of my study. Once in the unit, frontline staff used their microphone to ask (bark at, really) all girls to come out of their rooms immediately and congregate in the common area. Once out, I would inform potential participants of the voluntary nature of the study and hand them an information sheet. If they were interested, they would fill out the name and phone number of their legal guardian on the study information sheet, so that I could contact them for their consent. If the potential respondent was over 18, she would print and sign her name on the appropriate space on the sheet and would be interviewed within the following week.

During the course of the study, I recruited about 154 eligible girls. Of those, only a very small number (seven) did not return a filled-out information sheet. An even smaller number of guardians (two) whose daughters had wanted to participate in my study refused to consent. However, the response rate, as measured by the proportion of returned signed consent forms sent to guardians who consented over the phone was very small ($n = 15$). As mentioned before, attrition (respondents for whom I had consent forms but by the time I was able to interview them had left the unit) was also very common.

In addition to the qualitative interviews, my findings are based in part on the content analysis of 37 letters sent between May 2007 and March 2008 by girls released from Unit G to their *OE* counselor. These letters, with sender names reducted, were given to me months before my data collection started, by the *OE* Director, the only person who was also in possession of the senders' contact information. Due to the small number of letters, I did not sample them, but rather, I read and analyzed all 37 of them.

Participants

I ended up with a large amount of qualitative data collected through one to two-hour interviews (average interview length was about one hour and 30 minutes) with 28 detained girls,[4] ages 14 to 19 (average age was 16). A few of the respondents ($n = 3$) were interviewed more than once. Half (14) of all my respondents were adults at the time of the interview.

Regarding race/ethnicity, the majority ($n = 19$) of the girls identified as Latina/Mexican, and the rest said they were white ($n = 7$), and African American ($n = 2$). Interestingly, one of the black girls, as well as one of the white girls said that while their race label was assigned to them by others, they saw themselves as "Mexican."

With the exception of three first-timers, all other girls had been inside this facility multiple times in the past, some of them as many as 10 times. The average number of times served in this unit by the time of the interview was between four and five. Consistent with past research (ABA/NBA, 2001) this study showed that the most common reason for being locked up was probation violation, most often for a status offense such as running away, not showing up to probation meetings, or being incorrigible, coupled with a "dirty" drug test. Four of the girls I interviewed were pregnant at the time, and while nobody in my sample had kids, several of them had had experiences with terminated pregnancies in the past. Notably, all girls in my sample were or had been drug users. The most popular drug among my sample was methamphetamine. In terms of socioeconomic background, the group of my respondents was multiply marginalized (Vigil, 2008), and exacerbating the effect of this marginalized status, family dysfunction, sexual and physical victimization, educational neglect, and domestic violence were present in the narratives of all 28 girls I interviewed.

Procedure and measures

The discussion in the current study is based on the analysis of data collected through interviews and observations, and on content analysis. The purpose of this content analysis was to gain a rich, in-depth understanding of the experience of girls who had completed the program, and were at the time either back in the community, or had been transferred into a treatment camp following their incarceration. My aim was to analyze these written narratives in order to identify patterns and common themes that reveal information about the transition of these young girls from the controlled environment of secure detention to the less restrictive treatment facility, or to the free yet problematic environment which may foster conditions linked to delinquency and victimization. Another purpose was to discover how the *OE* program helped, if at all, in that transition, as it promised. This portion of the study was entirely exploratory. There were no anticipated outcomes or hypotheses to be tested by looking at these artifacts; rather I sought after patterns and recurring themes, which would sustain a more focused theoretical approach and perhaps help to interpret the findings of this study as a whole.

The interview process, as well as the wording of the questions in this study, draws heavily on Bellknap et al.'s (1997) method of interviewing delinquent girls in Ohio with the purpose of assessing the experiences and needs of this particular population. Although that study used focus groups rather than one-on-one interviewing, the current study applied similar techniques used by the focus group expert, in order to create a comfortable environment, and encourage open discussion of sensitive or not issues, while remaining focused on the purpose of the interview. Although I did not know it at the time, I intuitively (especially after the first couple of interviews) decided to use a method that Sue Cannon (1989) suggests is most appropriate when interviewing individuals who are undergoing traumatic situations about topics that are sensitive in nature. I used a conversational approach that would allow my respondents a choice as to how to tell their story and how much to reveal about their experiences and feelings. For example, having read the literature, I was expecting that many of my respondents would have been victims of past sexual abuse, and although I was interested in recording such experiences, I was very cautious, and self-conscious about bringing this up; I did not want to re-traumatize anyone, and to be honest, I was a little nervous about my reaction to hearing about it. I thought long about how to go about all this and decided to let things happen in my respondents' terms. I never initiated discussion of sexual abuse or of any sort of victimization topic, but those nevertheless made their way into the narratives. It turned out that my expectation was overly optimistic, as not only "many" but 25/28 of my respondents reported some form of sexual victimization and 27 of them reported physical abuse. These reports entered the interview narrative "naturally," if you can call anything about a childhood rape story natural. My first "interview" question after a light introductory small talk would always be something like: "Would you like to tell me what happened to bring you in here?" which would typically be followed by: "You mean, this time?," which evolved into a life-story narrative I had very little to do with structuring. As Cannon (1989) notes, this life-story method of interviewing produces an uninterrupted flow of rich qualitative data, and allows respondents "to fragment their experiences themselves if they so wish in order to evade difficult and painful issues" (p. 65).

Bellknap et al. (1997) also collected observations *while* their interviews were going on. In fact, researchers were observing participants in the focus group in an attempt to obtain rich and more in-depth information about them. The current study employed a similar method. Whereas only one researcher was present at the time of the interview, observational data were also recorded. Interviews were audio-taped in their majority (with the exception of two cases: in the first instance I forgot my recorder at home, and in the second the recorder malfunctioned). On the other hand, observations were written down in my note pad, although some personal notes mostly pertaining to my feelings were recorded in my car immediately before or after an interview.

Most interviews were audio-taped in my digital recorder and were transcribed within one week. For the interviews I was unable to record, I took detailed notes of the respondent's answers and I transcribed those within one day of the interview. Most interviews took place inside the unit in a private room upstairs, usually reserved for small group counseling sessions. Although there was a camera inside and glass windows in the entrance door of the room, it was otherwise a private space ideal for confidential conversations. A few interviews were conducted in the common, open-space area also (ironically) referred to as the "cafeteria," or "recreation" room. The room was loud enough, mostly due to staff conversations and the TV, which was almost always on, but we were allowed to sit in a relatively secluded corner, where nobody other than the respondent and I would be able to listen to the discussion. Whereas this space made it difficult for the audio tapes to be transcribed, it also provided me with an opportunity to collect a vast and rich amount of observational data as I was able to take notes of several interesting incidents that took place in the unit, and to better observe staff's interactions with the inmates.

As already mentioned, interviews were semi-structured and followed a storytelling approach. My prompts revolved around the following topics: the juvenile justice system, childhood experiences, familial and peer relationships, and views and attitudes about social institutions. Sometimes, if not volunteered, I would ask my respondents to give me some information about their experience inside Unit G, and in particular, their interactions with staff, counselors, and other residents, and the availability of treatment or recreational programs; their thoughts about their own offending (causes, consequences, justifications) and about their future. I would always end my interview questions by asking for their suggestions as to what should change or remain the same inside and outside the particular facility, and in society in general, in order for them and other girls in similar situations to succeed and become happy.

Similar to Gaarder and Belknap (2002), I also followed Taylor et al.'s (1995) method, and concluded the interview with asking each respondent to switch places with me, ask me any questions she may have concerning my role as a researcher, and my understanding or lack thereof of her answers, and to provide any comment, reaction, or feedback on the interview that had just preceded. This became one of the most interesting and important parts of the process, as it not only it countered the exploitative nature of social research, and perhaps leveled the field between my respondents and me, but also because it some times yielded the most insightful, while other times, the most rich and multidimensional data.

"Girls" and "young women"

You may have noticed that I use "girls" and sometimes "young women" interchangeably to refer to my study's participants. This work in all its iterations has been reviewed enough times in the past for me to know that many of my colleagues find the use of the tem "girl" jarring. I do not personally have a problem with it myself, as I belong to the movement that wants to reclaim the word and give it a new, positive undertone. I also personally find it less jarring than the term "young woman," which I have heard many male politicians and pundits in the US use to advance paternalistic, pretend-caring agendas aiming to regulate women. However, I do acknowledge that "girls" is a term that has been used to infantilize and consequently disempower women, and I do respect the concerns with my using it. I hope my readers assess the word in the context and intent it is employed, and accept it, perhaps get inspired to re-claim it as nothing to shun away from. But if you are still concerned with it, dear reader, I apologize for offending you as this was not my intention.

A note on going native

Another critique I have received in the past is that, similar to other field researchers before me, I have contracted the research disease known as "going native," a pejorative term to describe a process by which bias arises during ethnographic work. As someone who has read my fair share of research methods textbooks, "going native," or being a researcher who, in Bloor and Woods' (2006) words "adopts the perspective of their own participants and consequently may also adopt their participants' particular biases" (p. 26), is something I was concerned about.

It was partially with that concern in mind that when conducting interviews, I asked questions only when absolutely necessary to clarify my respondents' statements and to keep the conversation going and focused (although very often it veered off topic). I made a conscious effort to leave the interview structure up to the respondent as much as it was up to me. In presenting my findings, I tried to place my respondents' life-stories, thoughts and interpretations center-stage, although there is a lot of my perspective and inferences weaved in the analysis as well. I tried to be clear and honest about my analytical contributions to these stories.

I welcome critiques relating to "*erroneous*" analysis, and I am open to hearing alternative inferences made by anyone reading this monograph. But I take offense to critiques of "*biased*" analysis because I do not fake detachment from the reality I am studying, or because I color my discussion with personal sentiment. There is no value-free research, only research consciously attempting to mask the values, interests, and particular concerns researchers hold. As Stanley and Wise (1983) cautioned, social scientists who engage in feminist research should challenge "traditional" "hygienic" methodology that distances the researcher from the researched. My value-system as a researcher and woman is organized around social justice; it is why I chose to become a criminologist in the first place. So, yes, when I observed gendered injustices and abuses against my study's participants, I called them that, not something more diplomatic; I was honest about the fact that I was disturbed by these injustices; I did not pretend I had no reactions to them. I do not think that makes me biased, only a human.

Of course, my respondents' life-stories are filtered through my own experiences as well. Again, I do not claim machine-like accuracy and objectivity, but it is conscious subjectivity that I acknowledge, not bias. All research, even quantitative work, contains some autobiographical elements. I aimed for research that produces accountable knowledge. Because this research is grounded on life-stories it does not mean that *my* life-story is completely absent. As a feminist researcher studying other women I draw from the work of other feminist researchers:

> We draw in our own experiences to understand those of our respondents. Thus, their lives are filtered through us and the filtered stories of our lives are present (whether we admit it or not) in our written accounts. Surely it is better to acknowledge this and explore it rather than subscribe to false notions of "objectivity" or to collapse and confuse our respondents' experiences with our own.
>
> (Cotterill & Letherby, 1993, p. 74)

My experiences are, of course, shaped by my academic training and interests in critical criminology and restorative justice, and my familiarity with the

Gender-Responsive literature, which the current study triggered. I believe this is reflected in my analysis. But my experiences are also shaped by my personal background. I was and still am very conscious of the social distance between my respondents and myself; unlike them, I received great education and I acknowledge the privilege and power that comes with this; I have never been "in trouble with the law" nor have I ever carried a deviant stigma; I grew up relatively poor, yet enjoyed the social capital that my family's middle-class status conferred, and I was definitely nowhere close to experiencing the economic marginality my respondents had. I have experienced no kind of marginality at all. And, there's also the generational gap. I was an adult interviewing minors or just-turned adults.

I know these differences are seen as handicaps, but in my case, they worked in both the researcher and the researched's favor: I wore my "outsider" status on my sleeve and let girls guide me through a journey of an unknown territory: their lives. I listened carefully like very few if any person had before, out of sheer interest, not because I was trying to figure them out, or find out their needs, or determine which treatment program they should be placed in. And from what my respondents told me, that felt cathartic, like giving a confession of sorts, although better than that because the priest had heard all that before and also, priests judge. "You just listen; you don't judge; you are a good person," I was told, and although that was a little too kind, if you ask me, at least most girls believed it. I could also gather that by enlightening me, an educated grown woman about things that were common knowledge to them, they felt useful and somewhat empowered. So, social distance served this project and its participants well.

But it was not all distance. I shared many experiences with the girls I interviewed too. I am an immigrant, and although I have been told many times that I am "not that kind of immigrant" (meaning the target of xenophobic, racist sentiment), this status undermines the privilege I enjoy as a university professor. I am not marginalized, but I am an "other" and I will always be an "other." I look "white," but once I open my mouth to speak, I am placed in a racial/ethnic category (Latina, probably Colombian, is what I get most often, after "hi" changes to "hola."). I do not claim to live in the perpetual fear of harassment, disrespect, aggressive language, and deportation that many Latina immigrants do, but I *have* been publically and privately harassed in racist terms. I also have experienced insecurity, especially in interactions with federal law enforcement, because I know, even though I am a lawful resident, I am not "one of us." In that respect, I share some of the insecurities and fears that come with "otherising" that my respondents have been subjected to.

Last, I am a woman, an adult girl, if you will, and I was at one point a young girl like my respondents. There is no unified "woman experience," I know that. But despite differences, and there are plenty, among women, our views of the world are grounded in part on shared oppressions. I do not mean to write a diatribe about what it means to be a woman in contemporary society. I am just going to say that I cannot "go native" because I am not entirely foreign to girls' culture. I do not know many women who have not been victimized, as women, first, and then of course there are those worse and more salient crisscrossing victimizations, where age, race, ethnicity, sexual orientation, queer identity, poverty, and delinquent status meet all in one person. As I mentioned earlier, this research on a population harmed not singularly, as women, and as youth, and as persons of color, and as immigrant children, but as persons occupying identities in which all above statuses overlap to intensify oppression, lends itself almost naturally to an analysis framed by an intersectionality framework. With that said, it is my perspective, both academic and personal, that all girls and women as a group in patriarchal societies experience or witness gender violence – not at the level or intensity of the violence in my respondents' lives, to be sure, and definitely not of the quality that women of color do, but some form of gendered violence nevertheless that circumvents their lives and shapes their choices, their world views, and prospects. From rape and sexual harassment, to catcalling and objectifying images; from anti-choice policies and child marriage, to the feminization of poverty and the election of a self-admitted women's abuser as president of the US; macro-, meso-, and micro-aggressions against women keep all women in check, albeit some more than others. There is no more vulnerable developmental stage for humans than adolescence, where all forms of gendered violence thrive against female teens. I remember how it was, and it was not pretty. It was not as ugly as for juvenile hall girls, but it was ugly enough. I embrace that sameness as something to build on in my research.

My discussion of female delinquency is in part guided by that almost universal experience of gender violence[5] ugliness, especially during adolescence. Rather than assuming that delinquent, violent, and "bad" girls are "others" as we are often forced to, I try to ground my analysis on a "sameness" perspective. When "others" become "us" then they are humanized. Through humanizing "fallen" or "bad" girls and through voicing their points of view, I aspired to empower other women (and men) to collectively raise their voices against gender harm of the kind that the girls in my study have been subjected to. That my readers might not have been harmed in similar ways, is a matter of luck, socio-economic privilege, and opportunity, not some dramatic cultural or internal exceptionality. So, no, I did not study an unknown tribe somewhere in the Amazon, to "go native"; I was already part of the group from the get go. If you think that makes these stories and how I am making sense of them less accurate or worthy, then I would love to hear how you make sense of them. But why don't you read them first.

Notes

1 The title of this program is imaginary. The real title has been changed for confidentiality purposes.

2 Exceptionally, a small number of girls could and sometimes during my study were locked in a "special unit" for mentally disturbed or violent inmates, where they were under a 24-hour watch. That unit housed both boys and girls.

3 Read in informational pamphlet I was given during the fundraiser dinner.
4 These descriptive figures refer only to data I collected through interviews and observations. Such information was impossible to collect with respect to the letters, as all identifiers had been removed before the letters were given to me. However, based on the time period in which these letters were written, and on the situation of the senders, who had all been recently incarcerated in the facility under study, it is safe to assume that the content of letters I analyzed voices thoughts and feelings of a population very similar to that of my interview sample.
5 I borrow O'Toole, Schiffman, and Kitter Edwards' (2007) definition of gender violence as any interpersonal, organizational, or politically oriented violation perpetrated against people due to their gender identity, sexual orientation, or location in the hierarchy of male-dominated social systems.

References

ABA/NBA. American Bar Association and National Bar Association. (2001). *Justice by gender: The lack of appropriate prevention, diversion and treatment alternatives for girls in the juvenile justice system*. Washington, DC: Author.

Bellknap J., Holsinger K., & Dunn M. (1997). Understanding incarcerated girls: The results of a focus group study. *Prison Journal, 77*(4), 381–404.

Bloor, M., & Wood, F. (2006). *Keywords in qualitative methods.* London: SAGE Publications Ltd doi: 10.4135/9781849209403

Cannon, S. (1989). Social research in stressful settings: Difficulties for the sociologist studying the treatment of breast cancer. *Sociology of Health & Illness, 11*(1), 62–77.

Cotterill, P., & Letherby, G. (1993). Weaving stories: Personal auto/biographies in feminist research. *Sociology, 27*(1), 67–79.

Crenshaw, K. (1989). Demarginalizing the intersection of race and sex: A black feminist critique of antidiscrimination doctrine, feminist theory and antiracist politics. *The University of Chicago Legal Forum*, 139–167.

Gaarder, E., & Belknap, J. (2002). Tenuous borders: Girls transferred to adult court. *Criminology, 40*(3), 481–518

Mills, C. (1959). *The sociological imagination.* (GB 204). New York: Oxford University Press.

Stanley, L. *(*1990). Feminist *auto/*biography *and* feminist *epistemology*. In J. Aaron and S. Walby (Eds.) *Out Of The Margins: Women's Studies in the Nineties.* Lewes: Falmer Press.

Stanley, L., & Wise, S. (1983). *Breaking out: Feminist consciousness and feminist research*, London: Routledge and Kegan Paul.

Taylor, J. M., Gilligan, C., & Sullivan, A. M. (1995). *Between voice and silence: Women and girls, race and relationship.* Cambridge, MA: Harvard University Press.

Vigil, J. D. (2008). Female gang members from East Los Angeles. *International Journal of Social Inquiry, 1*(1), 47–74

Part I

Deprivation as intervention

Chapter 3

Disconnection as intervention

Yajaira, 18

The first time I was brought here, I was 11. It was for assault of a police officer. What happened is that my mom had called the cops. She didn't want my sister and I to go out to this party and my brother was like "I rather take them out and me be there." But she called the cops and they came in and they started screaming at us. They were like, "What the fuck are you thinking, you guys can't go out, you guys are minors and if you guys leave, we're going to blame it on him," and all this stuff. So my brother's like, "I'm sorry, but you aren't going to talk like that to my sisters in my house, you fucking pig!" And they had a big argument with him because he doesn't like cops. He just has issues with them. And then they went, "Come here!" And they took him to the room and we started hearing like commotion like bam bam bam and then my brother just called me. And I started kicking the door, ran to the room and then all my friends were trying to kick the door open and they were like, "Back up back up," and they called the SWAT team and closed the street down. I was mad and then like everybody just went crazy. Like my sister grabbed a bass and she like threw it at the cop. And she was just mad, she was raged and like once they opened the door, he was like bleeding, he was like fucked up. And they were dragging him on the floor. I was so mad and throwing stuff at them, and then when I saw the SWAT team coming in, I started to run around and then I felt somebody pull my hair and then they pepper sprayed me and I was like, "Oh you stupid bitch," and this and that. And then my brother, I was like, "I love you, I love you." And you know obviously he was my brother and he was like my dad at that point cause I don't have a dad, he passed away a long time ago. So you know at that point he's kind of like the only guy that I look up to. My mom, the whole time, cause she doesn't speak English, she couldn't really understand half of what they were saying. And her concern was for us to just not leave the house and to be safe and it ended up with like fighting and me being pepper sprayed, my brother beat up and going to jail. And I told my mom, "Is this what you wanted?"

My dad died when I was 5. He got ran over by a drunk driver and he got killed. We all had chicken pox that night. I remember we were all sick and we were in the tub with oatmeal and then my mom, I saw her throw herself to the floor crying. And we got out the tub and we were like, "What happened?" And she was just crying, was crying. And they didn't tell us what happened until like we went to the morgue. They told me he was sleeping. Yeah and I was like, "Ok, can I give him a kiss?" and they were like, "Yeah." And they said like, "He's going to take some vacations for a good time." and I was like, "Ok, but I want to give him a kiss, why don't you wake him up," you know. And they were like; they just started crying. So I gave him a kiss and I was like, "Why is he so cold, cover him, he's so cold." And that's what I remember. I don't remember his face exactly when I saw him. He had an injury on his head, but I didn't know; I was just like, "What happened to his head?" And they were like, "It's cause he got hurt that's why he's sleeping." My brother didn't cry. He was very resentful toward my father, both he and my other brothers, cause I have two other older brothers. My father used to punish them very harsh; he would drown them. He would be very harsh with them. He was very, very strict. And so that's why my brother and then like his teenage years, you know he was being rebellious and I remember one day, he had like this hair style, like a Mohawk? My father cut his little thing and he was so mad and he burned all his baggy pants. He was like I don't want you to dress baggy, dress like a normal person.

I'm addicted to meth. It's a drug that like your conscience crashes with your thoughts like: powww … I like to get cuddly, I don't like to go outside … I don't get paranoid either like "oh that's the cops" stuff like that … cause some people do. I feel relaxed … I'm a very hyper person but when I'm on it, I'm relaxed. I think I started pretty much cause of the whole rape issue; that was the biggest thing, cause regardless all the family issues that we had – my brothers' using – you know everything being out of control, I remember my bro sitting me down once and I was crying and he told me, "We all miss that sweet little girl." I did change when I did drugs cause I was very sweet, I was not afraid to show my love for my family. I knew right from wrong but not really, but when there was a family fight I would go in and tell them "stop" and they would. And all that has changed cause of the drugs.

I was raped when I was 10. Or maybe before that, I don't remember cause drugs mess you up, but I remember my 10th birthday so it was around then. My mom found out about it cause my friend's mom told her. I was talking to my friend and she said she was going through something like that and said, "I don't know how to tell my mom, I'm so embarrassed." [Until then] I put this face on all the time like I'm happy cause I didn't wanna seem stupid, but when she told me I decided to tell her; it felt so good, and she started crying with me, and we cried together. So I told her my story, but then her mom, she was hearing from the door and then the next day when she woke us up for breakfast (cause I never wanted to be home, it was kinda fresh then still), she told us and then she called my mom. My mom cried. I didn't want her to call the police and make a fuss, but she did cause that's how she is … but they didn't find him cause he had left to Mexico … but she put up the report and I remember they came to talk to me when I was in my house … and I was like … they sent two guys! *You know*??? I didn't wanna talk to these people about … I was … they were asking me all these questions! They tried to help us go into therapy but we refused, me and my sister. Cause she had gone through something similar too. Then my brother he talked to me and cried cause he told me, "Yeah we know about all this stuff," and I was mad … I was embarrassed but he said, "There's nothing to be embarrassed," and he told me, "If it makes you feel better, BS aside, I think everybody has been through that shit you know? So don't get weird about it." It was hard for me cause my brother is kinda strict and stuff and was like, "Don't let anybody touch you cause you gonna be a whore," you know … you gonna be a whore, this, you gonna be a whore, that. My sister kinda used to hear the same thing. I wouldn't have said anything if my friend hadn't told me and she just couldn't keep it inside anymore and she told me how embarrassed she felt just like I did. Although I was a little stronger, I feel so stupid too, cause he had told me, "If you say anything I will kill your brothers or your family," and then, as I grew older I had realized what they had done to me.

I had so much hate for my mom, and so much hate for my brothers and I told her, I looked her in the face and told her, "If you had been out worrying for me, I'd forgive, but you were not, you were too busy partying." Cause after my dad died, she was never home. She always worked and then she would go out to clubs and so we never saw her. We would be home alone crying waiting for her to come home the next morning. And then, these bad things happened to us at home. And now, years later, she didn't want to let us go out, when things happened at home?

But see, I didn't understand and that time I was so mad. I didn't understand everything that she was going through. She was working way too hard and sometimes she went out partying. I didn't understand the fact that what happened to me … I just wanted to kill that guy … I only cared about my pain … and my embarrassment, how dirty I felt, how is someone going to take the innocence away from someone like that, you know? Having his hands on you like that … that's not right … It ain't cool…

Yajaira's memories were blurred, and her narrative skipped back and forth between events, because "drugs mess you up like that," as she often repeated when she had trouble focusing. Yet the narrative always seemed to return to her childhood rape-related trauma and her mixed feelings about her mom. She was a young woman who had survived a tremendous amount of pain (family violence, parental death, neglect, sexual abuse, intimate partner violence, police brutality, and addiction) all while growing up in a marginalized, disorganized community, where social supports and opportunities to heal through healthy alternatives were unavailable. Exacerbating her experiences of collective isolation, Yajaira had been forced to suffer her individual problems alone as well: rather than healing, the intermittent presence of her mother, siblings, and friends had contributed to her sense of abandonment and insecurity.

Such experiences with damaged relationships, broken support systems, and vanished childhoods were universal among my respondents. Trish, an 18-year-old with multiple re-entries, summed up what most of her peers had communicated throughout their life-stories:

> I felt that I had always, like, grown myself. Like, I had been my own parent kinda or, like, I had made up my own rules and stuff, because I never really considered them, like, parental figures. It's not that they're really responsible themselves.

As a young child, social services had placed Trish in her grandmother's custody, while both her parents served time for drug-related crimes. Her mother also suffered from alcoholism and manic-depression, while her father drifted in and out of sobriety, unable to maintain a job, good credit, or a driver license. Trish became a chronic runaway and truant at 12, when she started hanging out with the "wrong crowds." She temporarily lived with a boyfriend's family, and eventually got taken in by another, older man with whom she committed check fraud, her only serious offense. She had been detained in the institution for a total of six times, mostly for probation violations. Similar to her parents, Trish had developed a drug addiction she kept drifting in and out of, and her inability to complete drug treatment programs always brought her back into juvenile detention. She felt detached from family, claiming there was nothing for her at home but the responsibility to take care of an aging grandmother and two physically and mentally disabled parents.

Tanya, a 14-year-old gang member, who had been living in her grandmother's mobile home since the age of five, related feelings of resentment toward her parents as well.

> My mom she's like, she's my mom but she's not really being a parent to me. Because she is always working or she's always talking with her guy friends. She never took 20 minutes to sit down and talk to me.

Her feelings toward her mother where nothing short of conflicted. On one hand, Tanya expressed admiration for her mother's aggressiveness with other women (although that aggression was often directed at her daughters). "My mom, she gets down easily; she's crazy." On the other hand, Tanya expressed contempt. She was mad that her mother was still engaging with her father:

> I don't like my dad. Cause my dad would drink and hit my mom. And she always had bruises and everything; and she still goes back to see him! I don't get it. I guess she has love for him. Me, I don't understand how she can love somebody that you know that's hit her. I don't believe in love anyhow.

Tanya's resentment of her mother and her relationship "personality" was also linked to long and frequent absenteeism. For example, she remembers the time when her mom, a local gang member herself, had strangely disappeared from their lives:

> And we didn't know she left. And like, she didn't want none of us to know she left. And like, my uncle would talk to her. And one day I got the number to my mom's cell phone and I called my mom crying to her, telling her I wanted her back home. And then, I guess she went to court. I couldn't go, but my brother and uncle went. But they didn't bring my mom home. So, I was worried.

During that time, Tanya also had to deal with her grandmother's abuse.

> I've grown up of violence with my grandma. Me and my grandma are not close. Because she doesn't like me cause of my dad. And like, she takes all the anger that my dad has given to my mom on me. She has a cane and she would hit me with that sometimes. And that's why I would always run away from my house.

As for her father, Tanya has no hope or desire for reconciliation. Describing a dramatic family fight between him and her older brother that followed a battering incident during a visit to Mexico, Tanya had decided to write him off. "And I told my dad, like, I told him: 'You're never gonna be my dad. You've never ever been there for me…' " Tanya admitted that these broken bonds, as well as several deaths in the family pushed her not only out on the streets, "doing whatever I wanted," but also into substance abuse:

> When I'm on Crystal Meth, my heart starts to race a lot. It's exciting. But like, I start to think about a lot of things. Like about my brother who died. My grandpa who died. My cousin who just passed away. I don't think about myself. I think about others.
>
> (Tanya, 17)

As already illustrated in Yajaira's life-story, estranged or tenuous relationships with loved ones were habitually referenced as sources of strain to which gangs, drugs, and alcohol offered relief.

> I don't communicate with my parents cause when I was a kid they never really talked to me so I kinda got used to that. My mom is a screamer and my dad is a cusser so that makes me not want to listen… And when I do try to communicate with them it's kinda weird to me, so I feel uncomfortable. My family they usually jump to assumptions … My family called me a slut before, or a prostitute and it's not even close to it.
>
> (Dora, 17)

> I just didn't want to remember anything anymore, like my whole life. Like I was self-medicating myself, really a lot. I had bad anxiety, I would get angry really easily. And you know, I hated, like my mind was always racing when I wasn't on alcohol. I was always thinking about my dad and why did my mom call the cops and why am I here or my mom and just all this other stuff for why that fat Kentucky lady would beat the crap out of me? It was all this stuff that I was thinking. Like, I was mad, like why is this girl sitting next to me hadn't had this bad in life?
>
> (Shelley, 18)

> You don't have no one to talk to. That's going to be there for you They're like oh I'm on drugs so I don't have to worry about that problem right now cuz when I used to … I used to do meth. When I had problems, I'd smoke. And then I wouldn't think about my problems no more.
>
> (Joy, 18)

These accounts show among other things that system-involved girls have been systematically subjected to rejection, neglect, and loneliness; they have grown up in what Laurie Schaffner (2010) calls "empty families," with irregularly present, or physically and emotionally unavailable parents, families where there was no childhood because the child was expected to be the adult and take care of, even defend herself against the adult. These are life-stories of disconnections and violations that created voids which young women often attempted to fill with alcohol, drugs, and relationships with older men.

In Chapter 1, I discussed relational theory's (Covington, 2007) contributions to developing appropriate responses/treatments for system-involved girls, like Yajaira, within the gender-responsive rehabilitative framework. One of the cited guidelines (#4, page 16, in this book) for working successfully with girls cautions against replicating disconnections and violations inside youth corrections. The juvenile justice system's responses, as detailed in the narratives I will reference in this chapter, are in direct contrast to this guideline, and to the propositions of relational theory. In fact, they reveal a systematic and systemic continuation of the abandonment, neglect, and "emptiness" that organizes these young women's childhoods and adolescence. My observations inside this county juvenile institution reveal that contrary to fundamental principles of rehabilitation, and gender-responsive reform, conditions of confinement build on, rather than upending the physical, psychological, and socio-emotional isolation that feeds young girls' negative self-image and despair. Despite theoretical and evidence-based arguments against correctional environments that perpetuate separation and disconnection in young women's lives, the female unit of this institution purposely fostered an environment that exacerbated inmates' fears by mirroring the neglect and disconnection that had caused them in the first place.

This environment was created by a wrongful understanding of the role relationships play in adolescent girls' wellbeing, especially to those who are at a high risk of depression and other mental health problems. Frontline staff had been instructed to be unapproachable and cold to inmates and to save nurture and warmth for children who deserved it instead. Often with the pretext of keeping the environment safe and fight-free, correctional counselors kept young women under their care physically and cognitively idle, room-confined, and mute. The only "care" they provided related to maintaining control, rather than fostering mutual respect and trustful connections in the unit. Even the very things that should be basic (e.g., exercise/food) became something that must be bartered for and something used as punishment/reward, in other words as governance.

The message this treatment intended to convey, was that these girls' offender status had thwarted their entitlement to humanity or basic rights, and that it was up to them to adjust their behavior in order to slowly get them back. In that view, juvenile girls were detained in order to be deprived of meaningful human interactions, because their criminal behavior had rendered them unworthy of such privilege. Young women knew that their "counselors" were not there to, well, *counsel* them, and had learned to accept this reality like they had accepted the reality of their life outside juvenile hall. It was just a consequence of being, well, being "she": Why would anybody want to listen to her problems? It is not that others had listened before, anyway. Young women in this institution expected nothing more than what they had received from their own families.

Emotionally and physically segregated in their unwelcoming, bare rooms, with very few activities to occupy their time, few opportunities to speak, and even fewer to be heard, detained girls were forced to spend long hours doing what they dreaded: thinking. Without self-medicating outlets such as drugs, alcohol, and thrills, they found no escape from torturing memories of violations they had both suffered and inflicted on others. However, this did not result in repentance, as correctional staff thought it might. It, instead, increased their depressive symptoms, and their anger against others and themselves, while diminishing their worth and self-worth. Feeling isolated in their relationships, unable to be heard and validated, stigmatized by the delinquent label, and overwhelmed with shame and self-blame, young girls continued to live in a state of *condemned isolation* that pervaded their lives outside the institution.

Consistent with the literature,[1] all respondents in this study entered the system already traumatized by unhealthy, disrupted, or abusive relationships. Furthermore, given the large number of young women in my sample living in the peripheral Latina neighborhoods in the county, my respondents represented a population characterized by multiple marginality (Vigil, 2008). Multiple marginality, the dislocation, alienation, and isolation commonly experienced by immigrant ethnic minorities, is stronger among young women; gender adds to their marginalization, which is a critical factor in crime, especially gang and drug related offending (Vigil, 2008). Because connections with others are particularly important to women (Surrey, 1985), these traumatic relationship disruptions had resulted in depression, loneliness, and hopelessness. The juvenile institution in which the young women I interviewed spent most of their conscious life, pretended to be a place of rehabilitation, support, and care. It had received funding for implementing GSP. Therefore, one would have expected it to put feminist theory (Covington, 2007) and evidence-based research on girls' programming into practice (Covington & Bloom, 2006; Koons, Burrow, Morash, & Bynum, 1997; Matthews & Hubbard, 2008; MS Foundation for Women, 2001; OJJDP, 1998; Zavlek & Maniglia, 2007) by working on building relational support, and that would restore girls' sense of safety and self-worth. That could alleviate their pain, and even reverse the long-lasting impact of past traumas. However, such opportunity was spectacularly missed.

Relational theory, one of the fundamental theoretical frameworks guiding gender-responsive practices, emphasizes the growth-fostering and therapeutic potential of mutual, empathic, and empowering connections for women. The systemic interactions inside this institution, however, were anchored neither on psychological development, nor feminist theories; they were in fact, in direct opposition to the suggestions of the National Institute of Corrections (Bloom, Owen, & Covington, 2003); and they re-created the "growth hindering or/and violating relationships that women and girls experience in the free world" (Covington, 2007). The methods of disconnection employed to re-create a world deprived of meaningful involvements ranged from lack of programming (either recreational or educational), to room isolation, segregation, and staff member's attitudes signaling unwillingness to engage in mutually respective, warm, genuine, or/and supportive interactions, while punishing such interactions between the inmates themselves. This chapter presents my respondents' experiential accounts reflecting how the condemned isolation that branded their life-stories was sanctioned, reinforced, and reintroduced as "intervention" inside the juvenile hall.

Boredom and educational neglect

One of the most salient expressions of the disinterest in caring for young women in supportive and growth-fostering ways was the fact that no serious effort was made to involve them in meaningful activities to counter the parental, educational, and relational neglect in their lives.

"There's nothing to do here!" was probably the comment/complaint that came up most frequently in the conversations I had with my respondents. The young women I spoke to during my volunteer work, recruiting sessions, and interviews looked tired of doing nothing. "Bored straight" was the most consistently implemented "intervention" inside the girls' unit (all other interventions were offered on an unreliable schedule). Although it was not always by design (remember, the manager had told me she *was desperate* for more programs), it served frontline staff's short-term goals well: they didn't have to do the extra work, as keeping inmates inside their rooms made supervision easier, and it communicated that this was not a "fun" place to be, and it was not supposed to be a fun place at all.

My observations during the time I spent inside the female unit indeed affirmed the fact that other than some scarce programs and activities, which were frequently cancelled for a variety of reasons (i.e. the counselor did not show up, one of the girls "went off" and so everybody was punished and had to stay in their room, there was an important game on TV, so the staff didn't have time for supervising recreational events, etc.), and part-time school sessions in the weekdays, there are very few things girls can occupy themselves with. Here is Trish's account of the weekend routine:

> We spend a lot of time in our room. Like today I think we're only out for breakfast and then we do nothing for the next four five hours and then it's lunch and then we do nothing until about three o'clock and then they have *LLM*[2] which sometimes it's like tae-bo and then I don't know whatever. And then we're in here until 6:30 besides dinner and then. We're just in our rooms a lot…

The weekday schedule is the same, but includes brief school sessions for some residents. It is worth noting, though, that not all girls are allowed to go to school every day. As with all other activities, with the exception of Bible study that cannot be withheld, it is ultimately unit staff who decide whether a client has been "good" and is therefore allowed to leave her room, even for school. It is no secret that educational services for detained and incarcerated youth across the US are sub-par, to say the least. A 2014 report published by the Southern Education Foundation (SEF) found that learning programs inside juvenile justice institutions are "profound and crippling," and rather than positively impacting the life trajectories of troubled youth, they effect major setbacks that increase chances of re-offending. Or, to put it bluntly, "School in here is a joke," as several of my respondents declared cynically, noting that the quality of classes was even lower than that of the continuation schools outside the system.

Consistent with the SEF (2014) report, classes are co-ed, unstructured, unsafe ("There are cameras in the rooms but they don't work," as one respondent informed me with a smirk.), and lack focus on the particular learning needs of each student. A few girls like it, because it feels like an escape from their room's misery, or because it is easy and they like "kicking" it with their "homies," their male acquaintances, and people they know from the outside. However, all, even the girls who like it, make derogatory comments about it. The teachers are talked about with resentment and contempt. As Vienna, a bright 15-year-old first-timer put it "That's not really teaching … they just sit there." I was told stories about teachers with obvious mental instabilities, anxiety disorders, and other shortcomings. Whereas most of these stories were told light-heartedly, they were nevertheless followed by complaints that all services provided in the facility "scratch the bottom of the barrel," which was interpreted as yet another way the justice system degrades the youth subjected to it. "My classes are seriously, like, I took these classes in ninth grade," said Shelley and continued with frustration: "I am being treated like a retard!"

This systemic mistrust of female children's abilities and desire for education is expressed in the juvenile justice system's attitude toward its own clients. Vienna was shocked by the correctional counselors' reaction to her "unlikely" academic interests:

> Well, the staff here make fun of me cause I tell them I actually like school … And they're like, "no one in here likes school" …

Despite the commonplace myth that delinquents are not into academic achievement, several of my respondents related that they liked school, especially math, and some used to be "A" students before probation came into their life: "I was dorky, I even had a wheel back pack," laughs Dora, reminiscing about her life before the age of 12, the year she started "messing up." Moreover, all the girls who were 18 or close to 18 said they were hoping to get their GED, and almost all expressed aspirations to go to college. In fact, three of the 18-year-olds in my sample had been attending community college just before serving their current sentence. One of them, Yajaira, had turned herself in voluntarily, in anticipation of creating a "clean" adult life with her boyfriend. Another girl's college life, Vera's, was abruptly interrupted when she was turned in by her probation officer. She was attending community college in a "rival" city – Vera was on probation on gang terms, and was prohibited from frequenting certain areas.

> He [my probation officer] said, "I don't care if you go to college," and he said I couldn't go. I would have my teacher email him; I had my counselor email him; I had people telling him I had papers I would write, I mean cause I was doing good, turning in homework, you know, I turned off my cell phone in class, I wouldn't just walk out, you know some people walk out you can pretty much do what you want in college, but my respect for my teacher was unlimited and I was going to do my work and I mean she noticed it and uh you know of course it was hard for me but I was there and I asked her and she was like "yeah have him call me if he has questions" but like everyone was working with me to work with my probation but he didn't...

Many of my respondents were fully conscious of and angry with the damage probation, of which the current institution was a part, had caused to their adolescence, as well as to their future, with education disruption being the major contributor to this effect. This emotion was reflected clearly in Trish's description of her detention experience:

> I feel as if like I've kinda robbed out of like my whole high school life and I really kinda ... cherish that you know, like, before when I first started getting into trouble, like, I was a truant, you know, like, I didn't go to school for my whole freshman year, but uhm, after that like um after my first time coming here I kinda realized, "hey, school is kinda cool," you know?

Shelley, another youth who had just turned 18 inside the facility, sounded even more frustrated with the juvenile justice system's undermining of her academic potential:

> You know I went all the way to Algebra II and Physics last year; if I was out, I probably be graduated already with my diploma. [This experience

> could be helpful] if I got a good education and was able to graduate from here with Calculus on my record and you know, just being here depressed shows the fact that I can't and there's nothing I can do about it. And I'm really into education. I love learning, I love … I actually want to do things with my life!

But there was another, less conspicuous, but in my opinion more powerful impact these "empty," "worthless," and "wasted" juvenile hall days had on my respondents' prospects. After all, gaps in education could be bridged, albeit not as timely as they could have been if school was not "a joke" in youth corrections; but what about gaps in one's self-worth? What these accounts say, more than "we don't care about your education" is "we don't care about you." Like parents, grandparents, and other adult guardians who had disappointed, even harmed children with self-interested attitudes, and inadvertent violations, correctional counselors signaled that they too, despite being paid to become these girls' surrogate parents, even if temporarily, showed no interest in comforting, entertaining, intellectually stimulating, or plainly respecting them as the whole, deserving humans that they were. They kept them physically, mentally, and emotionally idle and bored, and they did it systematically and with gusto.

They just leave us here

Girls want to do aspirational things in their life, but as the song-turned-cultural tagline asserts, they also "just wanna have fun." Leisure and recreational programs are essential to the general wellbeing of children, produce therapeutic effects for victims, and serve as protective factors against delinquency (UN Committee on the Rights of the Child, 2013). Because of the magnitude of the problems system-involved girls face, the lack of leisure in their lives might seem like a relatively small harm, the redressing of which should not be a priority. Recreational inactivity, however, not only negatively affects health, including mental health outcomes, but is also a by-product and a cause of social isolation. This type of isolation in the neighborhood, at school, and inside detention overwhelms marginalized girls, who sexist convention wants passive and less interested in sports and active recreation. Many of my respondents' disrupted family lives, persistent poverty, and underserved communities had deprived them of healthy recreational opportunities. Not to be outdone, the county juvenile corrections further deprive young girls caught up in its institutions of such opportunities.

Inside the girls' unit in juvenile detention, leisure activities are scarce. There are a few reading materials in a small dilapidated bookcase, AKA the "library," to borrow, or sometimes read after dinner. In theory, visitors may bring books as well, but they must first be approved by staff, and the recipient must keep them outside her room. She might lose the privilege of reading with no notice, if she is suspected of even the smallest wrongdoing, such as talking during meals. There was a TV in front of the control station where staff spent their shifts. Sometimes, depending on staff mood and resident behavior, residents were allowed to watch Nickelodeon, but for the most part, it was correctional staff who watched football games.

The institution features some pretty impressive sports areas: a few basketball courts, right outside the units, and grass soccer and softball fields. I was surprised to see these in a juvenile jail. However, although most of my visits took place in the weekends, I only saw them occupied a few times, and never by female detainees. The lack of recreation and especially sports activities is a complaint several girls in my sample discussed. Some of them described themselves as very athletic, acknowledged the physical and mental health benefits of exercise, and detested the fact that they never got to play sports while incarcerated:

> I know that they play a lot of sports and like I'm an athlete you know, like. I've played on many things. I know what I'm doing. But they never allow me to participate. And do you see all these fields, out here? Oh, no, they are great … We NEVER go out to play, they just leave us here (in the cafeteria) and some times they play music and we jump up and down, or sometimes we run outside in the little yard in circles…
>
> (Trish, 18)

For the few girls who were given the rare opportunity to participate in group sports (a couple of them in the male teams) in the past, this advantage was a source of anxiety as the fear of it being taken away in case of misbehavior was hanging over their heads at all times. Barbra explains, in a trembling voice:

> I am the only one who plays softball with the boys' team in here. I was the only one selected. I will not give them (the unit staff) the chance to take this away from me … That's what they want!

Again, services that both by law, as well as by the County's commitment to rehabilitation and restoration, young women are entitled to and would benefit from physically, mentally, and socially, are used in a perverse punishment/ rewards system, that casts correctional counselors in the role of law enforcer rather than adult caretaker. For some of my respondents, the fear that was distressing Barbra had been realized before:

> Before they had sports and stuff like that … like certain sports and like I would make a team and then, the one counselor who didn't like me wouldn't open my door so I could go. She wouldn't allow me to be on the team. I don't know, I thought that was really like unfair because, you know, like I was chosen to be on the team!
>
> (Shelley, 18)

"Sports keep you happy," said Barbra, a 15-year-old, who suffered several health problems, including depression. Yajaira shared a similar opinion:

> I want to get involved into sports, to get my mind off drugs, cause it will make me feel that high and then I am gonna be tired and relax but in a healthy way ... I love basketball ... Either that or some kind of martial arts or yoga kinda thing ... Cause it makes you feel good and I know it does sub the feeling of being high...

Opportunities for meaningful exercise and recreation depend upon the availability of funding, volunteers (such as coaches and group exercise instructors), and ultimately, the staff's discretion. The only times I witnessed girls in the female unit exercising, or having any fun at all, was when they were jogging in circles in the small back yard, and during a short-lived Zumba program offered by a volunteer. That program was clearly disliked by frontline staff because, as they told me, they had to watch "too many girls, too close together at the same time," and was soon terminated. By contrast, unit managers had told me that they were "desperate" to find such volunteer-run recreation. Perhaps it was difficult for volunteers to commit to something that was so frequently cancelled at a moment's notice. The set-up, right in front of the frontline staff desk, with correctional officers closely monitoring every move (and commenting on it), did not make this arrangement any less awkward than it already was.

The staff's lack of effort to increase recreational activities for their clients did not go unnoticed by my respondents, who frequently complained that while they were alone and unhappy, their counselors did not miss any opportunity to enjoy their time at work, an observation that increased feelings of mistrust and injustice.

> The other night when we were closed in our rooms they were watching Flipper. We asked them the other day and they said no, but we knew they were lying...
>
> (Macy, 17)

> Well, we're supposed to have exercise for an hour a day and I mean it's not that hard to take us outside and they don't ... They'll sit there and play video-games...
>
> (Lori, 18)

But there was another activity that doubled as a source of both stress and relief: being on kitchen duty, otherwise known as being "on cart." Being on cart is an informal privilege that is given to few selected girls in the unit, and it is, as far as I was able to observe in the approximately 18 months I was there, the only *one* "privilege." With that said, selection criteria were neither obvious, nor transparent: according to some of the girls, the fewer "early beds," the higher the chances of joining this select group; according to others, "kissing up" will do it. Either way, the staff used cart selection as positive reinforcement (be good and I will give this to you), as well as negative punishment (be bad and I will take this away). I am intentionally placing the discussion of this proxy rewards system in my "recreation" section, not because it was an objectively fun, or entertaining activity, but because the young women I interviewed viewed it this way. In fact, they viewed it as an indulging and status conferring activity. Girls on cart were responsible for helping in the kitchen, and cleaning up the common rooms, and they all loved the opportunity to do something instead of nothing.

> Yeah and when you're in cart like you're always outside. You're never in your room. Never ... Only to sleep ... And you get to see and talk to people...
>
> (Bertha, 17)

> Yeah, I'll do the work. Anything. Anything, to get out of my room!
>
> (Nora, 18)

Being on cart is consequently a point of tension among the girls, as it is considered by many a case of blatant favoritism, and discrimination against those girls who never get chosen, because they have been "bad."

> Well the girls who are on the cart who do like the food, they get treated better than we do. And that's not fair.
>
> (Tanya, 14)

Other girls discuss being on cart as a badge of honor, a way to be accepted, approved, and loved by the staff. They discuss their role with enthusiasm, their eyes lit up, their backs straightened, and pride in their voice. Some girls even consider the frequent reception of the privilege to clean up after everybody else in the unit, too fortunate, because it is an "easy way out," a relief from punishment, and a means of tricking staff into treating them better.

> It's hard work, but, that means I have no punishment while being here. So, I see it as if I go out and come back in, I don't mind, because I would know what to do and get on cart.
>
> (Victoria, 16)

Frontline staff seemed to share this attitude: they were more lenient to girls who go on cart and going on cart was a form of expressed leniency. Another form of leniency: roommate placement. On the books, room segregation was reserved for those inmates who pose a risk threat. In this unit, however, it was used profusely as punishment for the smallest infraction, and according to some of my respondents, as retaliation. This made most girls' stay traumatizing, especially when that stay was served within the confines of their small detention cells (rooms).

Trapped miserable

"We're trapped in our rooms, miserable," said 15-year-old Isla, voicing a sentiment most of my respondents shared. Room segregation is the "treatment" that girls most commonly received for the largest part of the day, the whole day, or for their whole stay. It is devastating to most, because it is seen as an often-unfair form of punishment for which they have no defense.

> Like I know for a long time I didn't have a roommate and it wasn't for any reason it was just because the counselor didn't like me…
>
> (Trish, 18)

Bianca, an assertive 15-year-old who talked to me at length about her hostile relationship with the unit staff, including her assigned "counselor," discussed various ways through which it was made obvious to her that she was being unfairly and discriminatorily treated. Whereas her narrative included a number of vastly more serious mistreatment accusations, she nevertheless discussed her room isolation as one of the most hurtful ones, and the most obvious sign of hostility:

> …the other day I asked [one of frontline staff] when am I be able to have a roommate and he said: *NEVER*, and I was, why, and he goes, we have our reasons … They hate me.

Being trapped in a room all day, with nobody to talk to, would understandably be punishment for any teenager, boy or girl, whose normal development justifies an elevated craving for action, excitement, and peer socialization. But it is especially frightening and traumatizing to kids who have recently gone through the pain and humiliation of arrest, adjudication, and confinement, and more so for adolescent girls who carry the additional weight of family dysfunction, violent victimization, and abuse in their memories. "They like put me with no roommate and I was, like so terrified of being alone at the time," explained Yajaira, describing her detention following her family's violent encounter with the SWAT team. Even "tough" girls like Tanya expressed fear: "Well, to me it's scary in here because like you're just in your room like behind these brick walls… "

The significance of a peer's company especially for girls with histories of abuse, and the potential amplification of trauma that room isolation might cause (Chesney-Lind & Shelden, 1998), is exemplified in my interview data. For vulnerable young women hit with the shock of first-time confinement, double room occupancy substitutes for the crisis intervention they never receive.

> And I came to [the institution] and Anna, the other girl too, she got arrested and she came in here with me too which was great … It was sad that she had to be in here but she helped me do time, like, different, you know what I mean? She was my roommate in here … because I was all hysterical…
>
> (Dianne)

In no other practice was relational theory and its propositions most severely undermined than in the practice of locking young girls up with no companion. Dianne, who is referenced above has navigated a life laced with relentless victimization and abuse (her story is highlighted in the next chapter). Like most of the peers inside juvenile hall, she has experienced family dysfunction and separation, violent relationships, manipulative adults, and neglectful guardians. What was exactly the point of exacerbating the impact these violations from others and with others had on her? Which theory were they informed in and what were they trying to accomplish? It could not be that these practices intended to cause more pain and distress, could it? The next section attempts to answer this.

We want you to be miserable

Frontline staff are well aware of the psychological distress and sadness room isolation causes to their wards. Victoria thinks they just do not care enough to make accommodations for them:

> Sometimes I feel bad, cause the staff doesn't really care. They would just say, "Alright, just go to your room, just go to your room. Just go to your cell," you know?

However, many of her peers believe that their counselors deprived them of anything remotely fun or uplifting, not (only) because they did not really care for them, but because they saw it as their duty to make young women under their supervision feel miserable and unhappy in order to deter them from recidivating. Several young women reported that the staff often yelled at them, saying: "We want you to be miserable. We want you to do your time unhappy!" This attitude is reflected in much of the staff's actions, detailed throughout several chapters in this book. It is based on a very dim perception about who these young women are and what they need or are able to accomplish. It is also based on a pervasive view of deterrence, a misunderstanding of juvenile justice's goals and the particular unit's mission, in the view that correctional institutions for youth are designed to correct through deprivation, and that delinquents are detained *for* punishment rather than *as* punishment.

> This is a facility, not a camp, you know? They're not supposed to treat you, they're supposed to just hold us accountable for our actions … it is a punishment facility.
>
> (Vienna)

Part of this punishment also includes relational isolation. Detainees are not allowed to talk to, or even look at one another, without first asking permission from staff. They are required to walk around with their eyes on the floor, and hands behind their back. And as mentioned earlier, most of their day is spent in their room, without meaningful contact with peers or counselors. The idea that separation and solitude are conducive to behavioral reform has its roots in nineteenth century penology and the Pennsylvania system of punishment. I am not quite sure why frontline counselors thought these long abandoned principles should serve as models for the treatment of adolescent girls today, but surely these girls knew they did not translate into effective practices:

> They say that being in your room all the time and staring at your four walls makes you think … I don't think that … It makes you think: Oh I don't want to be here and I'd do anything to get out … Like, and pretty much … you sit there thinking and there's so much thinking, that you are convincing yourself in your head that what you're gonna do is right, but when you get out it's not the same, you're not gonna do it, I'm gonna do this and I'm gonna do that, and you have all day to think about it, and you keep saying over and over again, and you convince yourself you'll do it … JUST TO GET OUT … To say it to your PO and the judge, you try to convince them, and sometimes they give you a chance and then you get out and you do the same thing…
>
> (Monique, 18)

It is important to note that the Probation Department management did not seem to share the "bored straight" model that was practiced in the girls' unit. In one of my first meetings with the institution managers, before I had even started collecting data, I was assured with pride, that "all sorts of programs and activities" are implemented inside the units, so that residents have no idle time. They seemed to endorse the rehabilitative mission of the system, and eager to have me see for myself. But somewhere between management and frontline staff, that mission got lost and substituted with another. I do not have enough information to determine where the disconnect emerged, but some of my observations point to the training of correctional employees. Since I was required to receive a volunteer badge in order to be granted access inside the unit, I had to attend training sessions offered by probation to newly hired employees. There, I learned that I did not want to get "too close" to the minors I would work with.

> They're clever, they're manipulative, they're opportunistic. They'll take advantage of your kindness and warmth, so do not show any. You are not there to be their friends; you are not there to coddle them.

I understand there was some advice that could be useful to those who were new to this. In fact, most attendees were young college students: interns, and volunteers. We were told to not give out our contact information (phone number, address, etc.), which I suppose is a good advice regardless of context. But the tone (hostile) and the rationale (delinquents are predators) only served to encourage an "us v. them" attitude among an audience that is generally interested in "helping" young kids reform. Why not harness, rather than undercut their empathetic, service oriented approach? The training was run by two male officers, one of them a retired veteran, who volunteered in probation. Per his own proclamation, his favorite part of the job was tracking parolees and probationers under electronic monitoring. "I spent last New Year's eve tracking this guy on my computer," he informed us. "Nobody gets away. I'm always watching." As for an evidence based discussion on causes of delinquency, demographic characteristics of the population to be served, risk and needs factors, or gender-specific differences, that never happened. If this session was similar to those received by frontline staff before they start their job, it is not surprising that they would fill in the gaps with their own pre-conceived notions about how to best help young women stay crime-free.

Condemned isolation

A pervasive sense of isolation characterizes the female detainees in my study. Most of them grew up feeling ignored and unloved, rejected by the very people to whom they looked up for care and support. These feelings were validated and reinforced by a correctional environment that fostered separation, frigidness, and indifference, thus mirroring the minors' life circumstances outside the justice system. That is particularly problematic from a program effectiveness perspective: it is well established that connections with others are very important to women (Surrey, 1985). Consequently, programs that emphasize relational support promote feelings of safety, a critical measure of success in girls' programming, (Covington & Bloom, 2006; Koons, Burrow, Morash, & Bynum, 1997; Matthews & Hubbard, 2008; MS Foundation for Women, 2001; OJJDP, 1998; Zavlek & Maniglia, 2007). Because delinquent girls typically enter the system already traumatized by unhealthy, disrupted, or abusive relationships, institutions that discourage or undercut relationships, such as the institution under study, are destined to exacerbate these past traumas and thus fail. Depriving these young women of human connections, however, results in something even more damaging and long-lasting than treatment ineffectiveness: it impacts the way these young women view themselves, with all the powerful consequences this view has on their self-efficacy and life-prospects. What happens with arrest and incarceration, intensifies a condition that encapsulates the lived experiences of system-involved girls, a condition known as *condemned isolation.*

Condemned isolation, a term coined by psychiatrist Jean Baker Miller (1976, 1990) refers to the emotional impact of chronic disconnections and violations, of the kind system-involved girls have typically experienced. It encompasses the detrimental effects of physical, social, and psychological alienation, to which detained girls are accustomed outside juvenile hall, and to which they are subjected inside it as well. Multiple alienation creates feelings of worthlessness, powerlessness, and desperateness; it is often accompanied by internalization of blame, so that the person is made to think that something is wrong with her personally; and it may result in destructive behaviors such as substance addiction (Covington, 2007). I cannot think of a profile that illustrates Miller's theoretical propositions better, than that of girls' whose stories I am sharing.

"I've got nobody to blame, but me," says Isla, regarding her drug addiction. "Nobody put a gun in my head," she repeats over and over throughout her interview. "I started using it for excuses, for being hurt for my past, you know, and then got hooked," she continues. Her "past" revolved around her step-father's arrest, an incident that had created a huge schism in her blended family.

> When they took him away my mom, she would just sit there and cry and cry and cry. I'd be like "mom" and she would just ignore me and I would just be like "alright" and I would just take off until one day she reacted to it and we got in a big fight and she started putting her hands on me. She'd tell me she loved him more than me, and my brothers and sister they all blame me cause they lost their dad cause of me.

The reason why everybody was upset with Isla is because she had reported the stepdad (and her siblings' biological father) to the police for having raped her. It is not that her family thought she was lying; they believed her; but they claimed she had reported him only because he "would not let her go to this party," and accused her of being selfish. The stepdad was their only source of income, and the only father his children had ever known, and she was taking him away from them, just out of spite.

> My sister told me a couple months ago, "Let's sit down and talk, let me tell you how I feel. Because of what you did my dad got taken away and I will never see him again, and you know, I was daddy's little girl." Cause when the cops came they were hugging, like, she was grabbing his feet, you know how little girls do that to their dad. So I was like, wow, like it got to me when she was telling me that, cause that was the only reason I hadn't want to call the cops on him before.

Isla felt both wronged and guilty all at once.

> I feel like he took my childhood away and I never got to be that girl that I wanted to be, uhm, but ... He was all like a molester and everything but we

> had a good family, we were happy; we used to go to the beach, to *Chuck E. Cheese*, we would go eat pizza a lot, but after that night everything went upside down; my brothers hated me and, I don't know, it was so bad.

So, naturally, Isla turned to alcohol, drugs, and her gang-affiliated friends for the refuge her family refused to provide, and preferred not to think about the fact that her own mother had decided to denounce her and refused to even visit or call her when she was locked up. But, she did not like using her "past" to excuse her addiction. It was all her fault, after all.

Similarly, Nora (18), a repeat detainee, with a history of violent victimization by her mother's partners, and a knack for school fighting, also blames herself for her substance abuse: "I mean I put myself here. It's not fair, but it's my fault," she insists, after casually mentioning both her parents' addictions, incarcerations, and physically abusive relationship. Self-blame and fatalism lace most of my respondents' self assessments.

> We are not worth anything and its like, when we die we are going to have nothing.
>
> (Isla)

> I should just stop trying.
>
> (Anonymous, letter)

> Why can't I change?
>
> (Barbra)

> We're all fuck-ups.
>
> (Monique)

> They say we're here cause we're obviously not good people.
>
> (Vienna)

Isolated from the world, their families, and each other, young women in this study have been encouraged to develop a criminal understanding of themselves and their actions and to construct a "fallen" self-identity which contributes to young girls' further marginalization and a powerlessness. They have come to see themselves as unworthy of the affection, care, and trust of conventional others, and accept the "deprivation intervention" the institution has adopted as a direct consequence of their badness. In the words of Brenda, a six-timer and gang member, whose father is serving a life sentence and whose mother comes in and out of her life to use drugs with her:

> We're not supposed to have nothing in here; cause we're criminals.
>
> (Brenda, 18)

Relational deprivation as intervention

Condemned isolation was but one of the several "interventions" employed inside the female unit of this county juvenile jail. It emphasized the necessity of keeping inmates away (from the outside world, the correctional staff, each other, and their own selves). It was rationalized as a security measure; a pre-emptive tactic to protect employees and volunteers; and by a penance doctrine. It manifested in physical, emotional, and cognitive idleness; in room isolation; and in absolute emphasis on separateness rather than community.

These manifestations were not entirely new to young inmates. As their personal narratives reveal, their most intimate relationships were laced with loss, violations, and abandonment; their lived realities were shaped by social exclusion and crumbling, ineffective support systems. This reality is not unique to my sample, but rather, it seems to be a universal feature in system-involved girls' lives. Schaffner's (2006) ethnographic work reveals an almost identical pattern of girls navigating "empty families" (p. 86), a by-product of broken down institutions who could, but did not, lift them up. Empty families are populated with "worn down," powerless persons who perpetually fail to successfully care for their kin. Similar to my respondents, Schaffner's too reported parenting younger siblings, even their own parents and grandparents, and were expected to fend for themselves. Often their escape and survival tactics impacted them in material ways, as they entailed affairs with older men whose crimes they would abet. Their connection deprivation inside juvenile hall only re-enforced the emotional damage inflicted by experiences of relationship dysfunction. That is true not only for California institutions, but also in other states such as New York. A joint Human Rights Watch and American Civil Liberties Union (HRW/ACLU) report (2006), also reveals that youth correctional counselors ignore female detainees, avoid speaking to them, lock them up in their rooms alone, and provide little, if any, meaningful programming.

The literature of psychological development and gender-responsivity guidelines provides excellent suggestions to help heal the traumas resulting from relational disconnections, and to even reverse the detrimental impact on self-identity and resilience. Juvenile corrections could and should have seized the opportunity to apply knowledge about what works with girls into practice. Instead, arrest and detention assembled young girls' past disconnection experiences into one, and even justified them as a natural consequence of the acts of an undeserving person.

The negative affect of this culture of "just deserts," the correctional system's exclusive focus on retribution, rather than reform, was reflected in many of my respondents' words. The perceptions that "There's nobody to talk to; Nobody is there for you; Thinking is painful; I'm on my own; Nobody cares," captured by my respondents' narratives were reaffirmed with a vengeance every time they re-entered detention. Young girls were subjected to systematic boredom, room isolation, and separation from loved ones; while counselors instructed them to avoid conduct with their peers, they also clearly communicated that they too, were not to be bothered. As a result, this "rehabilitative" environment not only did not heal, but rather it exacerbated young women's traumas by fostering frigidness, separation, and indifference. Girls' state if condemned to isolation resulted in defeatism and hopelessness. Research (Morash, Park, & Kim, 2010; Ness, 2004) has linked these attitudes, which are especially prevalent among system-involved girls from "bad" families and neighborhoods to increased aggression. In light of this scholarship, investing in more isolation seems to be making very little sense if we are looking to rehabilitate young women. If we are looking to problematize these young women's character and encourage them to self-sabotage and self-pity, and consequently to more inward and outward aggression, then isolation seems to be the right intervention. Dora, a 17-year-old runaway who self-describes as both depressed and violent puts this intervention strategy in words best:

> This place depresses you sometimes, you are used to being out and listen to music and all you hear here is yelling and … and you don't have really anything to do but to think about all the things and usually you remember things that make you feel bad … cause everything catches up to me, you have so much time to think here…

The following chapters will detail examples of yet other types of interventions that were used to "treat" system-involved girls. Though they target areas other than girls' thirst for connections to attack, these interventions are nevertheless all based on the same assumptions about the purpose of youth corrections, and the needs, challenges, and aptitudes of the population they serve. They were based on a distorted view about who these girls were, why they broke the law, and whether they were capable of living healthy, productive lives. Most importantly, they were based on the view that youth institutions were designed not to nurture, support, and assist, but to deprive any which way correctional officers found possible.

Notes

1 For a comprehensive summary of the most recent research on trauma and incarceration among women, see Joosen et al. (2016). "From Juvie to Jail" in Kruttschnitt and Bijleveld's, *Lives of Incarcerated Women: An International Perspective.*

2 LLM time is "exercise" time. Unless there is a volunteer athlete/gymnast coming in to lead a group exercise, LLM on a good day, means jumping jacks, and stationary jogging in the middle of the cafeteria, right in front of the control console where frontline staff sit. On a bad day LLM means watching some TV show, and on a really bad day, it means staying in the room.

References

Bloom, B., Owen, B., & Covington, S. (2003). *Gender Responsive Strategies: Research, Practice and Guiding Principles for Women Offenders*, National Institute of Corrections, US Department of Justice, Washington DC.

Chesney-Lind M., & Shelden, R. (1998). *Girls, delinquency, and juvenile justice* (2nd ed.). Belmont, CA: Wadsworth.

Covington, S., & Bloom, B. (2006). Gender-responsive treatment and services in correctional settings. In E. Leeder (Ed.) *Women and Therapy Journal, 29*(3), pp. 9–33.

Covington, S. (2007). The relational theory of women's psychological development: Implications for the Criminal Justice System. In R. Zaplin (Ed.) *Female Offenders: Critical Perspectives and Effective Interventions* – See NCJ-225923.

HRW/ACLU, Human Rights Watch & American Civil Liberties Union. (2006). Custody and Control: Conditions of Confinement in New York. Human Rights Watch.

Joosen, K. J., Zoutewelle-Terovan, M., Slotboom, A., & van deer Geest, V. R. (2016). In C. Kruttschnitt & C. Bijleveld, *Lives of incarcerated women: An international perspective*. Abingdon: Routledge.

Koons, B. A., Burrow, J. D., Morash, M., & Bynum, T. (1997). Expert and offender perceptions of program elements linked to successful outcomes for incarcerated women. *Crime and Delinquency, 43*, 512–532.

Matthews, B., & Hubbard, D. J. (2008). Moving ahead: Five essential elements for working effectively with girls. *Journal of Criminal Justice, 36*(6), 494–502. doi:10.1016/j.jcrimjus.2008.09.011.

Miller, J. B. (1976). *Toward a new psychology of women*. Boston: Beacon Press.

Miller, J. B. (1990). *Connections, disconnections, and violations*. Work in Progress No. 33. Wellesley, MA: Stone Center, Working Paper Series.

Morash, M., Park, S., & Kim, J. (2010). The importance of context in the production of older girls' violence. In M. Chesney-Lind & N. Jones (Eds.), *Fighting for girls: New perspectives on gender and violence*, 219–240. Albany, NY: SUNY Press.

MS Foundation for Women, Collaborative Fund for Healthy Girls and Women (2001). *The new girls' movement: Implications for youth programs*. New York: author. Electronically retrieved from: www.cpn.org/topics/families/pdfs/New_Girls_Movement.pdf

Ness, C. D. (2004). Why girls fight: Female youth violence in the inner city. *Annals of the American Academy of Political and Social Science*, 595, 32–48.

OJJDP, Office of Juvenile Justice and Delinquency Prevention. (1998). *Guiding Principles for Promising Female Programming*. Washington, DC: US Department of Justice.

Schaffner, L. (2006). *Girls in trouble with the law*. Piscataway, NJ: Rutgers University Press.

SEF, Southern Education Foundation. (2014). *Just learning: The imperative to transform juvenile justice systems into effective educational systems*. Atlanta, GA. Retrieved at: www.southerneducation.org/getattachment/cf39e156-5992-4050-bd03-fb34cc5bf7e3/Just-Learning.aspx

Surrey, J. L. (1985). *Self-in-relation: A theory of women's development*. Work in Progress No. 13. Wellesley, MA: Stone Center, Working Paper Series.

UN Committee on the Rights of the Child. (2013). *General comment No.17 (2013) on the right of the child to rest, leisure, play, recreational activities, cultural life and the arts (art.31)*, April 17, 2013, CRC/C/GC/17. Available at www.refworld.org/docid/51ef9bcc4.html

Vigil, J. D. (2008). Female gang members from East Los Angeles. *International Journal of Social Inquiry, 1*(1), 47–74.

Zavlek, S., & Maniglia, R. (2007). Developing correctional facilities for female juvenile offenders: Design and programmatic considerations. *Corrections Today*, *69*(4), 58–63.

Chapter 4

Suppression as intervention

Dianne, 18

This is my eighth time being in here. I've been coming in here since I was 14 or 15. And ever since, I've been on the run, but never from home. I would never run away from home … if I had one … I only ran from probation. But now I turned myself in … I need to stop running, because now I have my family again … I have a support system, now.

My parents were separated when I was 7. Until then, we all lived together; me and five other siblings. Together my parents had four kids, plus they had one kid each from previous relationships but we all lived together until my parents split. They don't talk anymore but I know that my mom loves my dad because that was her first husband and she was with him 17 to like 25. You know what I mean? So she was with him young for a long time and had kids. After him, she hasn't married or anything. And my dad loves my mom but they know they can't be together. They are abusive to each other. They used drugs also at the time when I was really young, so they would beat each other up. They weren't a good couple, you know? I remember them beating on each other and I remember them going to jail. Like, my mom, I found her one time when she was really … when I was in kindergarten, she was on the bathroom floor … after, she had a neck brace on. She said she fell in the bathroom but my dad did it. I found her on the bathroom floor, she cut her wrist and she was bleeding everywhere. I had to go like, "Mom, what are you…" you know? And she went to a mental hospital when I was in kindergarten…

That's when they started splitting up … My mom started dating the guy next door who was young. He was 19, but they stayed together. When she left my dad when I was 7 she went with him and she stayed with him for 10 years. I liked him, he was really cool. He was 19 and he got a telemarketing job and took care of five kids at 19 years old. It was wild. He and my mom split up when I was in seventh grade. He loved her a lot, but he had to leave her because she was using a lot of meth again. I still talk to him till this day…

My mom had a boyfriend and my dad had a girlfriend, so our family split. I lived with my dad, and so did my little brother Charlie, who is a year and a half younger than me. And then my two little sisters lived with my mom and my older brother Michael who is my mom's. With us stayed my dad's girlfriend too, who helped raise me also for 10 years. My dad was a big coke-head then (now he only smokes pot). One time, he got drunk and he was saying to his girlfriend that her son needs to go to work and that he is 18 and all he does is sit on his ass, you know what I mean? So they ended up, he got drunk, and he got in a fight with her son. And then she tried to get involved so, you know, he ended up going to jail. And for a week, *just for a week* though.

So he went to jail for a week and when he was in jail we went with my mom. And she messed up *during one week*! What happened is she got in a fight with *her* boyfriend. And she like threw a knife at him and I remember her throwing a knife at him and all this stuff, so … and I really liked Mike [the boyfriend]. I think, I don't know why they got in a fight. I think it was how I told him she was cheating. Yes, while I was there, I caught her cheating and I was mad at her cause I liked Mike, so I told him. She was in her room in the motel, cause we lived in the motel (My dad lived in houses … He did it nice, you know what I mean? But when I would stay with my mom we were in motel rooms). And I saw her in the room with another guy. He had boxers on, I think. And I remember I told Mike because I liked Mike and I didn't want him to be with anybody else. I was young. I obviously till this day wouldn't do that. But when I was young I did it. I don't know if that's why they fought, but I mean, they fought a lot and I could have been part of the reason. And then, she threw a knife at him and I was holding him and it almost like hit him and stuff like that … I mean, my mom, she drank a lot at the time. I remember I would throw the alcohol out so she wouldn't drink and she'd get mad … She was young and had so many kids. By the time she was 24, she had four or five kids…

But she ended up leaving the motel room with all of us in the car. She took us to a friend's house and she told them … "Can you watch them?" But that friend was a girl who had already had her kids taken away because she tried killing her kids. You know what I mean? And my mom didn't know, so she left us with that friend. So, then that friend took us to *her* parent's house cause she wanted to party or whatever. You know, drugs, stupid young kids with kids. So they didn't want to take care of us, took us to their grandparent's house and the grandparents took us to Payless Shoes … And me and my little sisters we all got some shoes and like, I remember all that. And four days later, I don't know how I got a hold of my mom, cause she didn't know where we were but I told my mom what we were next to and what I saw. And my mom ended up finding us and she told them, "I'm gonna press charges on you guys for stealing my kids." You know? So they were worried about that, so they called the police and said … And I don't like to admit it, but it's true, my mom was a wreck. And they said, well she's on drugs, blah blah blah … So I saw my mom get arrested and they took us in a van and they took us to Oceanview[1] right here. And we were there for 5 days and my dad was told while sitting in jail, also next door to here, that he was charged with failure to protect their children and your children are in Oceanview. My dad is sitting there like, you got to be kidding me. You know what I mean? Like he is pissed. He's already in jail, cause my dad doesn't go to jail often. He's already in jail and now his kids are being taken away? He was so mad at my mom!

After 5 days in Oceanview, my grandma, my mom's side, came and got us all and we were in foster care in her house for a year and a half while my parents got to see who gets the custody. My mom she just kept testing dirty and this and that. She said, "I don't know how I tested dirty for heroin, I ate poppy seeds." But, she probably ended up testing dirty. I used to believe her, you know? But I know she tested dirty, just like I would make that up too, later on. Like, "I don't know. I ate a poppy seed bagel." You know? "I don't know what I did." And cause my dad had a house and had a girlfriend and he had money and he had stability and he had a nice picture and he was testing clean, and all that stuff; cause he was trying, he ended up getting full custody of us. He even asked the judge, like, "Give [the mother] half custody." You know? But they said no.

For [a while] we lived with my dad … I raised my brother and sister and I was the one who would wake them up and take them to school. But when his girlfriend came around she told me I was no longer mommy. I liked her a lot though. She was strict, Caroline, but I liked her a lot. She was there for me when I first started my period, you know what I mean? She was there from when I was 7 till today. But then my dad and her started fighting and she also had five kids, so it was nine kids in the house. And because they wanted to figure things out and because I would always sneak out to go find my mom, my dad gave my mom another chance … Even though he wasn't allowed to, but since his social workers were gone, he gave my mom another chance and we moved in with my mom in a 2-bedroom place. And my mom was good. She packed our lunches every day; She was involved in PTA; walked us to school. She was doing good and she stayed sober; she cooked for us; she was a little mommy … You know what I mean? It was five kids in a 2-bedroom but we liked it. My mom had it really cute and she painted the walls even though she wasn't supposed to. She made curtains out of sheets … You know what I mean? Like, we didn't have any money, but we had money for food and to pay the rent. But my dad would still come around to see us. I remember I would always see my dad and with his Starbucks mints and his rent cars … He would come over on the weekends and he would have his leather jacket on. And he used to pick us up, take us to Jack in the Box and the drive was always so long, I thought. We were driving from "Verde Park" to "Rojo Beach." But it wasn't long. It was just like, it was funny. Like, we would just go.

But, my dad ended up getting all of us kids back and we had our own rooms then. Around Christmas, something happened, I don't know, and my mom started messing up again. Her and Mike were fighting again or something. My dad got us all back and he wouldn't let me go with my mom. Cause I look just like her and that reminded him of my mom for some reason, so he tried to keep me away from her. And long story short, we ended moving to a 3-bedroom condo that was upstairs and downstairs. I was in like seventh grade or something. Ever since then my little brother and sisters have lived with my dad. And all of us have lived together. And my mom was in prison from then. And then she didn't get out till last month. She had been involved in Hell's Angels. She was doing drugs and stole a car and all these crazy things. She got bad charges and then Mike left her after this. He left her and that's why she was all like twisted cause she was involved in that stuff and he was like trippin', you know what I mean?

This is when my mom started going in and out but not to prison yet. My dad didn't really let us outside cause she would get out and my dad would try to keep us away from her. One day I called her and she told me she was going to come see me after school, and I waited at Carl's Jr. after school till like 10 o'clock at night.

She never showed up. I was pissed. I was so mad at her that day. After that I didn't see her for 3 years. But then in ninth grade, when I started using meth, I got a hold of my mom somehow and she just got out. And I remember, my mom was this pretty little housewife before, right? And I see her 3 years later … And when I saw my mom, *pftt*, I was looking at my mom and, oh my gosh! She always had little tattoos like me, you know, but she had like these sleeve tattoo on her arm now and she was wearing this leather outfit and she had her teeth missing. And she had a bullet hole on her face from getting shot. And the first thing she says is, "Oh my god, that's my daughter, I need some heroin." You know what I mean? Cause I was all grown up now.

When I told my mom that I tried drugs she said: "Oh the first time you try acid you gotta do it with me." And she's all cool like my sister. My dad would never let me see her, but I used to sneak and call her on the house phone and hoped that he didn't pick it up and find out, but he always knew. He always knew when I was trying to sneak and see her … And she would always get picked up by the police and go to jail because she would come find us, although she was not supposed to. But she didn't care. She would stand in front of our house and she didn't care. My mom said I'm gonna see my kids no matter what. I know it was stupid because she was on drugs and I didn't understand why I could not see her then but it was how I wanted it, you know what I mean? Cause I wanted my mom. You know, I wanted her to try. But my dad kept moving us a lot, cause he didn't want us to be Hell's Babies and be watched by Hell's Angels all the time … But when she got out and we started getting high together, my dad found out. I actually ratted myself out to him. Cause my dad and I have a good relationship. But then my mom got locked up again, and I got locked up too. And when I got out, then I got pregnant. And that is when my dad kicked me out of the house.

I called my mom and told her I was pregnant and that I got kicked out. So she came and she ran from her rehab to come down here. And I moved in with her and her friend. I didn't really care to think about my dad, but I would always end up going home to him like 3 in the morning knocking on the door. My dad would stay up all night long. He'd be up all night long and then open the door for me and let me in the house and tell me, "Shh, don't wake anybody up. Don't make a scene." He knew I was on drugs and every time I was coming home, I was coming home cause I was tired. You know and I wanted to come down cause I had been up for days. And my dad always opened the door for me. You know? And then, when I finally decided that I had to get an abortion in June, I was 15 weeks pregnant. And I didn't want to do it. And I had gone in like seven times. I went one time to Planned Parenthood and I started crying to my dad on the phone, "Dad I can't do it." And he's like, "Baby, you can do it. It's ok, you have to." You know what I mean? So I am crying, "How are you gonna make me kill my blood, your blood? This is our blood. Blah blah blah," you know? I've only seen my dad cry like three times in my life and he cried one time when my mom left him and I remember I was holding him when I was 7. And then he cried when I had the abortion on June 5 last year. I finally did it, and I had the abortion and my dad picked me up and I was hysterical. Like, it was the hardest thing I ever had to do in my entire life. Like, nothing in my entire life has hurt so much emotionally in the world. Like I did not want to do it, I did not want to do it, but I knew I had to. You know what I mean? And I was just hysterical. I was using drugs too, you know? So, I didn't get to be put to sleep. So I sat there.

It was atrocious. I was hysterical. Right before they did, I said, "No I don't want to do it." It was already too late, you know what I mean? And I just sat there and I felt this … I heard this loud noise. And the pain was horrible and I stopped breathing. And they go code something cause I had stopped breathing. My whole body just … and my heart had just curled up in a ball and they took me out of there. Next thing I was sitting on the recovery room waiting for my dad to come and pick me up and I was the only one crying. None of the other girls were crying cause they weren't awake for it. You know? And I just sat there crying and crying. And then my dad sent my older brother Carl to pick me up. And my boyfriend was in jail, so I was waiting for him to get his call cause he called me right before it happened and I said "I'm gonna go in right now and get it." And he said, "Ok, baby I love you." You know what I mean? And he called me right after and he goes, "How was it?" And I was like, just talking to him on the phone and I was just crying and then I stopped crying and I was just like, "Dad, I don't know what's going on. Is this ok?" I sat on the toilet with the door open, I'm bleeding a lot, what do I do? You know what I mean? And he was just like, [panicked voice] "I don't know. I don't know. I don't know." He couldn't handle it and he went to the room and started crying. I was mad at him though, so I called my mom and go, "Mom I just had a miscarriage." Cause my mom wanted to help me have the baby. You know? And I didn't want to disappoint her. So I told her I had a miscarriage but she knew. She knew that I was lying, you know what I mean? So my mom picked me up. And 3 days later, I go, "Wait, mom. There's something wrong." I had to give a dry birth and I didn't know. So something starts falling out of me and I go to grab it with my hand. And I go, "Mom, something's wrong." She knew what was going on and she goes, "Come to the bathroom." I sat on the toilet and the pain really started. Like then it was just, uh dude, I was hysterical crying and I go, "Mom," and she goes, "Don't look, don't look." And my baby was coming out then. And my aunt Sheryl, she's not my real aunt, but I call her my aunt. She's been there since I was very little. And they're just sitting there like, "You gotta be kidding me." And I was like, in pain. And they picked me up and carried me to the bed. They just kept changing the towels and I laid there with no pants on. And my mom then got pipe and she started lighting it for me. She goes, "Man, I don't know what else to do. You just gotta get high. You just gotta get high. I am sorry baby. You just got to get high."

Dianne narrated her story with surprising ease, contrasting with the uniquely difficult life experiences she had endured before she even reached maturity. Her delivery was for the most part uninterrupted by probes or clarification questions. She was letting it all out, and even seemed relieved, rather than burdened by describing out loud the heartbreak she had been subjected to. Her life-story did not end where this excerpt stopped. It continued on with more hard-to-believe twists, which, however, always revolved around her relentless search for a stable, warm home: from living with her dad's former girlfriend to avoid interaction with his current one; to staying with her incarcerated boyfriend's mother (whose boyfriend was also serving time concurrently with her son) and her five children; to moving in with a middle-aged man, a "very nice sugar-daddy" who picked her up while she was mourning her boyfriend's prison sentence outside the courthouse; Dianne was always trying to find a place to call home. But, in the end, the one place she would always return to, by her own admission was the Juvenile Hall ... located right next to the orphanage she had spent time in as a young child, which is located right next to the local jail in which both her parents, all her boyfriends, and herself had been detained at one or more points in their lives. It is painfully ironic that the one place she had been most consistently coming back to stands against everything a home-like environment is supposed to be. Ironic also is the fact that theory, research, and legislation all highlight the importance of what Dianne intuitively understood to be her most basic needs: normalcy and stability.

Meeting those needs, which are shared by most young women whose life-stories resemble Dianne's, is an essential step toward effectively responding to the unique characteristics of system-involved girls. In order to meet these needs, female juvenile institutions must look like normative environments and simulate real-world contexts (Zavlek and Maniglia, 2007). That is a suggestion and a promise that evidence-based programming for girls allegedly practices, as mentioned in Chapter 1. Given the fact that female delinquents are largely detained for non-violent offenses, fewer restrictions are not incompatible with security or safety concerns inside those institutions.

Unfortunately, for what seemed to be non-utilitarian purposes, the design as well as the strict regimentation inside the unit where this study's respondents "wasted their childhood"[2] mark the environment as anything but normative; indeed, the routine and rules that dictate everyday life behind these walls make it unnatural, and opposite to what Zavlek and Maniglia (2007) recommend, oppressive to the point that not only is not female-friendly, but to the contrary, is "*human-hostile*." This observation refers to more than an absence of embellishments or design elements such as curtains, college-dorm accessories, and grooming spaces, all of which are cited as preferable additions in residential places for females. Although those features would without doubt benefit the wellbeing of detained youth, they nevertheless seem luxuries given that more essential commodities such as privacy, self-expression, dignity, respect, and control over one's environment are not only withheld, but punished. This chapter illustrates through my respondents' narratives how this represented a continuation rather than a reversal of the non-normative life-context that enveloped delinquent girls' circumstances outside juvenile hall.

Attacking privacy, personal space, and dignity

The visitation space is located outside the unit, but it is not private. That *could* be justified by security concerns; however, security could also be maintained with minimal monitoring rather than guard presence in such close proximity that people's interactions and conversations are easy to overhear. One of the unit staff was able to provide me with extensive details regarding certain girls' visitation with their parents, and showed no reluctance in criticizing their demeanor while interacting with their visitors. Sometimes detainees are forced to use the phone located on the control station desks, and the few times they are allowed to call a family member or a public defender, they are carefully and non-discretely watched by the correctional staff.

Privacy and dignity were also compromised in a number of other ways, obvious or subtle, necessary or unnecessary. Girls must shower in the common area, with their peers, while female staff keep an eye on them; they must ask for toiletries, even feminine products the moment they need them, even if no female officer is available. Contrary to showers, restrooms are not open to minors in the common area. The actual toilet seats are located inside the small double-occupancy bedrooms where girls are forced to serve most of their time. Awkward as this sounds, only a couple of the girls considered this accommodation design worthy of mentioning, and that happened accidentally during a joint interview. Not only had they said they were unbothered by having to use the toilet in front of each other, but they also seemed amused and shared interesting stories about it, frequently bursting into laughter.

Rooms are searched routinely on the pretext of safety maintenance. For as long as I was able to observe, however, room searches revealed only petty and harmless violations such as possession of drawings, or letters, and lip balm smears on the walls. As a result of such violations, personal effects were removed frequently, despite the sometimes detrimental consequences to girls' emotional stability. Other possessions were often removed from rooms for solely punitive reasons. For example, staff entered one girl's room to take away a sheet with song lyrics she had written, to punish her because she had been misbehaving during the day. Girls whose stuff was taken away, or who were punished with "early bed" or room isolation because "contraband" had been found in their rooms would often "go off" i.e., yelling, screaming, and banging at their doors in protest. The whole unit's welfare was compromised during these events, as residents and employees were forced to witness (and try to ignore) another girl's emotional outbursts. Several of my interviews were conducted while girls were screaming in the background and correctional counselors were "just standing there like nothing's really happening," as Veronica (16), the girl I was talking to at one of these times, observed. As I was informed, this was a frequent happening in the unit, and disturbing for everybody, even girls who had "gone off" in the past. Shelley blamed staff for not preventing foreseeable fights between girls that often end up in lockdowns and screaming sessions. Explaining the reason why another girl was screaming and banging at her door during my interview with her, Shelley described two recent fights between two different sets of girls who had caused and continued to cause chaos in the unit.

> I think this is the staff's fault. The staff knew that they [two inmates] had been yelling at each other all night long. The staff knew that Gomez was a risk. They let her out of the room with everyone else around. And as soon as she got a chance, she went up to the African girl and started fighting. There was blood on the floor and I mean they had to wash blood off the floor. They did the same with Banez. Like, it's of course the girls' fault for doing it but they … it could have been prevented. It could have been prevented. It's like they *wanted* it to happen.

Another way through which personal space and dignity are unnecessarily compromised is by frontline staff's censoring of letters sent to detainees. In fact, whether recipients will read the letters, which are their only means of communication with the outside world, depends upon the discretion of frontline staff. In some cases, staff take it upon themselves to punish girls over the content of sent letters, even though recipients have no control over it, and even though the content violates no laws, or poses no threat to security. In a characteristic case, a girl got in trouble with her counselor/staff because one of her female friends who had recently been released wrote to her and greeted her with a "Hey love I miss you. How you been in there?" As the story reveals, not only this was an invasion of privacy, but also a hit to the girls' dignity, and a judgment of the girls' morality based on discriminatory and heterosexist standards that staff were eager to expose, or impose.

> And they … If the staff look at it, it looks like wrong but that's how she talks … Like the way she said "hey love" all the time … but he thought … I was like "eww (Counselor's last name)" I was like, "She's my friend! We were like this!" … And I started crying. I … I was mad … because he told me, "I'm really disappointed of you" … and then when he started reading me the letter after lunch, I started pouring tears … and he's like, "You know the other part the way she wrote to you," and I was like, "But you know the way me and her were. She was my best friend!" And he's, "I believe you. I believe you but you know other staff would have read it and it would sound bad too." And I'm like yeah but everybody in this unit know how me and Sonia were and then … we all knew she was going to write to me cuz she told you guys that she was going to write to me when she gets out."

That was Bertha (17), who had been in the institution five times already and not only knew the correctional staff well, but had also formed a bond with the counselor who was assigned to her, the same counselor who opened the letter before sharing it with the whole unit, and had expressed disappointment at her alleged deviation. Bertha was in desperate need of an older adult to trust and to trust in her. She had lost her own father at the age of 8 and started running away and drinking heavily soon after her step-father moved in. Unable to bond with a man who had not only "replaced" her dad, and diverted her mom's attention away from her children, but also had children of his own who were substance abusers, she started running away, drinking, shoplifting, and fighting. This time she had been arrested and given a 9-month sentence for grand theft auto. Throughout her narrative, Bertha repeated "whatevers, I didn't care" 15 times. This time, she claimed she had started to care and wanting to change. Her siblings, both married and living in her mom's apartment were a source of distress for Bertha's mom, who although separated, was still involved with a man none of her kids approved of. Bertha felt it was her duty to step in and save her mom from poverty, financial dependency, and her abusive brother. First, she would begin by recognizing her mistakes. She admitted that running away had "messed her up." She also admitted that she had been irresponsible and immature and had betrayed her mother. She credited her correctional counselor for making her see what was right and what was wrong.

> I never had my dad to tell me things like that or my stepdad never told me nothing like what's right and what's wrong. The fact that he's a guy, makes me, I trust him.

When the same counselor whom she trusted and respected expressed disappointment in her for having done nothing other than receiving an affectionate note from a former inmate, violating thus a nonsensical, unwritten rule, Bertha was consumed by grief and guilt.

> I think that fact that he was disappointed bothered me so much. Because, like I said I never had a guy in my family tell me "oh I'm disappointed of you" umm ... él (he) structures me. He tells me what's wrong, what's right. He tells me that if it's wrong, it is wrong, and I believe him. You know? I ... and I felt bad.

Despite her efforts to become "good," during her jail time and once again in her life, Bertha was made to feel that she had betrayed an adult whose opinion she valued, and who rejected her for the sake of maintaining control over detainees, and allegiance to his co-workers. Enforcing such strict rules then, controlled not only young women's behavior, but also shaped the way they understood the world and themselves in ways that undermined their privacy, their relationships, and their own sense of direction and control.

Undercutting a sense of self

The previous case reveals not only a privacy invasion but also correctional employees' persistent efforts to shape young girls into a conventional model of femininity prescribed by the puritan ideology that has dominated the juvenile justice system's reactions to "bad" girls since its conception. Apparently, admitting or even being suspected of homosexuality while incarcerated elevates girls' risks of receiving differential, that is "unfavourable" treatment, of being scolded by the counselors for their deviant nature, and of being informally punished through room solitude, or through ineligibility to help in the kitchen (an activity that, again, is largely considered a privilege in this unit). As it was explained to me, a gay inmate is never "good," therefore is never considered for rewards:

> The girls who are in their rooms ... well some of them are doing good, but because they're pregnant they can't be cleaning ... or they're NR [No Roommate] because they're like gay or something like that ... like they like girls ... They won't let no girls liking other girls be in cart [kitchen duty] because they think that they're going to do something with the cart girls.

It is consequently not surprising that whereas I never initiated this issue, several girls I interviewed went out of the way to let me know that although they wanted a roommate, they just wanted company, they were not gay or anything, as if that would be something I would frown upon. Two of the girls in my sample, however, mentioned that they were indeed gay, and felt that "the staff here don't like gay people." When I asked how anybody could know the sexual orientation of each inmate, I was told that girls are specifically asked about that during intake. Both girls who identified as gay were among the most reserved and apprehensive during the interview.

This climate of course is antithetical to the idea that juvenile institutions for girls should be environments that encourage self-expression. In addition to this strong heterosexist attitude, the right to individuality, as well as even the smallest amount of control over one's environment that would promote healing, self-efficacy, and empowerment, are undermined in multiple other ways, some of which stream from formal codes of conduct that incarcerated girls are subjected to in this unit.

First, girls are obliged to follow a strict time schedule that cannot be bent for any reason short of illness: they are told when to sleep, wake up, get out of their rooms, exercise, or shower. Several girls complained that exercise, although a rare and desired activity, also poses a great dilemma: "I feel gross, I stink," one of the girls told me at the beginning of our interview, which started as soon as she was done running in circles in the small backyard. She looked genuinely embarrassed and uncomfortable in her sweaty clothes. To make her feel better, I told her that I could wait for her to take a shower, but she said that they were allowed only one shower per day, in the morning, and even after heavy activity, work in the kitchen, or other unfortunate mishaps that are common among adolescent girls, they were obliged to wait until the next morning to thoroughly wash themselves.

If such basic hygiene needs are prohibited unless part of the schedule, it is perhaps needless to mention that other opportunities for taking care of one's physical appearance are non existent. Most girls were obviously self-conscious about the way they looked, their hair in an uncombed bun, their face without any make-up, their eyebrows messy, their outfit comprised of ugly, baggy clothes, baby-blue pants and yellow/orange. Some even apologized to me for the way they looked, and assured me that this was not "how I normally look." Knowing from personal experience that convincing a teenage girl that she looks fine even when she wears hair, clothes, and make up of her choice is useless, I prompted my respondents to tell me what they felt was the worst thing about their appearance. They complained about how they all looked the same, and wore the same clothes – literally.

> We don't have our clothes here, not *our* clothes, like the clothes we were wearing and stuff – they lock those up with our personals. I mean we get anything that comes out from the washer, you know ... Every Friday it's laundry day, but you don't get to keep the pants you had, you know, you get whatever fits...
>
> (Barbra, 15)

Along with clothes, girls in the unit are also deprived of having their own underwear:

> Sharing underwear is the worst thing about this place ... Cause the underwear we wear are not our own. It gets washed and passed around ... It's yucky and not good cause let's say ... I don't know if they're clean and what people come in with ... It doesn't feel right ... And we only get to change our bras once a week...
>
> (Yajaira, 18)

This seems to be a common practice in California detention centers, and a common complaint among girl detainees elsewhere. Young women in Laurie Schaffner's (2006) ethnography for example, seemed as uncomfortable sharing clothes and underwear as my respondents, and whether it should or should not be, that is a pretty big (cultural and gendered) deal. Yes, girls and women, in general, have been trained since birth to construct their identities through their clothing items. But it is also worth noting that for these particular young women, personal attire possibly bears an even stronger significance, for these are girls who possess little in terms of material or relational property that is dear or valued to them.

It may be necessary to put such seemingly trivial complaints in perspective, in order to bring the point across more clearly. Barbra, one of the girls quoted above, was a strong-willed, athletic, self-proclaimed tomboy and "bad ass" who in her short life had been detained three times in juvenile hall. She was no stranger to deprivation prior to entering the system. She was born with a meth addiction, to a mother who as far as family gossip goes, was a street walker who walked away from her on day one. Her father had walked away from her too, eventually making his own separate, less embarrassing family with another woman. Barbra was left behind to be raised by her grandmother along with a cousin (another grandkid). The cousin was older and physically abusive. To add to the trauma of abandonment and physical abuse, Barbra also fell victim to rape by an older man: all that by the time she was 11. Her encounters with the police had not been soothing either. Running away had become a habit and an annoying one to arresting officers. Sent to spend Christmas with her father's family in Las Vegas, feeling left out and disrespected by his wife and kids, Barbra ran away and was found hanging out, using meth and alcohol with some older juveniles outside a gas station. "Do whatever you want with me," she begged the police officers who found her. "Just don't send me back to my dad's." "You don't get to decide what happens to you young lady," said the officer. That was in one line Barbra's whole life-story: she had no control of and no say in her body, feelings, or prospects; she got no input in decisions made about her. For "good" measure, like outside jail, she was allowed none of that inside juvenile hall either. She tried to hold on to whatever dignity she had left by asserting herself through defiance and violence. She was outspoken about what she saw as an unjust and sexist culture of corrections and she felt that sharing clothes was a humiliating manifestation of such culture. "The boys get all that stuff; they give us girls nothing!" she would exclaim referring mostly to recreation, programming, services, and goods.

The young women in this institution were denied a variety of seemingly harmless goods or actions that could be helpful in their coping with illness, emotional distress, or even dry air. Monique (17) described to me an incident in which she had been wrongfully accused and unfairly punished for the following "violation":

> I got early bed cause they switched me beds … And then, you don't know what the other girl before you had in the room, and the girl had Vaseline left in the wall, and I got early bed for that. And when he (the staff) wiped it out, it had dirt on it! And I was like, oh, yeah, that's mine [sarcastic], that's old! But they still punished me for it…

The most troubling part of this story is not even the unjust punishment, but the alleged rule violation. Girls' lips and skin often get dry due to weather, room, or personal health conditions. For example, several girls in the unit are medicated, or go through drug withdrawals, which may cause dry mouth and skin. Yet, they are not allowed to use Vaseline, more than once, or any time of the day other than in the morning. So in order to get relief from dry skin, girls must become creative.

> Some girls put Vaseline on the wall, to save it … Cause it's clear you know … But if the staff find it before you clean it out, that is bad news…

In fact, it is "bad news" if the staff find anything left behind in the room, even toothbrushes, pencils, anything other than pre-approved reading and writing material. It is made more than clear that nothing inside the unit does or should belong to its residents, and there is no such thing as personal space for as long as the stay lasts, whether that is 30 days or six months.

Catch 22

It is also clear, to all the girls but the "newbies," that certain otherwise normal behaviors and interactions are prohibited inside the alternate universe of the detention facility. Girls are required to walk with their arms crossed behind their back and their heads lowered toward the floor, they are prohibited from looking around, talking to each other, or even smiling – at anybody. Victoria describes how she learned to become accustomed to and accept these rules as legitimate:

> I used to like be bad. Like, I'd smile a lot. Like, I wouldn't care, so the staff was very hard on me. The staff would give me early bed every single day … You can't smile or you'll get in trouble … Like, we can't, it's nonverbal communication … and I'd get in trouble, like, I have a nervous smirk.

When I asked Victoria to elaborate more on the reason why she thought smiling was "bad" behavior, she admitted that the rule was unreasonable to begin with. Perhaps she had sensed my objection with respect to this and other rules and changed her attitude to please me, but I think that she just felt "safe" enough to challenge this and other discipline methods, once she figured that I was not accepting them at face value either. It was my impression that her ambivalence about nonsensical rules such as the one against smiling exhibited the pressure this environment applies onto young girls' minds that in order to become "good" and "straighten up" they must uncritically accept certain things as normative, even if they are purposeless, a juvenile hall version of "because I said so!"

> I don't think it'd make sense. If we're like bitchy, they'll be … they'll give us early bed. OK, so one time I got early bed and they said, "Poor attitude." Ok, so I get early bed by smiling, I get early bed if I have poor attitude. You know what I mean? I can never do right!

It might be helpful to mention that Victoria was one of the respondents who had most internalized her "badness," so her ability to sense this "catch 22" regimentation is noteworthy and came as a surprise to me. Throughout her interview, she kept repeating that she was a mess and in need of structure to straighten out; she used the terms "spoiled" and "monster" to describe herself, and "crime" to describe her offenses, mostly status violations and substance use, with one exception. Her first arrest and subsequent detention were due to domestic violence charges that were generated during this incident:

> Well my mom was trying to get me up to go to school, and I accidentally like back hammered her. So, I think she was fed up with all my stuff. I was already ditching school. I was already like being bad, so my mom was just tired of all the mess I've been causing, so, she just called the cops.

Victoria's "incorrigibility" had been "upcrimed," that is, upgraded into a misdemeanor offense by way of being re-labeled as domestic violence, a policy change that has helped law enforcement bolster parental discipline against unruly children and has shepherded many non-violent, non-serious adolescent girls into juvenile halls across the country (Chesney-Lind, 2002; Chesney-Lind & Pasko, 2004). Victoria had been coming in and out of detention ever since that "domestic violence" related arrest, running away being her most frequent probation violation and reconfinement reason. She never truly explained what it was she was running away from, especially since she was insisting that her family life was great. At one point she did mention that the reason why she had started doing drugs was to "run away from my pain." When I asked what pain that was, she was reluctant to respond and came back to "the pain I put myself in with my behavior." I did not push her to clarify. Her behavioral problem, according to her, was her inability to listen, conform, and obey directions, especially those set by her parents, teachers, and probation officers. In juvenile justice language that is called: "incorrigibility." In the US,[3] incorrigibility is a status offense, and constitutes grounds for arrest, which is typically initiated by parents who claim that their kid is out of control. As mentioned in Chapter 1, incorrigibility statutes disproportionately affect adolescent girls who are more likely than boys to be arrested for having violated them, because their parents insist so (Chesney-Lind, 1990). Inside the institution, Victoria, a minor who had already been convinced that she was too defiant for her own good, learned that conformity was nothing to get indiscriminately rewarded for either.

The feeling of not being able to "do right" was almost universal among my respondents, who were perpetually disciplined, especially during their first stays in the institution. It almost seemed as if disciplinary rules were intended not to shape behaviors by deterring girls from being bad but by setting them up *to* be bad. This finding is not unique to my study's site or population. It seems that such attitudes toward troubled, deviant youth are popular among a variety of "helping agencies." Currie's (2004) ethnographic study of seriously troubled adolescents reveals that some treatment centers' rigid rules parallel those of juvenile detention centers. Similar to my respondents, youth interviewed by Currie also complained that it was impossible to avoid rule violation, and thus the consequences attached to it. As one kid put it:

> … there are eighty-five rules, and you have to learn them all … You take one step, you break a rule. Take eighty-five steps, you break eighty-five rules.
>
> (Quoted in Currie, 2004, p. 157)

And although that study's sample constitutes a population demographically different from mine, it does offer reasons to believe that regardless of where, when, and under which circumstances, treatment providers respond to youth deviance in a universally unsympathetic manner, and one that "equates treatment with the enforcement of obedience." (p. 157).

This might be the reason why these obscure rules were never explained to young women in detention beforehand, yet, "ignorance of law" was not considered an acceptable excuse not to be punished in the case of a violation. This made girls' initial stay in the unit confusing and stressful. Here is Yajaira describing these feelings:

> It was just like the first time I had been there (when I was punished a lot). They were just like … I was really slow to understand what they were trying to tell me. Like they would pop the door to my room open and like they wanted me to immediately know what was going and I didn't know, so I would look out and I would be like, "What do I have to do?" and they would be like, "Shower!" and I would be like "Oh-oh OK, OK."

All girls' accounts regarding the way rules were made known to them were consistent: they would find out what they were supposed or not supposed to do either by trial and error, or from older girls who took the initiative to enlighten them. I, on the other hand, was told a different story by the staff, who insisted that the rules were clear and then proved their argument by showing me that rules were in fact posted on the walls. However, as I found out again from talking to my respondents, the posting is useless, because girls are not allowed to read anything that is on the walls anyway. Moreover, there are some actions that are not prohibited by the book, yet are disallowed and punished by staff.

The most commonly mentioned controversy regarding what is acceptable or not inside the unit, was whether talking during meals was allowed or not. Generally, girls are not allowed to address, or even look at each other. However, during meals it is practically impossible to separate each one of them, so depending on capacity, two or three, sometimes four girls may share the same table. In this case, it is unclear whether girls are allowed to have conversations with each other. Some of the older girls who have been in the facility often told me, and they make sure they tell other, younger girls who are less experienced with the justice system, that nothing in the rules prohibits conversations during meals, and that the staff made up this rule to make their own lives easier. "They want us to eat, finish and go back to our rooms, so they can sit back and have their own time," as Brenda (18) explained.

> Oh, you can't talk when you eat … Well, in the rules, you can talk when you eat but they [the staff] say, "No you can't talk," so I got early bed…
>
> (Janice, 15)

> Like, I've been here for so long I know how it goes … You know how they say we're not supposed to talk when we eat, and if we do you get early bed, so I tell the supervisors and the staff get mad at me … Cause we have the right to talk … When you are asked to talk to the girl you are eating with, you can talk … When you've been here a long time you know that … But the newer girls don't know cause they won't tell them…
>
> (Monique, 18)

I was told that everything is done by the book when the supervisors are present and that even when they aren't there are some correctional counselors who are nicer, or just in a better mood that day, and do allow conversations during meals.

Meal me out

I assumed that dinner conversations would improve the meal experience, albeit not its nutritional value or taste, both of which are extremely low according to my observations. The food in detention was often viewed with contempt, symbolizing yet another means of disrespect and devaluation. In fact, whereas the most common complaint about life in the facility was boredom, food was a close second. The food was described as "nasty," "disgusting," and "gross." It certainly looked unhealthy (frozen hamburger sandwiches were among the few menu items) and unappetizing to me, and every time I happened to sit next to a girl I was going to interview after dinner, I noticed that most of the food ended up in the garbage rather than in her stomach. Girls also complained that the meat was "fake." "It's like, soy, or something crazy like that," said one girl in disdain. Consequently, girls would get extremely excited with the prospect of extra, tasty snacks, like the ones the group counselors or volunteers would bring, but again, this joy was always reserved for the "good" girls, that is, those who were allowed to leave their rooms, or to participate in programs, or be on cart. I was surprised to discover that (yet another) form of discrimination, especially in light of the following incident. When in the beginning of my study I had asked whether I could bring snacks during my interviews, I was told that it would be OK as long as other girls did not see them or as long as I didn't eat anything in front of the girls, to avoid making them feel deprived. I then proceeded to state what I thought was obvious, that the snacks would be brought for the girls I would interview, of course, and initially they agreed, yet later on retracted their permission (along with other things they had initially agreed to) and said that rules were unclear as to whether I, as a researcher, was allowed to bring anything to the inmates, so it would be better to err on the side of caution. Nevertheless, such food and snack related privileges were given all the time to certain girls –"the favorites," as other girls would call them – and not only were they not hidden from the less fortunate ones, but they were even celebrated. In addition, frontline staff would display a myriad of snacks, drinks, and other food, such as chips and soda, which girls I interviewed were very fond of, on their console, which was centrally located in the common area and exposed for everybody to see, smell, and crave. Similar to findings from interviews with adult women in prison, in juvenile detention too, food consumption, a human right, was elevated from necessity to potent disciplinary or/and retributive scheme that perpetually kept young women in check.

Taking away a sense of control

Zavlek and Maniglia (2007) propose that allowing girls to switch the lights in their room on and off could be a good way to promote empowerment and healing, and to assist the reversal of the disempowering effects past brutal victimization experiences have had on most female offenders. In the site under study, such control over one's environment is unimaginable, and even when girls beg for it, it is crudely and without explanation denied. Having lights on because they are scared of the dark or lights off because they have a headache was mentioned in my interviews often during the discussion of problems girls face while living in the unit. Sometimes this becomes so important that girls fight for it, but to no avail, as described in the following incident narrated by Vienna (15), between an obviously distraught girl and her caretakers in the facility.

> … so she got an early bed … and this girl, she's not supposed to be in this unit even, she's supposed to be in the "special"[4] people unit, so she was really, really upset. "It's not fair," and she started banging the door in her room, so the med lady came, and popped her out to give her her meds, and then the girl asked her lights off and they're like "No, lights close at 9:30," and she's like, "You do it for others," and he's like, "I don't. Maybe other staff do but not me." Point is she walked where we used to have the tooth brush, she got the box and threw it on the desk and then she started throwing other stuff and yelling, "Fuck this place!" So right away they called code one and had to calm her down … So they tackled her and that big guy, and Jones plus eight other staff, and then they put her in the observation room (when the staff watch you, every little thing you do), so she started banging her head in the wall…

Incidents like the one described above are unfortunately not uncommon, and one can't help but wonder whether they could be avoided by manipulating the environment these girls are thrown into, especially since it usually serves as the immediate replacement of other environments, such as abusive homes, degrading schools, or dangerous streets, which surround and ultimately guide girls toward self-harm, delinquency, and detention.

Creating spaces that allow some privacy, dignity, self-expression, control, and that ultimately respect the young women who are housed in them, would not only be materially effective in creating a humane and therapeutic solution to these girls' deep traumas, it would also be symbolically effective, in that it would send the message that these detained minors are not "others," different from the "normal" good girls we call our daughters. They are children who should be treated as equals to their "free" peers. They are also children that suffer a tremendous amount of emotional pain resulting from past experiences, shaping what are nowhere close to being "normal' and definitely not "normative" childhoods. Juvenile institutional spaces must be spaces where such memories are put to rest, not stirred up – places where new, healing memories should be created.

By sheltering system-involved minors inside institutions that resemble home-like contexts, one would debunk the myth that these girls' delinquency is a result of having been spoiled rotten by their families or/and friends in the outside. Allowing formal and informal regimentation for the purpose of "hazing girls straight" sends the message that these children deserve neither sympathy, nor support. Consider this a unique version of "Broken Windows" theory, the idea that obvious signs of disorder (in our case pervasive order) send the message that nobody here cares – which invites real serious disorder. Similar to the policy implications of the theory, which emphasize aggressive policing of minor violations such as jaywalking, frontline staff's fixation with authoritarian regimentation only results in superficial order that masks a whole lot of harm. Setting young women up for failure though, may serve frontline staff another utility: inmate failure provides COs with a legitimate excuse to both physically punish girls they find difficult to handle and get them out of their hair by locking them up, especially on weekends when no supervisors are around and staff get to be more relaxed. I believe this is what Shelley meant when she argued that staff "wanted" fights to break out while at the same time pretending to show zero tolerance of fighting. This is consistent with Jerry Flores' (2013) finding that juvenile detention staff (and school teachers) cultivate a fighting ethos and co-opt fights among the female detainees as a means of maintaining control over them. I think this is a plausible explanation, yet one that at least as far as my analysis indicates, needs expansion: I argue that the occasional lackluster prevention of inmate fights combined with the constant hyper-surveillance and harsh punishment regimen around which life inside this unit is organized, represents how correctional officers view female delinquents under their care. That view dehumanizes young women who are treated as pawns, underscores their feeble character, and thus, excuses their suffering not only inside, but also outside detention.

Here is an anecdotal illustration in support of my point. Once, I presented my findings in front of a group of juvenile justice employees (including juvenile judges and correctional staff). After relaying the "Vaseline" story to them, one of the correctional counselors in my audience put her hand up, annoyed with my criticism over the "only once per day lip balm" rule. "If girls' lips get dry later on in the day, then they should just lick them!" she said exasperated. I was at a loss for words with what I viewed as cruelty on her part. I could not understand where her lack of empathy for children she had made a commitment to care for came from. Perhaps individuals of this character should not be hired for these positions, I thought. Then she continued on: "Have you seen *Locked Up*?[5] These girls are brats, manipulative, and spoiled. They need to be taught a lesson, not to be cuddled." I had to think quite a bit about that statement. I initially thought that this point of view was based on ignorance, that this woman was actually informing her career attitude from a TV show. Later on, however, I concluded that her attitude was based on actual experience (which is in many ways the opposite of ignorance). Her experience came from working for a system that systematically treats youth delinquents, boys and girls, as innately different and unworthy, a treatment that could not be further from system-involved girls' reality. This attitude finds expression in the architecture, design, and management of youth institutions, and in its turn, shapes the opinions of those individuals who are asked to serve in them.

Conclusion: no such place

So far, and as we have seen in the accounts of young women detained in this "rehabilitative" juvenile institution, the idiosyncratic elements of everyday life inside it turn what could and should have been a safe haven where young women can heal and grow, into a non-normative, and purposely disempowering environment in which self-worth, dignity, self-expression, opportunities to exercise control over personal space, independence, and personal health are continuously and viciously under attack. If one wanted to create an environment that defies all evidence-based suggestions for institutions serving delinquent girls, this would be it. Instead of "simulating" real world (conventional) contexts, this context offers an alternative universe that makes little sense to those who still view juvenile institutions as places where minors are sent to get help.

The rationale of all the idiosyncrasies that shape life conditions in this detention center is based on a very grim view of female delinquents and their character. It is based on the understanding of girls' law violations and other digressions as expressions of spoiled character, as consequences of having too much love, too much affection, too many material assets (money, cell phone, clothes), too much fun, and too few "no's." In other words, it is based on a caricature of the female delinquent, one that I did not find among the young women I interviewed. "They're spoiled. You got to see them when their parents are visiting," said one counselor once, her face grimacing in contempt. "They just sit there, silent, starting at the TV. *Did you bring me anything*? That's all they care for." Similar remarks were communicated to me often. "They just have no respect for nothing. They really don't care," is what frontline staff members would say. One counselor even referenced a young girl by name, while pointing to her:

> I watched (girl's name) the other day and I timed her … for a whole 60 minutes I swear to God, she didn't take her eyes off of the TV to speak to her mom. She didn't say a word. They don't care. They only want their money.

Correctional counselors certainly had spent more time with these children than I had, but there was nothing among my observations that corroborated their judgments. My respondents would sometimes paint a similar negative image of their peers, even themselves, but I personally never saw it in person. Where was that callous, materialistic brat? I had not met her in there. All I had met were girls like Dianne: girls who had frequently harmed or risked harm to others, but had themselves been harmed by everyone else and from a very young age at that. I did not see spoiled, unless domestic violence, sexual abuse, neglect, racism, unstable households, and broken relationships spoil a child.

In all my interviews I would ask girls like Dianne to describe to me a time when they were happy: what did that time in their life look like? Dianne, my most outspoken respondent had volunteered this: it was when her mom was doing "mommy" stuff and the whole family (including her many siblings) were together under the same roof, when there was a home to shelter her, and when her dad would drive her and her siblings in his car, destination not important. She was happy when she felt safe, loved, and cared for, and when she had a routine ("stability" was her exact word) to thrive on. Yajaira remembered a better time, a fun time, when she'd wake up really early in the morning to go into downtown LA to sell pallettas (popsicles) with her mom; a little girl and her mother, working a cart with popsicles up and down the streets of LA, tired, hands frozen, but heart full of happiness. That was her best childhood memory. And she was one of the few respondents who could even find those among the devastating stories that filled their memory files. But when they did mention these few glimpses of light in their lives, none of them talked about material things, or about getting away with being spoiled, or with living the high life. They all referred to memories of love, affection, and normalcy. Memories that the juvenile institution in which they were forced to spend a good part of their adolescent life seemed determined to not only make them forget but also, make them believe they do not deserve to re-live. "Most of us that are in here, the one thing we want is stability," Dianne had said. "Where do you think you and the other girls in here can find that place? Can you describe it to me?" I asked, in the hope that she would say something like: house arrest; camp; a half-way house; back home with dad. That would have definitely helped me write a good conclusion. But, instead, she said, "Nowhere; there's no such place."

Notes

1 Pseudonym for local orphanage, located just yards away from the juvenile detention center where Dianne was at the time of the interview.
2 Paraphrasing several respondents' view of their multiple re-entries.
3 Similar statutes resulting in state punishment and detention for "difficult" or "unruly" children are found in many countries, such as Denmark, Japan, Belize, and Nigeria (Child Rights Information Network, 2009).
4 As mentioned in Chapter 2, in my "Setting" description, the juvenile hall includes a unit for mentally impaired or seriously distraught juveniles who are kept under

one-on-one, 24-hour supervision and receive psychiatric treatment. This "special" unit may house either girls or boys, or both.

5 *Locked Up* is a "docudrama" series that goes inside various jail and prison institutions in the US.

References

Chesney-Lind, M. (1990). Female status offenders and the double standard of Juvenile Justice. *International Review of Criminal Policy, 39*, 105–112.

Chesney-Lind, M. (2002). Criminalizing victimization. The unintended consequences of pro-arrest policies for girls and women. *Criminology and Public Policy, 1*(2), 81–90.

Chesney-Lind, M., & Pasko, L. (2004). *The female offender: Girls, women, and crime*. Thousand Oaks, CA: Sage.

Child Rights Information Network. (2009). *Global report on status offenses*. Retrieved from www.crin.org/en/docs/Status_Offenses_doc_2_final.pdf

Currie, E. (2004). *The road to whatever: Middle-class culture and the crisis of adolescence*. New York, NY: Henry Holt and Company, LLC.

Flores, J. (2013). Staff here let you get down: the cultivation and co-optation of violence in a California juvenile detention center. *Signs: Journal of Women in Culture and Society, 39*(1), 221–241.

Schaffner, L. (2006). *Girls in trouble with the law*. Piscataway, NJ: Rutgers University Press.

Zavlek, S., & Maniglia, R. (2007). Developing correctional facilities for female juvenile offenders: Design and programmatic considerations. *Corrections Today, 69*(4), 58–63.

Chapter 5

Abuse as intervention

Lori, 19

I've been in here 11 times. I started coming when I was 12–13 for running away and drugs – heroin mostly. Right now, I'm just taking care of a warrant to get out of probation. I got the warrant on me cause I had ran away from camp. See, because my BF at the time, who I had been with since like 8 years, we used to play house, childhood friends, he was at camp for 2 years at 14–15 and was doing 2 years again. Well, Jason was getting out in a month, the second month I was in the camp. It was Christmas, and he was getting out, and I had a furlough and I had waited almost 4 years for him to get out, so I was like, I'm not gonna go back. Like with camp if they sign you off on a furlough, it's basically on them and it's on you, they are basically giving you extra 30 days – not a big deal, so I ran. My mom had gotten tickets to Baltimore for both of us cause he was done. But 3 days before his release he gets in a fight with this other guy (at camp). We had tickets, we were ready to go to Baltimore, and he is 19 going to 20, and that is the problem with camp housing kids who are 19, if you get into a fight with a younger kid you get charged. He ended up choking the kid, and you choke someone, that's crossing the line, so they charged him with attempted murder. So, they sent him to county jail and he was facing life, but he fought it for 4 months and I went to all his court days – and going there was a risk for me cause they had staff there and I had a warrant. Then they finally gave him one strike and 8 months so he's out in September. But, that's not good cause of the strike. His dad is already a third striker and he's doing life, and his mom is in for 4 years so his life is already pretty like, he's kinda like … he likes it in there, he is institutionalized, he wouldn't bother getting a second strike, he'd be totally fine with it. With him and me, we don't have the using, like I stopped heroin, I guess, like, he was my motivation to stop … he's the only person to get me to see what it was doing to me, you know? Like the only person that I really thought cared when I did it, but *he* is doing it now … in county jail. He's snorting heroin in county jail – they get it in there. Nobody thinks he can do it, nobody thinks he can make it and I have so much hope in him, like he' s got so much hope for me … He's very smart … He likes hands-on things, like construction, he's very built like tall, very big and muscular. We have a childhood together, I know him from so long, like when I went with everybody else, you know when you're with people and they're something different, like with him I'm myself, and he is himself. But when I was out, I was like OK well he's not coming home, what am I gonna do? I couldn't stay with my mom cause I had a warrant for my arrest so I was putting her job at risk, so I told Jason, well, what you want me to do, so I had to go out and figure out where I was gonna live, so I started renting out a room from a guy I know, who's a really good friend but he uhm … we started to like each other a lot and Jason wasn't there, and I started to get mad with Jason cause like how can you get in a fight just 3 days before your release, and then me and Matt we got really close and we had a 3-bedroom house. And my mom likes him a lot, and uh, I ended up getting pregnant (*laughs*), and I ended up losing it in 7 weeks. I told Jason right away when I found out I was pregnant, and he thought I might be pregnant by him, during his furlough but I told him, "I'm not, Jason, it's Matt's." Well, he knew that Matt was taking care of me … Matt knew that Jason was in prison, cause Matt would give me money for Jason's phone calls and all that, and Jason wrote to him and told him thank you for taking care of her and I appreciate it, but Matt was beginning to be like, well you know, hopefully she'll be with you when you're out cause you know, I am planning on her *not* being with you … And Matt was like, not doing drugs, he is straight, I mean he got picked up last month for a DUI so he's doing some time in like a work farm, but he doesn't do drugs. And he likes my mom, like he and my mom are like, you know when I got pregnant he got real excited. He said, "I got another chance." He's like, "I'm gonna have a baby," cause he's got two kids, his kids got taken away from him, both the babies' moms are like, they're crazy and they moved away far. And I was like, "Oh Jason," like cause Jason would like call me and tell me, "So, I'm joining *War"* – it's a white supremacist prison gang in there, and I was kind of like, "Well that's everything we talked that you weren't gonna do, Jason." Cause that involves him having to check in when he gets here and having to get into more trouble … cause that's exactly what his dad does, his dad runs gangs. So that shuts everything down for me … so when Jason gets out September and I get out December, I think I'll probably be going home to Matt, cause Matt, we have a 3-bedroom house and he works, and I'm gonna be going back to school. I do love Jason, but he had a … like, there was another girl he was … she was already calling … there were letters and stuff, which was OK cause like, I see it as like *what else*, I mean, I can wait for him only for so long, and stuff happen.

I got into drugs, well, my dad was always a crack addict and he would sleep in the garage and I remember seeing him use, never really wanting to use. But then, I just started to run away at like 11 and 12, and then I wouldn't have anywhere to really go, and then finally I found an older crowd who was using drugs and finally found a boyfriend who was way older than me. I was 12 and he was 20, he dealt drugs and he was just kinda, like, the easiest thing to go in and fit in and that was meth, and turning 15, I started using heroin. I was always against using needles, even when I started using meth, and I had friends using needles and I was always against it. But as I started getting older, I first started to slam speed and then I got into a really good relationship and really bad relationship. I really fell in love with somebody and he was using heroin and our relationship just revolved around heroin. He was 27 and I mean, I couldn't even do it myself, so I was like I need you to do it for me. Once I got to the stage where I could do it myself, I didn't need anybody else, like my addiction was already played out for me. I just kinda like forgot about him and it was only about me and heroin and that's all *(laughs*). My whole thing is, when I am using … I know many people say when they use it numbs them, and it covers it up, but I know when I use heroin, I know that I hurt myself and I'm killing myself slowly. That it's more like a pleasure toward me, like from the way that I look, like my eyes get really dark, and I get sick, and I love the sickness. Like my whole addiction, it's not just the high, it's just the process of everything, like from throwing up to like laying on the bathroom floor and just feeling the cold bathroom floor on my body and just throwing up and being sick … like, I know now that cause I still, like, smoke meth or weed here and there and it's OK, I won't get stuck to it, but as soon as I were to do a shot of heroin, I know I am stuck for a while, and I already had two ODs on heroin … When I ODed the second time on heroin, I had a really bad OD. The third time before this that I got arrested, I had a really bad OD and I was knocked out for 3 days at my friend's house. I was at my friend's house and I was knocked out for 3 days and, actually, had a really bad kidney infection and nobody really bothered to ask me if I was OK. Like, I didn't even get up to go to the bathroom for 3 whole days and I didn't eat nothing and I ended up, my boyfriend took my temp and I had a fever of 107 and I couldn't move. Then, they were really worried and I wasn't even throwing up – and that is really bad, and so, they took me to my mom's house. And my mom hadn't seen me for 3 months, and my dad was there so I was, like, why is my dad here, but they called my PO and my PO came and arrested me and she didn't believe I was ODed and she was pulling me out of the bed and I literally fell on the ground and that's when I ended up puking. I couldn't even talk, and that's when they ended up calling the ambulance and took me to the hospital and I was in the hospital for 12 days on IV. I had ODed another time on speed and heroin mix, and that was the third time – second on heroin, so they told my mom I was very lucky and that's when they brought me here and that's when I got court ordered to camp the first time. The *first* time I ODed was on 275 pills when I was 12. I took Motrin with a bottle of alcohol. It was Christmas morning, so just about a really bad day. I did that, I think. for my mom, just to be like "hey."

I started running away from home because it was bad. My mom was very attached to my dad even though he was using and then my dad would come and stay for a few days and then he was gone. But, there was always fighting, a lot of fighting, physical fighting, and my dad would leave but my mom would always take him back. I've got an older sister, and every time there was a fight, my sister would always take me to the other room, but we could always hear it, and I remember I was really little and we could always hear them fighting and my sister would always have to close the door. I remember always my sister covering my ears and stuff, but still being able to hear. My mom was always working but was very emotional, it was a bad environment; there were a lot of emotions, my mom was always crying, and I was going through my own abuse from my baby sitter and my mom was not really paying attention to me, so I just wanted to get out from my situation. My mom was so dedicated to working you know as a single mother…

My mom, she is sensitive. She is very caring, my mom is a very big hearted person. She is not an addict at all, she's totally like, which is totally a shock, because my uncles, her brothers who are friends with my dad, they are really heavy drug users. My mom would never bring any other men around except for my dad. Yeah, until this day, like she recently learned he was in jail and she started crying saying, oh I really love him; it doesn't make sense, because the way he treats her, but my dad does the things he does cause he's got lots of issues, like he went through a lot of abuse too growing up, so she's got this big attachment to him and he's tried to get over his addiction for a long time, and he can't and his addiction is really bad. And like, she cares about him, but she sees that it has affected her children bringing him back. That, she sees now that she can't see him. She hasn't talked to him for almost a year, this is the longest; she got a restraining order cause he gets really crazy with her like he goes to extremes with her, watching her, and stuff.

My parents sent me away to boarding schools. I was actually kicked out from four out-of-state Behavior Modification schools by 14. They're like WWASPS[1] programs, all these private facilities in different states; there's one in Montana, Utah, Idaho, and they're all connected. But my behavior didn't become better, my behavior was getting worse actually, for a long time. Then I was sent to a school in Jamaica that was like the last resort. It was a lock-down facility and the way they are teaching to modify you back to society was … beating up and starvation. They have no child protection laws in Jamaica; my parents had signed off custody to the Jamaican ambassador, so it took them 2 months to get me back in the end. I think that when I hit Jamaica, my behavior became really worse, like my resentment to my parents, at that point, I was 14 and the girls there were 19–21. There's like a whole website on that program cause kids committed suicide and they shut it down. The program is called Tranquility Bay Academy.[2] There were riots between boys and girls; they had us lying face down in opposition which is like for hours with no food and I mean it was just punishment and they don't have child protection laws. I was a kid of Jamaica. My mom was not aware of all that. I ended up getting a counselor who came from the US and in her first week there and when she saw the bruises and what they had done to me she got scared and called my mom saying, "I don't think your kid should be there." And I would send my parents letters about what was going on there and they didn't believe me. They had support groups for parents in the US, who had their kids there, and they were told "Don't believe your kid, it's manipulation," and I would get these letters from my mom saying: "You will not come home till you complete this program." I'd get the same letter over and over. We also had seminars the same exact like our parents were taking, like self-help, but they were basically brain-washing, totally ridiculous, really stupid stuff. So then when I came home my mom was like, "Sorry I should've listened to you," and I was like, "Well yeah, too late now." I was so upset. My mom, she didn't know what to do, you know, "My daughter is running away, using drugs, all that, I didn't know what else to do." I mean, I would not come home for 3 months…

My mom could have taken easier steps with me … I think she could have talked to me … she never tried to talk to me; she never tried to sit down with me, she always tried to buy me things and always tried to cover up. Cause I was sexually abused by my babysitter, and when all my abuse stuff came out, when I finally told her after 4 years I was going through that, she just shoved me into counseling with all these people I didn't know and she left for work, and I was only at the age of 9 when she dropped me off and went to work. I was having trouble at school, cause teachers were calling in saying, "Your daughter is not listening, we have problems with her." So actually, I told my sister first, and she told my mom, cause I still had to go to his house to be babysat and I just was not able to handle it anymore. Then we reported it and because some of it had started when he was a minor, he admitted it and there was not much they could do, because it started when he was 17 and I was 5, they said there's not much they can do … They said when she turns 18, I can go ahead and do something about it cause he was a minor when it started. I got held back at school, so she changed me from public to private school, and that was harder and then, she would go to work all day and drop me off to these counseling sessions where they watched me, babysat me all day and they were trying to just, like, get things out of me, getting me to talk about it, and she'd be gone all day… Like, I remember my mom was never there, so I had a lot of resentment toward her. I needed *her* the most. And she was also so involved with work and with helping my dad, helping my dad, helping my dad, like, at the age of 10 *I knew* that my dad would never change, so … I knew the path I was gonna take at that point like I knew, I think maybe the way I went about things was also the way I probably knew how to get my mom's attention, like, "Hey, I'm over here."

In my brief and informal discussions with correctional counselors, I was often told that young girls in their detention unit engaged in risky and delinquent behaviors for "attention." A few of my respondents even repeated this in their self-evaluations and evaluations of their peers:

> My mom would just ignore me and I would just be like, alright, I would just take off and she wouldn't pay attention to me, so I would just take off, come back, take off again.
>
> (Isla)

> The problem with my dad was that he was always with his girlfriend; he paid more attention to his girlfriend, you know, so I was always like my mom was busy with doing drugs and my dad with his girlfriend so I was, like by myself.
>
> (Nora, 18)

> Well, when I was younger I was being like all depressed all the time, cause I had two little brothers and people would not pay attention to me so I was jealous …
>
> (Dora)

> A lot of girls in here are deprived and they feel lonely and they want attention.
>
> (Shelley)

Whereas this hypothesis seems to corroborate Lori's multiple accounts of self-harm, I doubt that counselors' and minors' definitions of "attention" are similar at all. Yes, Lori, like the majority of young women I interviewed reported running away from home to get *someone* to care enough to go after them and pay attention to their needs. Often the people who did go after them were older men, drug users, and eventually probation officers, each interpreting their "needs" by their own self-serving standards. Running away and substance abuse were both young girls' tactics of calling out their troubled home life and calling for help. "I just couldn't take it anymore," often followed reports of family violence, physical or sexual abuse, and loss-related grief, and preceded running away events.

These tactics, however, had the adverse effect: by running away from trouble, my respondents ran into *more* of it, when, as I was able to gather by reading their life-stories, what they were trying to achieve was a run *toward* safety. So, what Lori meant by wanting her mother's "attention" was more complex than the staff's understanding of what these girls were desperate for: a place where their physical and emotional integrity would be respected and valued, an environment also known as "safe space."

The mutually causal links among victimization and coping behaviors such as substance abuse and running away, female delinquents' most prevalent offense (OJJDP, 2018), are in the epicenter of the pathways literature (Daly, 1992; Holsinger, 2000). It is that approach to explaining female delinquency that has informed guidelines for working effectively with system-involved girls. These guidelines take under consideration the prevalence of abuse-related trauma in delinquent girls' lives, and the influence it exerts not only on their health, but also on their behaviors and their likelihood of offending and recidivating after detention. For correctional programming to be effective, juvenile institutions for young women must constitute safe spaces. This is not limited only to security and physical safety provisions. Reducing the probability of accidents, diseases, suicide attempts, fights, and escapes is necessary, but not sufficient for qualifying as a safe space for female delinquents.

As Zavlek and Maniglia (2007) indicate, emotional and cultural safety precautions must be taken as well. There are three essential elements that promote feelings of safety for adolescent incarcerated girls: (a) trauma therapy, (b) revictimization prevention, and (c) relationship support (Covington & Bloom, 2006; Koons, Burrow, Morash, & Bynum, 1997; Matthews & Hubbard, 2008; MS Foundation for Women, 2001; OJJDP, 1998; Zavlek & Maniglia, 2007).

In Chapter 3, I examined the various ways relational needs and connections are systematically and intentionally undermined in the juvenile hall. Chapter 7 will detail the failure of the same institution to implement trauma-informed treatment that is responsive to the gender and cultural contexts of clients' lives. In the current chapter, I focus on data that reveal gendered attacks and violations that subject these vulnerable women to repeat victimization by their own counselors.

The types of violations to which I am referring are not (as far as my observations and interviews are concerned) criminal. My respondents volunteered no physical or sexual assault incidents inside the institution; neither did I witness any myself. I know that the official rules of the facility prohibit such actions, and these rules were carefully observed, at least in my presence. In extreme cases and only for the safety of others (clients and employees), staff *are* allowed to "tackle," mace, or handcuff girls. This was confirmed by several of my respondents:

> They will restrain you if you don't stop after the mace. The mace doesn't stop you, then they have to restrain you. But the mace is a way of them not having to get physical. And if the mace doesn't stop you, then they have to get physical …
>
> (Shelley)

> They can't hit you or they'll get in trouble … But they can tackle you … And yeah, it hurts a lot when they twist your wrist like this … and they hold your head on the floor.
>
> (Barbra)

While these options do not legally constitute physical abuse,[3] they still cause pain, and perhaps pain that is more harmful to girls' dignity rather than body, especially since they are always performed in other inmates' presence, by the male staff, who are usually much older and bigger than any female resident in the unit. Macy, who has received this treatment in the past, uses sarcasm to shield her dignity while relating her experience of being tackled:

> The staff here, they think they're hard … They think they are cool … Well, let me tell you, I'd like to see them work in prison, not here, especially in the lifers' ward … Cause they (the lifers) don't give a shit…

Macy is no stranger to physical abuse. A fighter herself, often tackled by counselors in response to her attacking peers who are "coming for her," Macy grew up with a mother who would beat her constantly and with malice. "One time she started punching my stomach, cause she thought I was pregnant" recalls Macy. So, being physically restrained by someone with authority and more power over her was the norm for her.

I did not observe any sexual abuse, nor was I ever told of any in my interviews. Several girls reported that police, as well as probation officers like to use language which may constitute sexual harassment. For example, girls are often called "bitches," and "hoes," and are compared to street walkers. A 15-year-old girl who was playing loudly with her tongue piercing during her arrest was called a "dick-sucker" by a male officer. Girls also believe that there is a sexual favors exchange taking place inside the juvenile hall, but none of them has engaged in or witnessed such a thing. Other than "making stupid little flirty comments," as I was told, and sometimes staring, or talking to girls in a tone that I personally found unprofessional, staff refrained from actions that would qualify as evidence of sexual abuse.

This is not to say that young women were safe from violations. On the contrary, system-involved girls in my sample were victimized throughout all stages of their processing, and especially, inside the walls of juvenile detention, where such abuses were invisible, along with the persons who received them. Verbal, emotional, and psychological abuses were routinely and unequivocally preferred over less harmful "corrective" treatments. I observed them directly, as the staff made no effort to hide them from me – they found my research and the possibility of its publication entirely nonthreatening to their job security (and they were probably right). My interview data are also full of such evidence. In fact, I have so much data on this, that it would take pages upon pages to describe the multiple ways in which my respondents were victimized by staff members. The most concise way to summarize them is by saying that the staff commonly practiced nothing short of psychological warfare against their minor clients, who entered the institution wounded, frail, and defenseless.

I found that only two responses were realistically available to these victims-turned offenders-turned victims: surrender to the attack, and you will eventually be left alone, even receive some privileges further down the road. Or, fight back, stand up and defy the attackers and you will find the entire unit, including many of your peers, ganged up against you, win no small or large battles, and serve your time in hopeless distress. In fact, the minors were grouped and more specifically divided into "black" and "white" sheep. Whereas their life-stories shared similarities that defied race and class, many young women "otherized" their peers, expressed antagonistic attitudes against them, and often sided with staff when discussing unit conflicts, despite having been subjected to staff maltreatment themselves. This division served staff members well: by turning young girls against each other, they continued to victimize all of them with little resistance, and without facing any accountability. This division further disempowered girls, who developed self-contradicting accounts about themselves, their peers, and the adults in their lives. These self-conflicting understandings obscured their ability to sort through their problems, reflect on the causes of their offending behavior, and the reasonableness of the responses with which these behaviors were met.

The girl that won't shut up

No other young woman resisted the conditions of confinement and the treatment she was receiving by staff more passionately than 15-year-old Bianca. I was intrigued to listen to her story long before I was able sit down and talk with her. Her notoriety inside the unit was indisputable. She was brought up as example of "how to not do time" by several girls I had already interviewed. After my first one-on-one with her I had a chance to do a double interview with Bianca and Vienna, another young resident, who followed a much more tamed attitude in her interactions with staff. I noticed that the two girls had an excellent rapport, similar backgrounds, and identical views about their counselors, which surprised me: Vienna herself as well as other respondents had presented Bianca in a negative light in our interviews, generally describing her as a stubborn, gang-obsessed troublemaker. This description coincided with that of correctional counselors who gave me the run-down as soon as I walked in the unit with her parents' consent at hand. "You're talking to Gomez?" asked one of the male staff. "How much time do you have? She'll chew your ears off," he continued. Two of his peers, both women, rolled their eyes, adding "Good luck with her! You know, she just won't shut up!" Sounded perfect to me. At the same time, it contradicted my personal experience a day or two before, with Bianca's family. This was one of the many cases of minors whose parents I had to physically track down in their own space, in order to get the required written consent. Bianca's mom was kind enough to let me into her home, a small house she shared with her parents, in one of the largest Chicano communities in California. A large family portrait, mother and three children, hung across the dining table where we sat. Bianca's mom's broken English and my broken Spanish somehow managed to facilitate our communication. Mom burst in tears as she spoke about Bianca, glancing over at her image in the portrait. "She is my little one," she said. "And I know she is having a terrible time in there. They treat her really bad. And I don't know what to do about it. I am helpless." She also expressed concern about her daughter's risky behavior outside detention. "I don't know how to help her. And I love her so much. If you could tell me how to help her…," she kept repeating.

I am not sure what I was expecting to see, but I think a bold, hardened gangbanger with a cheeky attitude must have been it, because I was slightly surprised when the little smiley girl from the portrait walked inside the interview room and gave me a shy "Hello." Bianca informed me that she had been high on a weed-crystal-meth-cocaine combo the day the portrait picture was taken, and then proceeded to talk about her various adventures with her "homies," her dad's cautious support of her gang affiliation, her run-ins with the cops, and the stolen-vehicle arrest account that preceded her current detention. She *did* have a lot to say. She admitted that she talked back a lot and that police officers always got ticked off, calling her a "smart mouth." She had a knack for smiling as well:

> When I get arrested or when something happens I always have a smile on my face. I'm always happy. Everybody always says that [I smile cause I'm nervous], but to me, I'm not, like, to me, I'm happy. I don't know why, I always have a smile on my face, it's like, "Fuck it, whatever happens, happens."

Bianca seemed to relish in the idea that she drove police officers mad with her talking, due process knowledge, and sharp tongue.

And so he's all like, "Oh, so you got jokes." I was all like, "No." He was like, "Step out of the car." And he pulled me out the car and he threw me against the door and he was going to search me and I was all like, "You can't search me, sir." And he's like, "Yes I can." And I was like, "No, you can't, let me tell you something, you search and we'll be going to court like I'll make sure we do." He goes, "Alright, alright." So, he sits me down. They're sheriffs so they can't search me and he's a guy, I have to be searched by a girl and like he thought I was like, "Oh, like she won't know," you know? And I was like, "No sir, you can't search me," you know. So, like my homie gave all the drugs to the girls and the girls stashed it and everything and when they got searched they didn't find nothing. They arrested us but like they took us to the sheriff's department and the cops were acting stupid with us, they were all like, "Oh you fucking little Mexican girls." And I was like, "You fucking white piece of shit." And I started telling them shit, because they were acting like dicks and they were disrespecting my race and they were disrespecting me. You know, and he was like, "Hey, what're you going to do about it, I'll fuck you up right now." And I was all like, "Officer, you better recognize who you talking to, you're not just talking to one, you talking to all of us." I was like, "You know he's from G street, we're all from G street, so you better recognize who you talking to." He goes like, "What're you going to do, shoot me?" I was like, "No, but if I had a strap I would." And he goes, "So, now you want to threaten me." And I was like, "No sir, but you're disrespecting me, so I'm disrespecting you." And he took us to the sheriff department. But first, cause when he sat us out, he called a tow truck and they were towing my mom's car away. And we were sitting on the curb and the officer, cause I had my tongue pierced, we all had our tongue pierced, and we were playing with it and I guess the noise was getting the officer irritated and he was like, "Shut up." and we kept on playing with it and he was like, "You're not going to fucking shut up." I was like, "You can't tell me to shut up because I'm not talking, I'm playing with my piercing." "I'm going to take it out." I was like, "Try to take it out, I want to see that." He goes, "So you got a smart mouth." And I was like, "You know what, whatever, just shut the fuck up." And my homegirl started laughing cause I was basically the only one talking, I was like talking for everybody. Like they were all like, "Yeah that's right." And I don't know, I told them shady and fucked up shit and I guess one of them took it personally, one of the officers, and he's like, he turned all red and he's all like, "You can deal with them, I'm not about to deal with these fucking little bitches dadada." I was like, "Shut the fuck up, leave bitch, that's what you're good at doing, you're good at just talking shit and just leaving, you can't do shit." And he got mad and he just took off and the other officer was like laughing at him and we were laughing too and, yeah well everybody's parents came for them and except mines. Mine didn't come until the next day. Until Saturday morning.

I could see how adults assigned with the duty to correct Bianca would have trouble finding her endearing and loveable, I really could. I must admit, however, while astounded at the unnecessary risk she and her friends created for themselves and others in the stories she related, I still found her personally adorable and charming. Perhaps this had to do something with the fact that she was immersed in a culture that, knowingly or not, enabled and even rewarded her "rebellious" behavior. Her dad as well as her friends' dads were often described as "kick-back" "OGs" who knew "what's up" and would laugh at and make fun of their daughters for failing to escape arrest. Bianca always called her dad, separated from her mom, to let him know what she was doing, and he knew all her homies who seem to have great respect for him. My sympathy for Bianca was perhaps also qualified by the fact that she too acknowledged her actions as harmful, irrational, and embarrassing. She felt shame, and regret at her inability to control herself.

> I'm weird. I think before I do things. I know what's good and I know what's bad. I know what's going on, I like doing the bad things, but I like doing the *good* things. I don't know I'm confused. I'm in the line.

I thought her good nature and the love for her mom would constitute protective factors against her delinquency, so during our discussion I kept pressing her for an answer as to why she engaged in behaviors she knew would jeopardize so many things she cared about. The morning after her arrest and subsequent release, she and her friends stole a car from a driveway in a "rival" street. The engine was running, a young toddler strapped in a car seat, while the owner was inside the house. Bianca and her friend took the car seat out, placed it in the doorstep and drove the car away, keeping it for four days. They were both high on meth, and her friend who sat behind the wheel had not even learned how to drive.

> I tell you, I know I'm smart, I think before I do things when I was getting when I was going, when I was walking toward the car I was like to my homegirl, "Nah, that's fucked up. Her kid's in there, you know, like that's pretty fuck up. Her kid's in there. She's probably going to take her kid to the doctor or something, you know." Like she's like, "Fuck it, fool she's a fucking enemy," and so I was like, "Ok fuck it fool let's go then."

Some serious intervention was due for Bianca, and her friends, to be sure, perhaps an intervention that addresses a multitude of factors, both micro and macro-social, relating to the perpetual and pointless gang conflicts among different streets in the same neighborhood, and the very real consequences these conflicts have on people's lives. No matter how likeable she came across to me, she was a very difficult adolescent to control, by her own admission. Nevertheless, she was still a child whom adults, *professional* adults should be able to handle in ways that were productive and humane. Unfortunately, the adults who carried the responsibility for doing just that, saw that they did the exact opposite. Every time Bianca returned to detention, and she had been there three times in the previous year, the abuse she received escalated further. Bianca was subjected to constant verbal assaults and humiliating treatment:

> The staff here treat me like shit – I can't stand them, basically all of them, except for three. I don't get along with my counselor. He doesn't like me for shit. He always tells me: "You freaking evil child, go back to your room." He tells me things like … let's say … he treats me like shit, he calls me names like evil child. He calls me something, I don't even know what this word means. I asked this other girl and she said, "You don't know?" I've never heard this word. We used to have dogs in the unit, and one day the dog took a shit and he pops me out of my room, like I was in my room, and he goes, "Come here Gomez, what is that?" And I go, "Shit!" And he's like, "What are you doing on the floor Gomez?" … I'm like, "What the fuck is that, eh, are you serious, you pop me out of me room just to tell me that?"

Bianca is rarely allowed to attend school or group counseling (although she meets with the unit psychiatrist). Her frequent eruptions disqualify her from participating in the already limited programming. She is placed frequently on lock-down, and never in a double occupancy room.

> And they don't let me have a roommate … the other day I asked P [frontline staff member], "When am I be able to have a roommate?" and he said, "NEVER," and I was, "Why?" And he goes, "We have our reasons. If Miss A [Unit supervisor] wants to give you a roommate, lemme tell you, right when she walks out that door, we're taking the roommate out. We don't want you to have a fuckin' roommate."

Along with verbal abuse and isolation, her protesting results in physical restriction, as well. Most recently she had been restrained after refusing to change rooms. Bianca claimed that frontline staff used a room-changing tactic as a form of psychological abuse, to which they knew she was going to respond aggressively, providing them a justification for physically hurting her.

> And it got me mad cause on Wednesday I was in room 7, and Thursday I was in room 22, and then Friday, I was in room 6, and then yesterday they moved me to 7. And you know, room 7 is in the corner and sometimes cockroaches come in, so I asked for a towel to put under my door, and they're like, "Oh you don't need it you'll be moving rooms tomorrow again," and I was like "WTF? Why do you guys do that?" "Oh It's our job." No it's not! And I was like, "You guys have been fuckin playing me and I had patience

> with you guys. I'm not gonna lie, either you keep me in this room or I don't know what I am going to do."

What she did was to spin out of control. She "got off," was restrained, and placed in 24-hour lock-down.

> I went off on Friday, cause they got me so mad. One thing that bothers me here, is when girls go off, you know, and they start banging at their doors, that really irritates me. Friday, when *I* went off some other girls went off on *me*, and one girl started banging on her door and I was like, "Don't fucking bang your door; I am not playing around," and she stopped. I have a lot of anger inside me … Like, when someone tells me something, I take it out on them, you know?

Gathering from her own account of the events following her melt-down, Bianca's poor anger management skills were not the sole, or the deciding cause of her behavior.

> Yesterday, they were banging my door every time they would go by. I was sleeping and they would bang my door. They know how much that irritates me. First I was scared but then I got mad … And then they would get on the speakerphone and they would put their cell phone on it and they have this ringtone play that says: "*Wake up Bitch, Wake Up Bitch*" … I don't know who that was but I was like, "WTF," and then Ms. M comes and was like, "Who are you talking to?" And I was, "You need to stop." And they started banging on my door. They just do that just to irritate me.

This account was nothing less that horrifying. Why would so many adults think agitating this already distressed child was a good way to restore order in the unit? Bianca and other respondents who corroborated this event (which had taken place only a few days before the interview) described this as the collective action of frontline staff, rather than the deviant behavior of one unruly employee. Was there not one grown up in the unit to stand up against that borderline torturous treatment of Bianca? She had mentioned that there were three at least with whom she got along, so I asked her what their role was in all this. In brief, other staff were just too scared to side against their peers.

> They listen to what the others say to me but they don't say anything. Cause they know that I tell the supervisor everything, and Miss M, I get along with her, but sometimes I tell her what is going on, but she says, "I don't wanna get involved," cause I told her I am gonna write them up, and I am gonna put you in as a witness and she's like, "No don't get me involved," so I understand you know, she wants nothing to do with it.

Fine. The other staff members opted for washing their hands of rather than for standing up for children's rights. But how about the supervisors? Bianca's attorney? Bianca's parents? The therapist she was seeing inside the detention facility? Were they not aware of the situation, and what had they done to protect her from it? Bianca made sure everyone *was* aware. As mentioned in the previous quote, she had filed several grievances against her counselor – that was, after all, the formal procedure to be followed. She had also taken the informal route by verbally complaining to the unit supervisors.

> I get really along with the supervisor … I get along with both supervisors, but especially with Miss A. Cause Miss A, she's basically like you, like she is here to talk, what I am going through, and I trust her, I know everything I tell her stays between us, so I tell her everything … but right when the supervisor leaves, they treat me like shit, like they don't let me get out of my room, they tell me shit, like call me "lil snitch," or they talk shit behind my back.

Here's the even more terrifying part: all adults in a position to help her were very much aware of her abusive relationship with unit staff, and had each offered a response; it had done little to improve Bianca's conditions of confinement, but had placed a large enough target on her back for all unit staff to take a shot at. The moment Bianca made use of the grievance process, she became a "snitch" and a "rat" and her issue was elevated from a minor conflict with her counselor to a full-fledged war against the frontline unit staff. It was now her against them.

> I let the supervisor know about it, and I also let the public defender know … and the staff get in trouble for that. They still tell me shit but not as much as they used to cause I told me public defender and I had my dad come in here and talk to the administrator, and I had miss A talk to the administrator, and then my dad told me they had someone come in and check how they treat people here. You can ask other minors about it cause some of them have complained for me saying, "That is not right how you treat Gomez," and I even asked the other girls, and they said, "Yes I'll be the witness" … I also have a CU who comes and talks to me … well he hasn't been here for a while, he has some family issues … but, he's been helping me a lot, he's been checking with the staff … You know CU is one-on-one, everything stays in between you and the CU, and he told me that other minors tell him about what is going on with me.

It seemed as if Bianca had convinced herself that her conditions of confinement had improved since so many caring others had intervened on her behalf, yet her most recent lockdown incident stood in direct contradiction to that belief. She quite possibly found solace in the idea that fighting for one's rights, something that her narratives showed was empowering to her, resulted in positive change.

Her lived reality did not warrant such optimism. I did not dare point out how badly resistance had worked out for her on Saturday (the day after she went off):

> I declined all day yesterday, I didn't eat breakfast lunch anything, I was sleeping all day and they kept coming and banging on my door. I haven't told them a word today.

So, finally, the "girl who just doesn't shut up" was silenced, even if temporarily. I wondered how many girls had been silenced the same way before her. At the time of the interview, Bianca's detention experience was unique in that most of her peers were not attacked with such intensity. It did serve as a blatant warning to others, however: want the whole unit ganging up on you? Be a Bianca, if you dare! No supervisors, CUs, attorneys, or administrators will save you; they always leave; frontline staff are there 24–7, and they are patient, united, and vengeful. In Bianca's abuse, staff send a clear message to all minors that deterred them from speaking out against the smaller scale aggressions they too faced. Young women in the unit were no strangers to threats and attacks; they knew what they had to do.

> Other girls say I am weird cause no matter the way they treat me I am still happy and I'm like, I'm gonna be here for a while, I am not gonna let them put me down, and wake up every day unhappy you know…

Other girls did think Bianca was weird for not breaking down, or for hiding the fact that she, even she had broken down a little. "When I first came here, I was horrible," she concedes. "Now I am trying, I've been trying to do good, to improve my behavior, to improve my anger and my patience." If she had reached that point, I had little doubt that others had too, at much earlier points in their juvenile hall time.

The girls that shut up

Most girls used self-degrading language to describe themselves, even in the face of gross violations they had been subjected to by others. Very few had continued to resist those violations, even as they acknowledged that they partially deserved them. Barbra (15) and Macy (17) still were defiant enough to get restrained and locked-down quite often, although their reaction was much less passionate and more cynical than Bianca's. Monique (19) was a strategic fighter: she was experienced enough to know how, when, and for what to fight; she understood the consequences of filing grievances to get back at staff for mistreatment: "Staff are with staff, they won't go against each other unless they don't like each other which is very unlikely," she shrugs. She files grievances only when there is a utility to it. Having been disqualified from using the payphone to call her boyfriend, Monique knew that she was nevertheless entitled to use the staff phone for legitimate phone calls:

> So I'm supposed to use a staff phone cause I am monitored, which for me it's better, cause it's free. But the staff are like, "I don't know anything about that." And I was like that's BS. I didn't file the grievance the first day; I waited, and I asked each day. Then I filed. So now, I get my phone call.

Monique argues that staff do not like her talking to the "newer" girls in the unit because having been in detention so many times in the past, she poses a threat by enlightening others. Staff do not like that, she argues, because it strips them of the opportunity to take advantage of the fear, immaturity, and inexperience of newcomers.

Monique has learned to adjust and survive, which I supposed Bianca, Barbra, and Macy would eventually learn also. Most of my respondents had, albeit in different ways; some, like Monique, had learned to pick their battles, and play the system; others had given up fighting back altogether, not because they saw staff behavior as justified, but because they had learned that nothing good and everything bad would result from complaining to them about their abuse. In conceding that, they shared no allegiance with girls who did protest.

> Well, there's no really talking to them like once they kinda make up their mind on something; it's like that but I mean, I just kinda like ignore it now and just, you know, do whatever. And then I know that I'm going to be transferred to camp soon so this is only like a pit stop.
>
> (Trish, 18)

That was one way to look at this institution. But for young women who were on "placement" or on "gang terms,"[4] this was not just a pit stop; it was their adolescence. Most of them chose patience nevertheless, and engaged in covert microresistance, like gossiping, sneaking in valuable goods such as lip balm, or placing phone calls without prior permission. And yet, they were still not entirely insulated from abusive behavior. Even compliant girls were commonly targeted with attacks that were not only intentional and purposeful, but also, masterfully gendered. It is as if juvenile correctional counselors employed all their knowledge of female adolescent psychology in crafting gender-specific insults rather than programming. Such insults included mocking girls' physical appearance and posture, yelling, name-calling, and constant cursing.

Once, I asked frontline staff to point out to me the girl I was supposed to interview. The girl, who had braided her hair up in pigtails, was standing very close by, so the employee told me loud enough so that she, and everybody else could hear: "Do you see that one, with these two things sticking out from her head? That's her!" Another time, I observed frontline staff watching and correcting young girls' performance during a short-lived aerobics program. This exercise program combined cardio and dance movements, and it was obvious that certain girls were body conscious or shy to perform some parts of the routine in fear that they would look awkward, or be laughed at, a fear that was not unfounded. The program was carried out in the day room, right in front of male and female staff, who would stare at the girls and make derogatory remarks when they were not doing the exercises "the right way." "Why don't you try a little more [girl's last name]?" a female staff member once asked aggressively. "You look all stiff," she continued, before the girl took one look at me, standing close by, and put her head down with a shy smirk. No wonder half of the girls who participated stood in the back trying to hide, or moved as little as possible in an effort to not attract attention.

My interviews were also laced with accounts of insulting acts and words staff used against my respondents. "People here pick on me sometimes and that would bring me down," remarked Isla, a 15-year-old I interviewed. Trish describes an incident that made her file a grievance:

> One of the counselors, well, she was degrading to me … she would be like, "Oh yeah children this is why you don't do drugs," or something cause I'd come in and I'd be coming down and like, you know, I'd be like wooh, like, you know…

Trish, who had been battling a meth addiction since she was 12, did not appreciate being made fun of in front of her peers, for going through withdrawal symptoms. She knew it was unprofessional and against the rules yet her grievance resulted in further mistreatment. Trish was denied participation in group programming, either counseling or recreational, and was never given an explanation as to why. She understood that as revenge for having filed a complaint. She found staff cruelty objectionable and damaging:

> I think a lot of them sometimes can be immature. I think they all have their own reasons and then um I know my reason why the staff didn't like me kinda, uhm, a long time ago I filed that grievance. I try to see things from their perspective but I think that there's a lot of people who are working here that don't care. A lot of them, they love to pick favorites but they also kinda do psychologically mistreat us and it's just kinda hard, cause some girls are more like vulnerable than others. In here, they can really psychologically kinda mess you up. We're juveniles like, you know what I mean, and like, they're adults like they freaking ugh, this is supposed to be their job like, who are *they* to like, ugh…

I could see the struggle in Trish's demeanor and hear it in her words: She *was* trying to put herself into correctional officers' shoes and understand where they were coming from. It was an attempt at empathy that I had expected but had not seen from the grown-ups in the unit. It seemed as if she was trying to force-fit a cruel reality into a made-up world: detention was not as bad as other girls made it out to be! "Some girls here, they're in self-pity," she claimed at the beginning of the interview. Self-pity was not something Trish was interested in steeping into. Trish had (even if temporarily) participated in enough counseling programs that teach coping skills, to know that self-pity and complaints were counter-productive and disempowering. So, instead of scorning the sources of the problem, she turned against those who did:

> A lot of the girls like to complain about everything, and oh my gosh and this and that, but it's like, you know, you don't really have control over the situation. I've kinda learned that from coming back so many times...

The more Trish shared details about life outside and inside detention, however, the more this initial attempt to distance herself from her peers' feelings and side with the staff fell apart. That shift in her narrative emerged when she was relating an incident about her friend and roommate Lori, with whom she shared similar backgrounds (age, race, addiction history, and parental addiction). Lori, like Trish, had also expressed favorable views on correctional staff:

> I love the staff here ... they're like my family, like they're more out to help me than the PO. When the girls first come in here, they're not nice. But with the girls that have been here for a long time ... it's like family here ... I can talk to any of the staff that I know and I can joke around with them and that's totally understandable, like they're only 21; they're not that much older than me.

Later on, though, Lori contradicted herself when describing an incident that had taken place just two days earlier.

> The other day a staff I was just walking by and she's like, "Ewww, would you look at that," and she looked at me disgusted and I knew ... I get a lot of crap from the staff, cause I'm the only girl here with so many tattoos...

Lori's arms are covered with tattoos, and the name "Jason" is displayed in large fonts across her neck. Trish, who was walking behind Lori explained:

> It was not right! Like she has a lot of tattoos and stuff, but like none of them are bad or like you know, like, racist or anything like that, so you know, *why*?

Lori was even more disturbed:

> I was very upset cause like these staff they're not that much older than me you know? A lot of the staff are degrading to me, and it's totally against the rules, and I can file a grievance for that. They look down on me cause I have tattoos in my neck and they think, oh she's skin, she's racist ... so I was like, oh she's being very judgmental, like why is she judging me, and I was like very upset.

Lori did not file a grievance but continued by generalizing her accounts of staff's demeaning attitudes, which now included some whom she had previously referred to as "family."

> I don't know, I mean some of the staff are real nice and some others aren't; they're rude and I don't know why they work here really. Some of the male staff are real cruel and degrading; some of the female staff are degrading to the girls too. They look down on us, they like to pretend they have a lot of power, you know and to me, I'm very uhm, they call me, here in my unit they call me "auntie" cause I've been here for so long...

Pet-names like "auntie" are used as terms of endearment by correctional officers. Intentions notwithstanding, they trivialize and ridicule stigmas these young women are trying to overcome, such as Lori's chronic failure to stay put and complete her probation, or Dianne's susceptibility to small yet recurrent status injuries: because it rhymes with her last name, yet matches her non-damaging compliant demeanor in the unit, staff call her "fender bender." "They're cool with me," she notes. "I don't cause any problems" (Dianne, 17). In other words, she never complained for being mistreated, even when she was. The CO's work was done with Dianne.

"Better people needed"

My respondents understood abusive staff behavior as a "bad apples" type of problem, individualizing thus what seemed to be a routine and pervasive reality inside the institution. The common thread among all my respondents' suggestions about what needs to happen in order for the institution to qualify as an environment where verbal, psychological, and physical abuses are eliminated, and where minors feel secure enough to express their dissatisfaction or discomfort regarding their confinement conditions without fear of retaliation was "Hire better staff."

> I think maybe the people who hire these people should kinda look at like people they're hiring like their character traits or like whatever, like interview them a little bit better...

The fault that young women seemed to have assigned to frontline counselors was that they lacked work ethic:

> I mean some of the staff, I just don't get why they work here, cause like, we're supposed to have exercise for an hour a day and I mean it's not that hard to take us outside and they don't ... They're lazy ... Some of the staff will sit there and play video games, and they also tell us: "Just don't ask questions!"

> They're lazy! [Our] unit staff ... I'm serious. One day I was sitting there waiting for 45 minutes straight after visitation ... They would call them every 5 minutes, "You have a minor for pick up," and they wouldn't come ... damn these staff are fuckin lazy...

> Cause ... I don't know, but I think it's cause they're lazy ... Do you see what they do? They just sit there, you know ... And then they're like ... "I'm tired, I'm stressed," and it's like, WTF ... you've been in your cell phone for like 8 hours! What do you mean you tired?

Young women made sure to clarify that it was this particular unit, the *female* unit that employed the least desirable personnel.

> Everybody knows we have the worst staff here. Control staff will talk smack on them all the time.

My respondents felt that the reason why frontline staff were "so mean" and "derogatory" was that, lazy as they might be, they mostly hated working with female delinquents, and took all their resentment toward their job duties out on the young girls they supervised. There might be some truth to that argument. Attitudinal research reveals correctional officers' disdain for working with female inmates (Baines & Alder, 1996; Britton, 1999; Chesney-Lind & Shelden, 1998; Kempf-Leonard & Sample, 2000; Pollock, 1996). Such attitudes were communicated during my discussions with frontline staff, who rationalized their preference for working in the boys' units with old-fashioned accounts about girls being "difficult," "manipulative," and "too dramatic." It is possible that these stereotypes about women's weak and inferior status served to enable misogynistic attitudes, and, as a consequence, actions like the ones described in this chapter.

It is also possible that correctional officers' own employment status augmented their resentment and consequent mistreatment of their detainees. As far as qualifications, pay, and experience go, frontline staff are on the bottom of the Probation Department pyramid: theirs is an entry-level job, with an entry-level salary, that requires only a high school degree, and minimal training and experience. On the other hand, these low-paid, minimally qualified employees are vested with the huge responsibility of advising and maintaining order among other people's children, children whose communication, self-control, and emotional skills are severely compromised. Most importantly, they enjoy discretion to exercise those responsibilities as they see fit, and away from the supervisor's or the public's eye.

There is certainly an argument to be made about the importance of individual traits detention workers must possess; indeed the job description emphasizes some. I am not trying to argue that there is no personal agency involved in the decision to torture a distraught 15-year-old girl by banging at her door while she is in lock-up. As my respondents said, "some staff" are bad. What I am arguing is that individualizing the problem misses its systemic nature: whereas only a few staff members engaged in abusive language and behavior, *all* of them tolerated it at minimum, and in some instances, rewarded it with their support. Once a minor filed a complaint, good and bad staff members alike retaliated against that minor. There was no consequence for their abusive or retaliatory acts: nobody lost their job, was transferred to a different department, demoted or otherwise penalized except through a verbal reprimand by the supervisor. Bianca's testimony, corroborated by several of her peers, as well as supervisors, effected no positive change for her, or for other girls. This, then, does not sound like a case of bad apples. It sounds like a system deficiency that extends further than the particular county. Even though there are very few studies that have focused on the treatment of young women inside juvenile detention facilities, past findings (Acoca, 1998; HRW & ACLU, 2006) seem consistent with mine in that detained children are perpetually subjected to emotional, psychological, and verbal abuse against which there is no effective recourse. Such reported experiences of course constitute child abuse for the direct victims, and as such, violate international law provisions. The United Nations Convention on the Rights of Children [CRC] (1989) reads:

> Every child deprived of liberty shall be treated with humanity and respect for the inherent dignity of the human person, and in a manner which takes into account the needs of persons of his or her age.
>
> (Article 37, section C)

The systematic violation of this rule in the institution under study creates not only a legal concern but also a personal tragedy for all inmates, regardless of the frequency or severity with which it happens. Young girls who are treated "favorably" as compared to the juvenile institution's "Biancas," are victims as well, by way of witnessing the abuse, by being forced to remain silent in the face of their peers' maltreatment, and by being reminded that one day, they too, could possibly face similar consequences should they displease their counselors. In other words, even when they are not harassed, young women are threatened with imminent harassment.

Learned helplessness

Abuse, suppression, disconnections, and neglect were omnipresent in young women's life-stories before they entered detention; and they persisted inside detention, as well. In fact several girls referred to past experiences using tone and language similar to those they used when they described the trauma of their first incarceration. For example, this similarity was obvious in Shelley's discussion of the time when she and her sister, five and three years old respectively, were removed from home and taken to an orphanage, ironically located next to the juvenile institution where Shelley would eventually waste most of her adolescent years.

> I hated it there. The way that it was, like, I don't know why but I just have memories of me screaming and crying all night and I was afraid of the dark. And they gave me a bunch of shots, and like, I was afraid of shots, because they had to update us on our shots, you know? And they didn't have any records … I remember I couldn't sleep, I was just crying all night, every night…

Life inside this juvenile institution, thus, was not an interruption, a change of trajectory, a pathway twist; it was its continuation. Because abuse is so regular inside and outside this unit, some detained girls have learned to normalize it and even excuse it as "not a big deal" or even as "deserving." "Whatever, it's the same shit … I'm used to it now, I don't care," is what Macy often repeated throughout her interview, whereas others were even more lenient, taking the side of their abusers, like 18-year-old Eva: "It is what it is … it's their job, they are trying their best." I found this attitude disturbingly reflective of *learned helplessness* (Seligman, 1975), the perception that one has no alternatives that results in passivity and an inability to effect change. Learned helplessness is a concept which has been used in the past to delineate the attributes of battered women (Follingstad, 1980), and one that I believe is applicable in the cases of these juvenile hall girls. It provides a theoretical basis on which detained girls' perceived, but also actual lack of power in and out of the juvenile justice system is grounded.

But an unwillingness to stand up for oneself was not the only consequence of girls' mistreatment by staff. More disturbingly, several young women I interviewed had become numb not only to their own plight, but also to the suffering of their peers, whether that suffering was caused by staff or by other causes. Their demeanor, even their comments on other girls often resembled the attitude of staff. While during my interview a girl was screaming behind her locked door, while everybody else, including the staff was acting like business as usual, I asked my respondent, Shelley, whether the screams bothered her. She said that several girls act this way to get attention. I persisted in asking whether she thought there might be another reason, perhaps depression or desperation that was the source of girls' outbursts.

> I actually feel sorry for … not sorry but I understand there's always a reason for something that happened in their life and that's why they're like that. I think they're just hyperactive and that they want attention. I think that they really want attention and because they're stuck in that room they're not getting any of it, so they'll do anything to get it. Most of the girls in here are attention … what's the word … Like they want to be in the subject.

For example, while I was interviewing a girl in the common area, another girl inside the room across from our table was crying and groaning. A couple of staff members were going in and out of her room nonchalantly. They would even crack jokes among them. When I asked my respondent Yolanda (18), what was going on she shrugged and said:

> Oh, nothing. She's on her period. She does that all the time. They just called the nurse to come with her meds.

I was surprised with the dissociated tone in her response. In later interviews, I came across similar reactions from my respondents when other girls were sick, suicidal, or "going off." They would roll their eyes, or dismiss their peers' anguish as "drama" or "brattishness." I was interviewing Veronica when the young inmate whose lyrics had been taken away was banging at her door screaming. I asked Veronica if she knew what was going on and she filled me in. She seemed both understanding and unconcerned about it.

> She does that like, every other day or every night. Like, we'll be sleeping and she'd be doing that … singing, screaming, banging on her door, so to punish her they go in her room and take away her lyrics. She writes poems and songs, and the staff take them away for punishment. But she doesn't learn, like, she keeps on. She's doing dead time. She's gonna have a release date, She's gonna go to placement. But placement hasn't came and talk to her. So pretty much she's waiting until someone comes – that's dead time. So she's upset.

I wondered why nobody (no adult) tried to talk to the girl to calm her down. Maybe someone had, though previous observations and interviews indicated that this was improbable. "No; they won't try to calm her down. They don't do that," I was told previously, so this time I thought I'd ask my respondent's opinion about this.

AT: Veronica, what would you do if you were working here and this was going on?
V: I would go talk to her.
AT: Would you give her the lyrics back?
V: I would.
AT: I think I would do.

For a moment, I thought I had discovered a side Veronica had been trying throughout our interview to hide. Her responses had revolved around the same account: personal responsibility. She and all other girls in there deserved what they were getting, and until they changed themselves, they would continue to be treated unfavorably by the justice system and by their families. It was the first time she had dared to show compassion for a "bad" girl. But as soon as she did that, she reversed course, again.

> Yeah, I feel bad. But then again, she knows what she needs to do. She knows she had to be good to get them. But she just doesn't learn. She never learns.

A similarly unsympathetic attitude against distraught peers was expressed by 18-year-old Nora:

> Sometimes girls here "go off" ... why should you be mad? Just be mad at yourself you know, like, you got yourself here, you know...

The incidents I witnessed were so intense that it made it extremely difficult for me to concentrate in my interview, which I once even came close to canceling. Yet, everybody else, including the inmates, seemed apathetic to them, an observation I can only relate to the social context of the correctional setting, and staff's subliminal message of antagonism that is transferred to the girls. It seemed obvious to me that staff preferred to pit girls against each other, by modeling contemptuous behaviors, showing favoritism to some, punishing the whole unit with an early bed or a lock-up for another girl's misbehavior, or simply mocking and bullying certain girls in front of others.

Despite the fact that my respondents' lived experiences had been depressingly similar to one another, correctional counselors' divisive, targeted harassment had resulted in obscuring these similarities, hindering reflection and self-reflection. Perfectly complemented and perhaps reinforced by the discouragement of relationships, girls' inability to empathize with their peers in a universal rather than case by case basis,[5] reduced their power and further diminished their well-being.

Trauma-informed and gender-specific treatments that focus on mutuality, empathy, confidence, and critical consciousness raising, could have counteracted and even overcome the impact of negative life experiences before, and during detention. According to the gender-responsivity literature, such treatments could have done even more: they would have contributed to healing, self- and collective efficacy, and empowerment that would extend beyond the walls of detention and would assist system-involved girls' reintegration once out. In fact, Probation had reassured me that they had "many great" programs in place that did precisely that. As I will discuss in the next two chapters, they did not.

Notes

1 World Wide Association of Specialty Programs and Schools.

2 Tranquility Bay was shut down in 2009 due to allegations of child abuse.

3 The American Civil Liberties Union would most likely reject this statement, citing US court decisions and international law standards as evidence that such actions, as well as other disciplinary methods (i.e. room isolation), are indeed illegal. What I mean is that

correctional staff have been advised to engage in them when someone's safety is at stake.

4 Several detainees, regardless of offense, had received sentencing enhancements because the court had identified them as gang members. These inmates were deemed too dangerous to be transferred to a less secure institution such as a camp, so they were forced to serve their whole sentence in juvenile jail. Bianca was one of them.

5 Strong friendships *had* been formed inside the unit between some young women.

References

Acoca, L. (1998). Outside/inside: The violation of American girls at home, on the streets, and in the juvenile justice system. *Crime and Delinquency*, *44*, 561–589.

Baines, M., & Alder, C. (1996). Are girls more difficult to work with? Youth workers' perspectives in juvenile justice and related areas. *Crime and Delinquency, 42*(3), 467–485.

Britton, D. (1999). Cat Fights and Gang Fights: Preference for Work in a Male-Dominated Organization. *The Sociological Quarterly, 40*(3), 455–474. Retrieved from www.jstor.org.sonoma.idm.oclc.org/stable/4121337

Chesney-Lind M., & Shelden R. (1998). *Girls, delinquency, and juvenile justice* (2nd ed.). Belmont, CA: Wadsworth.

Covington, S., & Bloom, B. (2006) Gender-responsive treatment and services in correctional settings. In E. Leeder (Ed.) .*Women and Therapy Journal, 29*(3), pp. 9–33.

Daly, K. (1992). Women's pathways to felony court: Feminist theories of lawbreaking and problems of representation. *Southern California Review of Law and Women's Studies*, *2*(1), 11–52.

Follingstad, D. R. (1980). A reconceptualization of issues in the treatment of abused women: A case study. *Psychotherapy: Theory, Research & Practice, 17*(3), 294–303.

Holsinger K. (2000). Feminist perspectives on female offending: Examining real girls' lives. *Women and Criminal Justice, 12*(1), 23–51.

HRW, Human Rights Watch & American Civil Liberties Union. (2006). Custody and Control: Conditions of Confinement in New York. Human Rights Watch.

Kempf-Leonard, K., & Sample, L. (2000). Disparity based on sex: Is gender-specific treatment warranted? *Justice Quarterly, 17*(1), 89–128.

Koons, B. A., Burrow, J. D., Morash, M., & Bynum, T. (1997). Expert and offender perceptions of program elements linked to successful outcomes for incarcerated women. *Crime and Delinquency*, *43*, 512–532.

Matthews, B., & Hubbard, D. J. (2008). Moving ahead: Five essential elements for working effectively with girls. *Journal of Criminal Justice, 36*, 494–502.

MS Foundation for Women, Collaborative Fund for Healthy Girls and Women (2001). *The new girls' movement: Implications for youth programs.* New York: author. Electronically retrieved from: www.cpn.org/topics/families/pdfs/New_Girls_Movement.pdf

OJJDP, Office of Juvenile Justice and Delinquency Prevention (1998). *Guiding Principles for Promising Female Programming.* Washington, DC: US Department of Justice.

OJJDP (2018). Girls in the Juvenile Justice System, Juvenile Justice Statistics National Report Series Bulletin, Washington, DC: Office of Juvenile Justice and Delinquency Prevention.

Pollock, J. M. (1996). *Sex and supervision: Guarding male and female inmates.* New York: Greenwood Press.

Seligman, M., E. (1975). *Helplessness: On depression, development, and death.* New York, NY: Henry Holt & Co.

United Nations. (1989). *Convention on the rights of the child.* Available at https://digitalcommons.ilr.cornell.edu/cgi/viewcontent.cgi?article=1007&context=child

Zavlek, S., & Maniglia, R. (2007). Developing correctional facilities for female juvenile offenders: Design and programmatic considerations. *Corrections Today, 69*(4), 58–63.

Part II

Programming as if girls do not matter

Chapter 6

We're all hurting

Blame-therapy as intervention

Vienna, 15

It was 9 p.m. I was walking with my two friends, and my one friend, she was already really upset cause her boyfriend had left her, you know? So, she was crying and was drunk and she was yelling. And there was this lady walking with her daughter and their dog, and I guess she didn't like the fact that my friend was loud, so she started telling my friend stuff that would upset her even more. Like, she told her, "You need to shut the fuck up!" I was, like, ahead of them and when I looked back, that lady was with her hands like this, "Be quiet!" and then I went back and asked: "Marianna, what did she tell you?" And my friend didn't wanna tell me everything the lady told her, so I obviously got mad and I was like, "Ignore her," but the lady comes back at me and keeps going, "She needs to shut the fuck up blablabla," so I was like, "Oh, hell, no!" I didn't like that cause, that's like my lil' sister, although she's older than me, but she's one of these girls that everybody likes to push around cause she doesn't do anything, so to me, she's like my lil' sister, so I was, "She's not gonna tell her anything." I was like, "If I don't do it myself, I'm not gonna let anybody do it," you know? And especially if my friend is not doing anything to her, why should this 43-year-old lady come up to her and tell her things, like, *who is she*? So, I was like, "First of all, you're coming down on her, now you not gonna come yell at *me*!" If I don't let my mom yell at me, especially, I'm not gonna let this white lady come at me like that, so I socked her. She fell on her knees and she got back up and she pulled my hair, she pulled me to the ground somehow, cause I was drunk too, and we had blazed it that day, and somehow I got on top of her and started swinging at her and then she scratched me! Like she put her hands all over my face, and I had a lot of scratches, and so I bit her and then after like 10 minutes – my friend was trying to stop us all this time – I finally got up and she got up too and started running to the neighbors and started banging at their door, and her daughter was just standing there. Well, the thing is, I didn't know that her daughter was special. So they left, and I bumped into them again on March … and I guess all this time that lady had been stalking me. She had all these pics of me, so one day I finally saw her but didn't recognize her at first but she called the cops so then the cops came. And so, they got me arrested. Then they dropped me off at my mom's house, they told my mom everything and they told her I could not be anywhere near the city of Eastcreek, for the safety of this lady. I still go though, cause, they can't do that! I still go, but the point is we moved cities, and everything was good, I was doing good, and I guess court papers had been coming but I wasn't living there no more, I had no idea, and I had forgotten about it, but then it became a warrant. So one day I was with my boyfriend and another friend and got pulled over, cause we had been kicking it in an ally. So, the cops came and they let everybody go … and then they asked me for my name and I gave it and then, "Hands behind your back you're getting arrested," and I'm like, "For what?" and they're like, "For a warrant." And I'm like, "What's the warrant for?" And they're, "Cause you didn't show to court three times," and then they brought me here, and then they told me that I had charges: Criminal threats – which was not true – great bodily injury, cause I broke her hand, and she had a crack in her bone cheek, assault and battery and assault with the deadly weapon (my arms). She put a RO on me, I can't be 100 yards from her, and I got 3 months, and that's why I'm here. And this is my first time in detention. Do I feel bad? No I don't feel bad, I don't regret it, no. Like I mean, the reason I feel bad is for her daughter cause I don't want her to get traumatized. I mean after I saw the pics I did feel bad, I was like, "Damn!" cause I wouldn't want that to happen to my mother, you know? But then, she came after me and if anything *she* should be in jail cause I was 14 at the time, and she came to me looking for trouble … And obviously me, as a minor I will respond to whatever she does to me!

When I got arrested, I started laughing cause the cops were like, they were pissing me off cause they called my aunt – I was living with my aunt cause my dad lived there – and said that they caught me drinking, that I was drunk. I had been smoking weed, so that was not true, and I was like, "I'm not drunk!" Cause there were open bottles there in the alley, and I was like, "You can't charge me for that, you got no proof that that was mine," and I said other things cause I was mad. I wasn't disrespectful, I was just mad, I was, "That's a fucking lie, you're fucking liars!" And then they didn't read me my rights, so I was like, "Where are my rights?" And they were like, "You're a minor we don't have to." And when I go there, my lawyer asked me, "Did they read you your rights?" and I was like, "No." And then, another thing they searched me and I know they can't do that since they were both guys. And I was in the back of the car, they were, "You're really pissing us off," and I was just laughing – I was just going against them, you know, they can't do anything! And I told them, "You guys are being liars … you can't do that," and they were like, "You can't tell us what to do," and I was like, "Exactly, I cannot tell you what to do and you cannot tell *me* what to do!" So, when I got here, I would look at them and laugh and they'd be, "What's so funny?" and I was like, "I just think it is funny that you guys think you are so badass and think you catch everybody even the slickest person, and it took you 6 months to catch me." And they were like, "Yeah, but we finally did," and I was like, "Yeah, but after *SIX* months," so they put me in another room cause I wouldn't shut up. But in the end, they got over me and they were, "Have fun in there," and I was, "Trust me, I will," and they're like, "How are you gonna have fun in there?" And I was like, "I have my ways." But, no, it's not fun in here (laughs).

My boyfriend gangbangs. He came here 2 years ago from Mexico. He knows English but he doesn't like to speak it; when he does, though, he speaks as good as me. I guess he's uncomfortable speaking English. I met him at school; we were set up by his cousin. In the beginning, I didn't like him, I don't know why, but one day someone told me he had a girlfriend and I got jealous. He's in a lot of trouble with the law, but hasn't been here, never been arrested. The cops go to school and talk to him all the time, and he has been pulled over, for fights; cause where I live, it's pretty much known as the "hood" so that's where he and his friends kick it so when there is another gang … I just heard 2 days ago he just got into another fight. A lot of his homies are here and I run into them; they're here cause they shanked another guy. On May first, I had a homie, he passed away, they shot him, and the homie who is here, he got shot in LA, and my boyfriend would have been with him, but I had told him not to go, so I *do* worry about him, but I know he knows the risk he's facing, so that makes me lay off on some things. But he's worried about me too. One time, I went to the enemy's hood – cause my cousin lives there – and I was wearing his gangs colors, burgundy, and the enemy gang colors are orange. But, I know all these guys I am really close to them, so they started dissing me, and I started dissing them, and I was gonna get down with one of the girls but I didn't. Her homies took her away cause she was drunk, but I was just standing there, I was not gonna leave, and my cousin, he kept on getting mad and he's like, "Let's just go," and then three guys came from the ally and took out a strap. I was telling them, "Do it," you know, "pull the fucking trigger, I don't care." I knew they were not gonna, cause these guys know me and my cousin lives there, they just wanted me to leave. My cousin started panicking but I laughed, but then I felt bad for my cousin so I did leave in the end. What a freakin color can do huh?

My mom thinks I bang. She doesn't understand the colors, but she thinks I bang. But I don't; It never got my attention. The thing is that … I don't know … uhm, there's a difference between representing the color and being from there, you know? But my mom, she trips about the fights, cause I fight a lot, but it's not fights because of gangs. It's cause like a girl doesn't like me or goes after my boyfriend. And they come looking for *me*, they always throw the first hit or they'll be like, they'll like my boyfriend. And I actually tell him, "I'm sure there's better girls out there," and he's like, "If I wanted to leave you, I would." But the girls will be like, "Get away from him, leave him," and they'll come looking for me in my house. They're coming out of cars and be like, "You need to leave him alone, cause pretty soon he'll be with me," and I'll laugh, and they'll be, "What's so funny?" And then we'll start an argument and pretty sure there'll be a fight. My boyfriend has done it a couple of times too cause guys will come up to him and tell him, "Hey that's my girl." There's this guy who's obsessed with me – he's 22 – and he'd stalk me like every day after school, and he went up to my boyfriend and said, "You need to let her go, she's my girl," and they got in a fight. Or, sometimes the fight will be … well, I've been to two fights with a 19-year-old and the 19-year-old's mom. Cause they told my mom things and it's like, this is one of my rules: no matter *who* you are or who you *think* you are, you don't disrespect my mom. This is one thing I'll never let go, slide by, period. And this girl, she had a 3-year-old, and I was barely 13, and she came and told my mom that she might abduct her daughter and my mom is, "Why would I do that when I have a daughter of my own? I don't do that to kids." So I went down there, cause she told my mom, "Let's get at it," and my mom is like, "You're nothing but a 19-year-old, why would you wanna fight with me, I am 34?" So I said to her, "Why don't you come looking for me?" and I socked her, you know? My dad came and broke us up. And I did threaten her cause

I told her, "If I see you around," – her house was right in front of us – "even outside *your* house, I'm gonna hurt you," literally, I told her I was gonna kill her, and the mom came and told me, "Don't talk to my daughter like that," and I socked her too, so when the 19-year-old saw me going after her mom, she came after me and somehow I got her to the floor and I told her: "You are gonna apologize to my mom," so I kicked her in the face three times and then she apologized and the next day they moved out. I got angry cause she had just told my mom all these things and called my mom a whore and I was like, "At least my mom didn't sleep with at least nine different guys to have nine different kids like your mom." And then she slapped me, and my dad kept holding me back, and then her three sisters came out of the house and I was like, "Oh, why are you so hurt?" And I was laughing and said, "At least I have my dad, my daddy is right here," and they were telling me to shut up. I like to stand up for people I love; I feel they are a part of me and if I let someone disrespect them it's like disrespecting me, especially when it comes to my mom, that I don't let go by. You know, in the past I have treated my mom bad but … and I don't let that go, I feel bad, I have no right to talk bad to my mom.

I love my mom, although I know I haven't shown it to her. I'm the type of person that doesn't show my feelings. My mom she'll be like, her birthday is on the 20th and I'll act like I don't know, or she'll be like, "Have a good day at school," and she'll expect me to give her a hug and she'll ask me to and I'll be like, "OK I have to go, bye." I guess, a lot of people say I am like my dad, cold blooded, that I don't like to show any weakness, but I don't know. She knows I love her. Like in the past, I was really bad to her; never put hands on her, but I'd talk back to her – really bad, we would be like enemies. She has hit me a couple of times. There was a time I did want to hit her cause she had hit my mouth and made me bleed and I wanted to slap her but I was like, "Who am I?" and it's something I don't do with other people, if you hit me, I'll hit you, you know? So for me to calm down, it's just like, you're lucky you're my mom. So my mom was like, "Hit me, go for it!" But I was like, "Trust me I want to but I can't." All that changed this year, but last year? It was damn, *so* bad!

I hate being in my house … Like when I was out. There was not one day I was in my house … The only time I'd go would be at night … I mean I'll be around the house cause that's where I am at, but that house is so burned out, everybody gets caught up … And I do drugs, I didn't until sixth grade, though. I was a big pothead … I started smoking cigarettes and I would do it every day; I also drink every day but not to the point of being drunk. I mean, my whole family drinks. Me and my cousins we'll go rent movies and we'll each drink a beer. My aunt wouldn't mind you know, but we do it every day. My cousin who's now in Mexico, he'd buy me Cobras. And I don't get buzzed right away so, we'd have one of those every day. But I never told my dad. I think he knew but he never said anything. And I smoked meth maybe two times, but that's not … that's not my thing, my cousins don't do that … And I fight – though this year I've only been in three fights. This past year I did bad at school, though. I got lazy. I was like you know what? I'm not gonna do this … I'd walk out of class, I wouldn't do the work. Half a year, I'd go to school but not to classes, so I had 68 truancies. And I only showed up 23 days and the rest were truancies, absences. I got suspended for a week. cause I was truant. But I'd still go cause the teachers like me, you know … And they were like, "You're gonna get in trouble, we'll tell the principal," and I was like, "So? I already said hi to the principal." I'm just messing around with them…

My parents split up December 2006, a day before New Years – 3 years ago. And it really affected me cause at that time, I could not leave with my dad. That's how I started living with my dad cause we had too many problems with my mom. They split up cause my dad hit my mom. To the point where she was bleeding. Cause my dad, like, before that would hit my mom, but he would just slap her, to make her shut up, you know? My dad he's really calm, like, you can do whatever and he'll be calm. It's really really hard to piss him off, so finally, when my mom would push him and push him … Cause my dad, when he's mad, he's really mad you know? He's never hit me or my brothers, never yelled at us. He'll still treat me like a little girl. He spoils me and my brother and sister. To him, there is no negative, there is no nothing he cannot do: You want this? No problem! He's just a positive person. But that day, he really lost it. He got arrested and went to jail and got out January first, 2007. And he's been in jail two other times before because for the same reason, 2001 and then again 2003. And then, two other times cause he himself had been in fights. He has a nephew, he is 43 right now – my dad is younger, and he really loved this guy and everything this guy wanted my dad would be like, "Sure!" And back then, when I was a little girl, 1995, I guess my dad had let him borrow the car, and he crashed into an old lady and she passed away, and because the car was under his name he got arrested, obviously they thought he did it … but the longest he ever did was 2 years. See, that's another reason I don't like gangs, cause they jumped my dad. Cause these guys had a problem with his brother, my uncle, and we lived across from each other, so they came and started talking to him and my brother stood up for him. And that night, my dad and my uncle had been drinking in the ally, and my uncle he end up going in, so my dad was alone and they came at my dad. These guys got my dad, and they pulled out a knife on him, but my dad managed to take it away from them, and then he beat one of the guys pretty bad, and the other two run away once they saw that this guys was tough … Yeah, he showed me the knife. At the time my mom had left to Nevada with my brother and my sister, and that day she left, they got him. But I stayed with my dad cause I didn't want to leave. But I am really close to my dad. I can tell him anything. When I first got my period, I told him, not my mom. When I needed bras, I told him not my mom, I was embarrassed to tell her – I thought it was weird to tell her. She is not strict, I mean, she does yell at us more. But, If I tell my dad I don't wanna do homework, he'll push, but then he'll tell me, "OK, do it later," but if I tell my mom she'll yell.

My parents always had problems. They stopped when my little brother was born in 1999, and they were doing good, and they started again having problems in 2006 after my baby sister was born, and then they split, cause the fights were affecting my little brother. He was getting traumatized. He turned 10 last week, and he's already getting kicked out of schools, he's really aggressive too. My parents are weird. They're acting like little kids. They've been dating since 16. He was my mom's first boyfriend. My mom, I guess she's like me, she doesn't like to show her feelings. When they're arguing, he'll be, "I don't need you, I can find someone else," and she'll be, "OK then, go!" And when he leaves, my mom would be like, "Do you think he'll do it?" And I will be like, "Mom, he's just trying to get to you." And then, my dad will call and be, "What is your mom doing?" And some times, I'd be, "I don't know." And my mom would ask me, "Did he say anything about me?" They don't see other people, hell no. I mean, they're planning on getting back together. Cause ever since my dad came out from jail he had a restraining order, but he was like, "I don't care, I'll still go see her." And even up to this time, he still is not allowed, but he goes to the house, sometimes he sleeps over, and they talk like nothing happened. To me, that's normal, cause they're my parents. But at the same time I see my little brother and I understand that is not good. It never affected *me*, I was never traumatized and that is what the teachers saw on me, cause my brother was going at the same school and he would tell them what was going on. They would ask me all these questions and I would answer them like [shrugs], "Yeah, they fight." I never cried, it never affected my school, I was always on the honors role, straight-A person. I was always active, had all this energy but, they said that the way it affected me is the way I am now … I am an aggressive person.

Young, petite, but feisty, Vienna was not the only adolescent I spoke with to self-label as aggressive and violent. Exceptionally, her behavior and attitude while in detention were tamed: no talking back, no quarrels, not even complaints. She is on cart, and her relationship with her counselor, though cold and unsatisfactory, is diplomatic. Whereas, unlike other peers, like Bianca, Vienna is able to stay collected while incarcerated, she admittedly carries a lot of anger as well. She is by no means proud of it, and she acknowledges it as a problem warranting a solution.

> I know I have a problem, I don't see it as normal, cause I am always willing to fight, if someone comes and they want to fight, my reaction is to kill them not walking away, and when I am tired of hitting them in the face, I start choking them, and when the person starts not breathing they pull me off and I am not comfortable … And when I realize later, I am like, wow I could have been a murderer!

Similarly apologetic declarations of anger and "anger management" problems were made during my interviews with other inmates. In fact, 20 out of 28 respondents described themselves as angry and acknowledged difficulty in controlling their aggression:

> I don't know, I was just mad … I would just be fighting and then like in first grade I would always fight … I even remember like in kindergarten I would pull some girl's chair each time she'd sat down. I was so bad, it's embarrassing.
>
> (Bertha, 17)

> I was always mad at people, like, why is this prissy cheerleader sitting next to me, smiling all the time? What's so great about her life?
>
> (Shelley, 18)

> I have like the worst anger issues … My mom says I am bipolar, cause I'll be one mood and then I'll change, instantaneously.
>
> (Monique, 18)

Such testimonies were also prevalent in the letters I read, such as: "I find myself trying not to explode," "My anger gets to me," and "Why do you think I have so much hate for people?" It was painfully obvious that although young women were "in touch" with their feelings and understood the impact their outbursts had on others and on their own lives, they were unable to explain, and largely unable to control them. "I don't know!" Vienna kept repeating, when I asked her why she thought she did this or that. Everybody (mostly counselors) had been asking her the same question, she said, looking frustrated, "You tell me!" She exclaimed, "I'm only 15!" Whereas I do not possess counseling credentials, I believe the therapists that had treated Vienna, were working on her reaching a breakthrough on her own.

> They ask you, "Why, why do you do this?" Or "How did you realize you had this problem…?" Like they tell me, "What gets you to be in this mood?" and I would be, "I don't know I just react like this," and they'd be, "Why?" and I'd be, "WTF, you're the doctor, do your job! If I knew, I'd stop." So I stopped going … and my dad didn't want me to go either, because he also had been to anger management before too, and it was a joke.

Without claiming any specialization on this, I too, wondered whether Vienna's point was worth examining. Perhaps children who had been though similar experiences as Vienna, that is, deeply traumatizing experiences, and who were currently facing the stigma of "violent juvenile delinquent" processing, needed a different type of therapy, that is specific to age, gender, class, ethnicity, and delinquency status. Like Covington (2007) argues, system-involved girls face not just a few problems; their lives are crammed with multiple sources of trauma such as witnessing, delivering, and receiving violence and "the trauma of stigmatization because of poverty, racism, incarceration, or sexual orientation" (p. 6). As the introductory narrative shows, Vienna's whole life was organized around violence and oppression, and thus her identity was intrinsically shaped by definitions and justifications of violence. These features were staples in all my respondents' lives and as we have seen previously, many of these features continued to exist inside the pretend-safety of juvenile detention. Real healing should encourage young women to view these types of oppression as the underpinnings of social and individual dysfunction (Freire, 2000). Real trauma healing could be possible through intense programming that encourages among other things, self-affirmation and positive thinking, and, consequently, allows girls to see the strengths and their qualities, and develop a strong, positive, and resilient self-image (MS Foundation for Women, 2001).

Most of the girls I interviewed had never been encouraged to do any of the above. Interventions based on a valid needs assessment instrument appeared to be non-existent, whereas aftercare considerations and strengths-based evaluations were not only absent, but also incompatible with the dominant view of delinquent girls in this institution (the view being that these young women were destined to fail once released, because they possessed no real strengths to build on). Furthermore, trauma-informed therapeutic interventions that targeted the omnipresent violent life-stories of system-involved girls were sporadic, temporary, and disorganized. Consequently, as the findings in the current chapter reveal, treatment interventions offered either too little, or too much direction toward cognitive, behavioral, and emotional resolve and restoration; they also offered nothing remotely close to critical thinking and consciousness raising. I found that counselors often left girls' fundamental questions unanswered, while at other times pushed them to accept uncritically a self-image that reflected their own opinions and privileged circumstances.

As a result, their clients were left frustrated and confused, unable to clearly understand what went wrong in their lives that brought them to jail. Although some intrinsically acknowledged the impact of social context and multiple adversity on the lives of *others*, they were nevertheless unable to connect those to their *own* legal, mental health, and addiction problems. Instead, they individualized the causes of their behavior, and engaged in what sometimes I viewed as vengeful self-blame. Young women who exhibited symptoms of post-traumatic stress disorder and other mental health issues relating to past violent victimization were offered incomplete, inadequate, or even damaging intervention.

I'm good, but I'm bad

Illustrations of guilt, insecurity, and self-deprecation were abundant in both the letters I analyzed and my interview transcripts. These reveal a serious identity crisis, a desperate need to fit a personality that others have constructed for these young women, and powerlessness resulting from a perceived inability to change, to become better, or in their words to be "good":

> I am the kind of girl like, as you [counselor] say that gets bored and goes to drugs and trouble.
>
> (Anonymous, letter)

> I am afraid one day my parents will be gone and I will be nothing but a bad memory in their mind.
>
> (Anonymous, letter)

> I am doing good in the program, but yet I am struggling with how I feel.
>
> (Anonymous, letter)

> This other part of me keeps telling me to just give up and go back to drugs … I don't deserve better.
>
> (Anonymous, letter)

> I let the little voice in my head control me!
>
> (Anonymous, letter)

> I am working on myself … I want to change … I wanna become a better person than when I came in …
>
> (Anonymous, letter)

> I'm good, but I'm bad…
>
> (Anonymous, letter)

Whereas judgments, and consequently punishments by parents, teachers, counselors, and justice system officials were standard responses to exhibitions of "badness" and unruliness, reality-informed responses that would clarify and validate girls' feelings, and ultimately alleviate the embarrassment, angst, and troubles those were accompanied by, were never provided. Instead, these feelings were condemned, trivialized, or treated through inappropriate means, such as medication and one-size-fits-all counseling, which problematized the angry individual rather that the *reasons* why she was angry. Others, mostly doctors, offer solutions that (over)treat the symptoms, but do little to alter the factors which cause them. As Shelley poignantly explains:

> When I started seeing a psychiatrist, and they put me on meds for a while, the meds did what the drinking did without getting me drunk…
>
> (Shelley, 18)

There is no question that many young women I spoke to, were going through mental health problems that required medical attention of the kind that a correctional institution was ill-designed to offer. This gap in service seemed unfair not only to minors with mental illness, who were penalized as if they were somehow responsible for it, but also to other girls, who saw detention as a dumping ground for the different, the "crazies," and the undesirable, a place one is sent to when all other hope has been lost and other responses have been exhausted. This function of the detention center was most clearly illustrated in the case of Sylvia, a 15-year-old under "lots of meds," a rape victim who had been diagnosed with bipolar disorder and depression, and had recently attempted suicide. The daughter of drug addicted, formerly incarcerated parents, Sylvia and her three siblings had been removed from their custody after a domestic violence incident. All four kids were adopted by her mother's sister, who sent Sylvia to a group home when she was 11.

> My (adoptive) parents couldn't deal with me. When I was 10, I was crazy. If someone would talk to me, I would scream at them, I'd throw bricks at them. I was angry. People would hold me down, and I get up immediately, like, I still had the energy to get mad and would get mad again. I was so crazy!

According to their website description, the group home Sylvia had been sent to at age 11, was a residential treatment program offering intensive therapy to sexually and physically abused girls. Sylvia had never mentioned having been abused as a reason for her placement. As far as she could tell, her behavior is what forced her parents to send her away, and to keep sending her back after her treatment concluded. Sylvia was sent back home after 18 months in that first group home, but her re-entry to the family was not smooth. Not only did her parents send her away again, but they also qualified their decision by placing all the blame on 12-year-old Sylvia.

> My sister was mad the way I was acting when I was back home. My mom said, "Your sister tried to cut her veins, cause of the way you treated us." Cause I was home for a month or two, and that is when my sister got really depressed and she started cutting herself. When my mom told me, I was shocked, cause I love my sister. I was like, "I can't be acting like this any more."

However, Sylvia's behavior worsened the second time around.

> I went back and I was back for 5 months, and I became worse, I got real depressed. Because now I was 13, and they put me in the big girls unit, I don't know why, and I had to be more of a leader. The girls, the little ones, with whom I was before, they were different. In the big girl unit, I would get restrained a lot and all the other girls hated me. I was so depressed. I didn't understand why my mom was sending me away all the time. I just felt like I wanted to be home, I thought my mom could take care of me and I missed her. But they couldn't take care of me.

One of the reasons why her parents could not take care of her, was the volatile relationship with her adoptive father. During one of her furloughs, a violent incident between the two seemed to have started the downward spiral that eventually landed the now 15-year-old inside the juvenile correctional system.

> My dad would yell at me so he would get me worse. It was a bad relationship and it was getting better, it really was, but a month ago we got in a real big argument, it became worse, like he had to hold me down, and my dad didn't wanna do that, and I was crying – it was sad. And the group home came to my house so they had to take me back, that's the rule, and that's

> when I tried to kill myself and run away. I went to a lot of psych hospitals and that's when they decided they had to kick me out of there. And as soon as they sent me to this psych hospital, and that was the 15th time I was there, they left me there for like a month, they sent me to a new group home and was there for 5 months and then I ran away, cause I didn't really care, and that's when I went to Compton and got raped.

After that, Sylvia's parents tried unsuccessfully to find a lock-down group home that would accept her, but the only secure detention facility available for a girl with her circumstances was juvenile jail.

Although Sylvia's case was uniquely tragic, it is nevertheless, one of many among the female inmate population in the United States and elsewhere. In fact, the vast majority of female detained youth meets the criteria for at least one mental disorder, which more often than not is accompanied by substance abuse (Teplin et al., 2002; Veysey, 2003), a co-morbidity factor that exacerbates violent offending risks (Monahan et al., 2001). Depression and anxiety reportedly affect more than half of detained girls (Cauffman, 2004), whereas suicidal tendencies are significantly higher among locked up girls, as compared to boys, or/and the general population (Suk et al., 2009; Trulson, 2005). Due to the prevalence of sexual abuse and other violent childhood victimization experiences among this population, post-traumatic stress disorder (PTSD) symptoms are also unusually prevalent (Dixon, Howie, & Starling, 2004). What makes Sylvia's and other young women's path to recovery so difficult is that in addition to the complexity of their personal and social statuses, they find themselves trapped in a system designated for penal harm rather than therapeutic intervention. Based on the testimonies of my respondents, this punitive ethos involves attributions of blame for one's victimization and/or neglect, similar to those Sylvia's parents conveyed to her.

Adolescent women, whose defiant, aggressive, and/or self-harming behavior was often symptomatic of psychological and contact disorders that research has long connected to distressed childhoods (Chesney-Lind, 2010), were treated as the sole wrongdoers during all stages of criminal processing. In a characteristic instance, for example, 15-year-old Jackie, perpetual runaway and a regular in detention, was visibly hurt when police arrested her.

> My dad, we got into a big fight, and my dad busted my left eye open and called the police on me.

That was the norm for Jackie, who frequently got in fist-fights with her father, and admitted that she wanted to hurt both her parents. After all, she self-proclaimed as "evil" and admitted she had "major anger issues," without hesitation. When I asked if the police arrested her father for injuring her, she denied.

> They asked, "What did you do this time?" Cause the cops in that PD, they have all this information on me, they know me. They know how bad I am.

> And then when I told them about my dad beating me they said, "You deserve it."

It is difficult to rationalize such reaction to child abuse from a public official, regardless of context. This reaction, however, becomes outrageous once you place Jackie's aggression, heavy meth use, and delinquency, in its proper context, which law enforcement had meticulously documented over the years: Jackie, who considered her family "good," was born to a blended Mexican immigrant family. Her parents, caregivers to several children from multiple previous relationships, were employed sporadically with low-income jobs, drank heavily, and fought constantly. Brenda grew up amid poverty, social exclusion, and a chaotic family environment. She would witness her dad hitting her mom, and often would get in the middle trying to break them up. She had begged her dad to stop drinking repeatedly, but to no avail. When she was 11, she was raped by two cousins, yet her parents refused to believe her. She started "being bad," drinking, using drugs, and running away, until one day her dad kicked her out. She then went to stay at a friend's house, at which point her friend's dad raped her (Jackie suggested that her friend most likely "sold" her to the father, for money). It was this child, who police officers found deserving of beating. When I asked Jackie if she agreed with the officer's remark, that she deserved the black eye her dad gave her, she said: "In that case, I don't think I deserved it, but generally, yes, cause I broke so many rules and I wouldn't listen."

Jackie's self-assessment is *also* the norm among delinquent girls in the detention facility. As with her, most other girls have been already stigmatized as "bad" and incorrigible long before they are incarcerated, so the ground for planting seeds of self-respect, confidence, and empowerment is already barren. Dora's (17) words illustrate the desperation and hopelessness that pervades young women's attitudes:

> I've lost hope; I don't think that I will ever catch up to whatever I … you know school, my family's trust and stuff like that? I've done so much and I've lost so much, and people give me so many chances and I always fail them…

Unfortunately, there is nothing that happens inside the institution to reverse this negative self-image. To the contrary, this attitude is reinforced by the very people, who are supposed to treat girls with such traumatizing experiences.

Needs, risks, and strengths assessment

Whereas female delinquency is determined by a combination of factors that are common in the lives of incarcerated girls (Holsinger, 2000), an individualized and comprehensive assessment of the risks, needs, and strengths of each girl is nevertheless essential to the planning and implementation of effective programs (Covington & Bloom, 2003; Matthews & Hubbard, 2008). While risk and needs assessment instruments that have been afforded scientific merit and are considered objective predictors of future behavior are very popular in male or female correctional settings, they use quantitative measures that sometimes ignore the uniqueness of the female experience. Because of this differential in the level and extent of risk associated with female misconduct, feminists argue that *needs* rather than "risks" need to be assessed for boys and girls separately in order to provide appropriate treatment, and they suggest that qualitative rather than quantitative measures are better in capturing these needs in detail (Covington & Bloom, 2003).

Another important call made by scholars who have studied delinquent girls for a long time is the implementation of a strengths-based approach in developing appropriate, empowering, and comprehensive programming for female adolescents. Consequently, comprehensive assessments must identify not only needs, but also strengths, employing age and culture-specific instruments such as Hurtes and Allen's (2001) Resiliency Attitude Scale or Ungar et al.'s (2008) Child and Youth Resilience Measure, and in-depth interviews with each girl separately (Matthews & Hubbard, 2008). Unfortunately, placement decisions in this county are based mostly on prior delinquent behavior, especially running away risks, mental illness seriousness (with detention serving as a secure mental facility), and institution crowding. Young women's preferences remain unsolicited or largely disregarded when offered:

> I don't know for some reason I wasn't allowed to be in their drug court program or anything like that, like, they really didn't give me much of an opportunity and when I did get to go to rehab it was because I really fought in court for it ... I had to convince them, I brought a bunch of documents to convince them to send me somewhere where I could get help...
>
> (Trish)

Most importantly, there is no evaluation of what types of treatment programs fit the personalities, backgrounds, and experiences of each girl. Several of my respondents, for example, told me that they preferred to have one-on-one rather than group counseling.

> I feel closer one-on-one instead of with 50 girls, when we're all talking. You get to [be] individually known, like, what is going on with you. You have to work on each individual girl, hear other stories closer up and more detailed, like, you know what I mean?
>
> (Dianne, 18)

Conversely, others appreciate the sense of solidarity and validation group counseling settings provide:

> I feel in group, it's good cause they'll see (the girls), even though there's this woman in front of me telling me, "You shouldn't feel weird about having been raped," you still do, mentally … But when others girls say, "Me too," then it's different, you know you are not weird.
>
> (Isla, 15)

Most importantly, due to the lack of comprehensive assessment at time of entry, there is no continuation of care for girls who need therapeutic or/and rehabilitation help, and the little programming they do receive is compartmentalized, interrupted, and often unsuitable to their specific situations. As Dianne incisively points out:

> What they do is toss girls around a lot. Say for instance this is a girl, and she goes to this house, this house over here, ok? This girl right here, she goes to this house right here. Well, this girl did "bad" over here so they're gonna put her over here. And then, oh she's doing "bad" over here, so they put her over here. How about if you start here, you talk to that girl and find out where she's gonna fit good and you can tell there's people like her there. And then you put her here so she doesn't do "bad." You know? If they're gonna put us in this hell hole, you know? Keep us here, find where we should go!

A comprehensive, case-by-case approach to aftercare assessment plans for previously detained girls that would perhaps eliminate their multiple returns seems to be lacking as well, despite Probation's lip service to reintegration goals.

> I think the POs should come in [the detention facility] more and sit down with the girls and say OK what needs to happen, where do you want to go, instead of just mucking you with time … Nobody ever asked what I want … Like, "Is going home a good solution for you?" Cause some of these girls will tell them flat out, "I don't want to go home," or they'll say, "if I go home I'll start using drugs." But the PO won't listen or say, "We can't find funding to put you anywhere, like in a group home," but there's always funding out there!
>
> (Lexi, 18)

Indeed, "I don't want to go back home cause I'll start using" was a fear that was iterated both in the interview narratives as well as in the letters. As one young woman characteristically wrote: "My house is like a trap; I can't go back!" she wrote, a few days before she was released back home.

Restoration is compromised also because girls' strengths and qualities are ignored. Frankly, my observations and interviews suggest that nobody who works with these young women believes that they have any strengths at all.

Most counselors are, instead, either consumed with efforts to change *entire* personalities, or have given up pretending that there are prospects that do not involve some form of correctional supervision. If past research on resiliency (Benard, 1991; Bjerregaard & Smith, 1993; Burley, Barnard-Brak, Marbley, & Deason, 2010) is correct in pointing out the positive correlation between adults' high expectations and children's triumph over adversity, then my respondents' repeat troubles with the law should come as a surprise to no one.

Several times in my interviews I heard girls saying that "everybody has given up" on them: parents, teachers, social workers, probation officers, cops, and correctional counselors made sure to let the girls know that they doubted them, and their ability to resist temptations, such as running away, drug use, or other violations that would bring them back to detention. Both Vienna and Bianca laughed out loud when I asked them whether counselors in the institution gave them a "you can do it" pep talk at their release day.

> Are you serious? You know what they say? Every time a girl is released here they say: "OK, see you in 24 hours!"

But low expectations are not only shared by staff members in the particular unit; it seems that that doubting clients is widespread among other juvenile justice employees. When Lori was at the treatment camp, she and another inmate got into a verbal altercation. Until that day, her behavior record had been impeccable, and she was in what she saw as a "high phase." However, the moment she got into this fight, she automatically lost her "reformed and ready to be good" standing, and was informed that she was determined to live a life of crime and incarceration:

> They don't give you the support … After I got into that fight, everybody, all the staff were like, "well, you're gonna fail once you're out."

Her probation officer was not one to stand by her side, either:

> Yeah, my PO was like, "I predict that I'm gonna send you to county next time, I guarantee I will have you in the back of my van, taking you to jail." He was just very stereotypic and just very rude and judgmental. He was like, "I know how girls like you end up … Girls who slam heroin and speed, and I'm sure I'm gonna find you in a motel in Costa Mesa one day … It's typical for me to have white girls like you who hang around guys, like you hang out."

Other probation officers, suspicious and fearful of being manipulated by their minors, would often remove rather than adding rehabilitation. Amy's PO, for example, did not allow her to participate in a tattoo removal program that was offered during a field trip that would take her outside the detention center because as he said: "With your record, we don't know what will happen," meaning that she was not trusted not to run away. Another probation officer warned a different girl with a running away record that he was "on" to her and her tricky ways, although, as the girl told me, that was the first time they had met:

> He's like, "Oh well, I know you're a runaway person and so don't BS me and come to me and telling me this and that ... Cause I will put you in there [the detention] for a long time."
>
> (Nora, 18)

Staff members inside the unit also make sure to let their clients know that they view them as untrustworthy and intrinsically corrupt trouble-makers. Yolanda explains:

> They think we're bad. One day that I was downstairs, the counselor told me: "What are you hanging around my office for? Are you gonna steal something?"

As a result, some girls were socialized to accept that "messing up" was a permanent feature of their character, felt bad about themselves and were more likely to use self destructive methods to cope with their feelings of shame and helplessness. Other girls recognized the futility of trying to stay out of trouble and jail, and saw no point in trying to fight against the odds, and in the end disappointing nobody but themselves. In explaining their engagement in actions they knew were going to bring them back to detention, several of my subjects responded with something along the following lines: "Well I'm gonna screw up anyways, why not do it sooner?"

In sum, the lack of a comprehensive assessment of female delinquents that identifies each girl's individual needs and acknowledges that differences in personality, family and cultural background, age, and delinquency context as important to designing programs and services, causes as negative an impact as the dated and imprecise profiling system that is followed in this institution. Moreover, the justice system's constant skepticism about the innate strengths and talents of the young women it supervises, and the employees' bizarre use of "reverse psychology" and degradation, not only fail to motivate girls to stay trouble-free, but push them further out into the margins of society, where they are made to feel they belong. This is regrettable considering the importance that the literature on female psychology gives to encouragement and emotional support, from which many girls could have benefited. In the current study, support for this argument is provided through Shelley's account of a positive experience she had with one of her private therapists, the only person who according to Shelley was able to get through to her and help her deal with her self-destructive feelings:

> I don't know how to explain it. Like, she knew exactly, like the way she talked and the tone of the way she talked, the way she looked at you, the way that she wanted you to look back at her … Like, she saw someone intelligent, she saw someone, she just really wanted me to know that there's nothing in this world I could not do. And I had a complex; I didn't think I was pretty till probably a year ago … She made sure I knew that I was beautiful and that I didn't need to be loved for me to love myself. Like, before she did anything else, she just made sure that I knew who I was.

Let it go

Many girls needed help figuring who they were and how their past experiences had molded their current sense of self. In this juvenile hall, there is absolutely no counseling program specific to girls' past victimization, especially rape, for example. Furthermore, the sporadic and generalist counseling offered by CUs, frontline staff, and affiliated group counselors, individualizes and decontextualizes young women's problem behaviors, locating both causes and solutions within them. Although this is not done in the precise and direct way the police employed with Jackie in the example referenced previously, it is nevertheless realized in a more subtle and elaborate way. Patronizing clichés such as, "You have control only of yourself and the choices you make," or "We must try to make the best out of our situation," were abundantly repeated in my respondents' descriptions of said programming's content. When asked about the objectives of counseling programs, either inside or outside detention, all my respondents had the same answer: "They teach you what is wrong with you." I would always follow up by asking them, to tell me, then, what exactly *was* wrong with them. Many of them stumbled trying to articulate a satisfying answer.

> They [counselors] help you see your faults, your negativities, your depression, your anger. And that's good, cause it pushes me hard to see the things I need to change…

> All the counselors I had, told me I need to change…

> I learned a lot about myself … I learned about my different issues I have due to the drugs, self esteem and how decisions are affected…

In addition to using girls' delinquent and inmate status as convincing evidence that something "was wrong" with them, sometimes counselors would also trivialize the gravity of the girls' life tragedies. I asked several times during each interview what counselors who lead one-on-one or group sessions suggested as an alternative to drug and alcohol use, or even to running away, which are common strategies system-involved girls use to cope with the multitude of problems facing them. However, it seems that while these sessions focused heavily on identifying the clients and their coping methods as unhealthy and illegal, they hardly ever provided viable solutions to the reasons why the coping was needed in the first place. In fact, those reasons were minimized, depreciated as "excuses," or all together unaddressed. "She [the counselor] tells us. "You guys have to stop it, just forget about it," explained Yajaira when I asked her how counselors helped her effectively alleviate her grief. When "just forgetting about it" just did not work, counselors would suggest more "new age" solutions, such as yoga, rock climbing, astronomy, or meditation, and of course, religion. Given the resource-limited, and economically depressed organization of the neighborhoods in which most of my respondents lived, these options were not only unavailable, but also unknown.[1]

Counselors and other justice officials, then, repeatedly chose to disregard the criminogenic conditions surrounding their clients, and would instead encourage or require them to live through these conditions. In another illustration of "treatment" that holds minors accountable for adults' mistakes, Joy describes the kind of intervention offered by counselors inside the detention:

> They will ask, "What's going on at home," like, "have you talked to your parents," and, "what did they say?" Like say I was arguing. "This is what you could do … tell your mom you're sorry," like they tell us what we could do to make our relationships better with our parents…
>
> (Joy, 18)

As discussed previously, relationships are indeed important to adolescent girls' well-being, and relationship building assistance must be an integral component of delinquent girls' rehabilitation regimen. In other words, generally speaking, counseling daughters on how to reconnect with their parents is compatible with both theoretical guidelines and evidence-based practice. However, the risk with relegating relationship building to a risk-management strategy, which is precisely what counselors seem to be doing in this juvenile hall is that young women are both personally blamed, and assigned with the responsibility of fixing unhealthy/broken bonds with others (Hannah-Moffat, 2010; Sharpe, 2016). A very important pre-requisite of gender-responsivity is tailoring counseling options, goals and methods to each client. Rushing to minimize Joy's risk of re-offending, her counselor's normative assessments of familial bonds seemed to have missed or disregarded significant elements of her family life. Joy's birth father had been absent from her life. In fact, he had been in prison "like in forever." Joy's mother, a habitual drug user, had three other children, an older son who was involved in gangs and had been in and out the juvenile detention for most of his adolescence, an older daughter, who was in prison for drugs, and a younger son, whose father (Joy's step-dad) was a felon. Joy started running away when the step-dad and his two other children, who were "already bad and in the system," moved in. Her mother could not handle Joy's bad behavior, predominantly consisting of running away and drug use.

> My mom was yelling at me, she would take away my phone, ground me, and all that, but she never hit me – only my brother would. But I couldn't really talk to her. She was on drugs too, so…

Eventually, Joy's mother gave up on her, and whereas she allowed all other siblings to stay home, she placed Joy in a group home. At the group home, Joy started getting into fights, until she ran away for good, moved in with someone, and "fixed" her life by finishing school, enrolling in college, and is currently expecting her first child. Surprised that counselors had told her before that she, when she was 14–15 was the one needing to apologize, I asked Joy if they had been aware of her family situation, her mother's addiction, and the communication difficulties in which that addiction resulted:

> I used to tell them that, and they used to tell us that not everybody's perfect. And that everybody changes and my mom is doing real good, now so…

"So, they were right," is what I understood Joy was implying. Encouraging empathy and forgiveness for others, especially parents facing substance abuse and family dysfunction problems similar to one's own, does not warrant strong criticism. What makes this advice problematic, is that these vulnerable children were asked to be kind and forgiving to everyone, even those who had hurt them, except to themselves. Joy was to acknowledge that parental mistakes such as exposing their children to crime, gangs, and drugs, then abandoning them for getting involved in all three, could and should be excused. On the other hand, excuses for her own misbehavior were rejected. "I think I deserved a lot worse when I was younger," she conceded. Subliminal messages of blame communicated through counseling are much more potent than downright accusations in turning girls against themselves and against each other. The "no excuses" language was spread throughout most girls' narratives and at times resembled a little too much the "tough love" approach to child rearing that is frequently adopted by justice agencies, school administrators, and counseling professionals.

> I wasn't doing the right thing, you know? Like, if I was going to school, if I was coming and cleaning up, if I was doing everything I was supposed to be doing, they wouldn't always be on me, you know … I don't think nobody could, like, try to force me not to do drugs, like it's all up to me. Like, it's up to me if I wanted to do drugs, you know? I really didn't care.
>
> (Victoria, 16)

> "They're around me," that's no excuse, like, to me, I used to use, "it's around me," "oh they gave it to me," or "they made me do it." Did they put a gun to my head? No. It was my choice.
>
> (Aimee, 15)

"I know it's my fault you know," explains Nora, a four-timer with a history of aggression, school fights and drug abuse. At 18 years old, she seems to have been conditioned into accepting sole responsibility for her troubled life: "Before, I used to blame others too but it's like, you're the one … I put myself in situations." Nora neglects to connect the situations (fights) in which she puts herself, with the situations in which she was placed. She had lived her whole childhood in home environments crippled by violence: both her father and older brother had been sent to prison for abusing their spouses; after separating from her biological dad, Nora's mother had moved in with four different men, all of whom hit her, and occasionally hit Nora as well. At one point, her mother, addicted to drugs, vanished for two years "doing drugs," and lost custody of her kids, so Nora was sent to live with her dad and his girlfriend, who was only a few years older than her. Yet Nora thinks *she* is the who failed when she tested dirty for marijuana: "I let my parents down." she says referring to her current return to detention. After repeat counseling sessions in camp, she thought she had done away with her weaknesses: "I used to cry a lot, like, I'm an idiot, you know?" she said about her pre-therapy self.

> I started crying for no reason you know? But with the therapy, I stopped feeling sorry for myself, like for what I did this to myself. So, now I'm disappointed; I was out only for two months! And that's why I don't wanna be here, I wanna go back to camp, so I can see my therapist.

Yajaira (18) was so eager to not come off as "untreatable" or as selfish, that she found it more plausible to justify everybody else's behavior but her own, and to discharge her emotional state after her rape as misplaced anger and resentment.

> [What I want from the group is] looking for not to lie to myself, to know who I am, what I feel, what are my addictions, my problems, pretty much to not lie to myself … And also, why we feel the need to use or, and to not use excuses for all the things we do…

When asked to imagine a treatment that could have actually kept them from (re)offending, my respondents argued that there was none, and often rejected their own and their peers' capacity to self-correct. Sometimes, and only after my prompts, they managed to acknowledge a connection between what had happened to them and what they had done to themselves and others. After hesitation, Joy admitted briefly:

> I don't know the reason I was doing all that exactly. It had to do with stuff at home. Like, my mom used to do drugs … And my dad was never around … Just all … a lot of stupid stuff that went on at home … Made me, like, rebel and I didn't want to listen to anybody.

But even in those few instances, my respondents never forgot to reassure me that they didn't consider these connections as an excuse for their "badness," and that ultimately, the fault of their actions fell only on them and on their wrongful choices. Most girls learned in counseling sessions to make similar interpretations regarding their delinquency. Embarrassed, they often attributed it to stupidity and misplaced self-importance, and argued that thanks to the counseling they had received, they were now mature, and changed.

> They [counselors] made me realize why I was messing up. I was … I just thought that I was a little bad ass. I was on drugs and just not doing good…
>
> (Yolanda, 18)

> I learned a lot, like how to like hold my patience … And like my temper and not to snap on everybody. I used to think I was a gangster and back in there [in the counseling] I noticed, "I ain't nothing" … How stupid I was…
>
> (Valentina, 18)

And yet, here they were, locked up in juvenile jail, despite having grown out of the mentality they thought landed them in trouble in the first place. Other girls seemed oblivious to the impact of the myriad of problems plaguing their family life, because family had after all managed to fulfill their most basic needs, such as housing and food. One example is that of Brenda, who grew up with her grandma, because both her parents were out of the picture: her dad was unknown, and her mother, who gave birth to her at age 15, was always either in jail or in rehab. Brenda repeatedly beat herself up for her "bad choices."

> It's all on you … It doesn't matter I was 14 … Everything in my house at the time was OK, like the bills were paid and my grandma wasn't sick.
>
> (Brenda, 18)

Amy, who at the time of the interview was pregnant and had been in detention four times in the past, another girl who had been abandoned by her drug addict mother at a young age, was often asked by her probation officer to explain why she was running away and doing drugs. The probation officer could not comprehend Amy's delinquent choices because her adopted parents were wealthy:

> … She just didn't understand like … for me she was like, oh your parents are so nice, you have all this at home like why are you messing it up, so … she didn't understand…

Amy had trouble understanding her behavior in non-pathological terms either. Nevertheless, accidental and sporadic breakthroughs were reached here and there, either during one-on-one psychotherapy, or during small-group counseling sessions, when girls were given the rare opportunity to talk about their victimization.

> [My therapist] she really did unlock a lot of my anger, a lot of my regret, even though I was so vindictive toward my mom, like when I first came here, because I had to do the cooking, clean, and laundry, you know, my sister tugging in on me telling me to help her with her homework and all that kind of stuff, walking her to school, going to school, I was so vindictive toward her. Like, my psychiatrist really, really helped me empty that out in my brain…
>
> (Shelley, 18)

> She asked me to imagine that the people who had hurt me were sitting in the room. I imagined my mom, my dad, my grandmother, and the guy who raped me when I was 14 … And I was crying, cause I had never talked about it … And I hadn't want to talk about it cause I didn't want to hurt, but she said, by not talking about it doesn't mean you don't hurt about it … I did it, and it felt like a burden was released from me.
>
> (Monique, 18)

Although Monique was encouraged to identify and correctly place her negative emotions that included anxiety and anger in the context of her rape, she was nevertheless left to fend for herself against the feelings this memory evoked. Job done, but only half way through …

> I was like, "How do I turn it around, how do I deal with it?" … And she said: "You just let all that go."… And that brought up a lot of emotion … And I did like … the week before I was OK, I was smiling and stuff, and then after I did that, the smallest thing would piss me off…

This reaction illustrates how difficult it is for victims to process emotions resulting from their traumas without professional help, especially inside an environment that often exposes them to secondary victimization. Perhaps this explains why young women in my sample were easily amenable to putting the blame for their troubles on their defective characters, rather than to looking back and reliving hurtful situations. Having been denied control over their bodies, their lives, and their environment, my respondents found owning up to their badness as the least painful way to at least control their identity. However, this coping, again, encouraged by juvenile corrections, in the end left plenty of emotions unresolved. Whether masked as anger, addiction, defiance, or delinquency, girls' trauma was deepened by their unaccounted shame, their helplessness, and their conviction that they were to blame:

> No one cares for me … I am a piece of shit … I should just kill myself

> Have you ever tried to hurt yourself and then laugh about it?
>
> Pain and me are attach[ed] or glued.
>
> Conclusion: the personal meets the political.

Few girls understood that their problems were bigger than them, especially after hearing from other girls inside the facility about experiences strikingly similar to their own. Some girls acknowledged and even denounced the pervasive sexism and racism women, and especially women of color, are subjected to, the ineffectiveness and impersonal nature of juvenile system processing, the counterproductive placement on juvenile probation, and the incongruity of the particular or any other secure confinement facility with drug, alcohol, or trauma treatment. And some of them understood crime and delinquency as a social rather than individual phenomenon. Joy in a very insightful remark said:

> But I noticed that a lot of girls that are raped, that grew up around their parents do[ing] drugs and stuff have more of a problem. Getting … they get in trouble a lot more because they think that's the right thing cause that's what they see when they grew up. Like, "I'm not doing nothing bad; what the hell; that's what I've seen growing up."

Of course, Joy applied this learning theory to others only, yet resisted offering it as an explanation of her own offending. Then, in voicing her opinions about programming, always as it applied to these other girls, she correctly made references to the politics of spending allocations.[2]

> There's a big budget cut specially this last few years … There's been that big old budget cut so I noticed like schools are cut shorter umm … Programs are cut, music is cut. All those things that students used to do when … on their free time they're not allowed to do it anymore. There's no money for it. So they'd rather go do a drug and do something stupid then to go find something new to do … Cuz it's not there anymore.

Similar to Joy, Lori identified social-cultural factors at play in several social institutions that devalue and restrict young women's prospects:

> I think schools, public schools are just cruel, like society everything is so screwed and twisted … like just everything like the world, TV and the way that they portray everything, especially girls.

These are the types of attitudes that gender-specific, empowerment-focused interventions should and could have built on. Critical consciousness, the ability to think critically and act individually and collectively to challenge oppression, inequality and marginalization (Freire, 2000) was conceptualized and employed as a tool toward the empowerment of marginalized, oppressed groups (Watts et al., 2011), and I cannot think of a group who would benefit more from a program focused on raising it than my respondents.

The juvenile detention unit, in which this ethnography was conducted, promoted an innovative program that promised to do something like that. It did not call it "critical consciousness," but gender-responsive empowerment. It was administered by counselors dispatched from a community organization that advocated women and girls' emancipation, strength, and success, and touted feminist ideology and practice. Chapter 7 will examine in detail the theoretical underpinnings, and the stated goals of that specific program, and will present a qualitative assessment of its implementation and its effectiveness that is informed by the voiced testimonies of the young women who participated in it.

The current chapter offered a general assessment of the prevailing blame-based therapeutic ethos in juvenile corrections, and the counter-healing impact it has on system-involved girls. The lack of effective and targeted therapeutic treatments perpetuates and even adds to a negative, gloomy view of self, which is widespread among the population of female inmates, while failing to address the single most persistent element in delinquent girls' life-stories. As Dianne, an 18-year-old who has had more traumatic experiences than anyone ever should, noted characteristically:

> We're all the same. We're all hurting, you know what I mean? We're all hurt. We're all in here because we're hurting about something.

This universal experience of pain in which juvenile hall girls trafficked their whole lives mattered to counselors only with respect to the impact it had on their status or delinquent offending. In other words, the concern was superficial, disingenuous, and self-serving all at once. They were there to help girls fall in line, and if stitching their wounds was necessary, that is what they tried to do in the most efficient yet barely comprehensive way. Girls did not *really* matter. The laws they had broken, the norms they had violated, and the institutions they had disrupted mattered more, and thus, the therapeutic strategies employed to reform them were informed in what mattered to the system rather than what mattered to girls.

Notes

1 Religion was an exception to this, as many young women I talked to expressed a strong religious sentiment.

2 During my interviews the US and many of the world's economies had entered a period of economic recession.

References

Benard, B. (1991). *Fostering Resiliency in kids: Protective factors in the family, school and community*. Portland Ore: Western Center for Drug-Free Schools and Communities.

Bjerregaard, B., & Smith, C. (1993). Gender differences in gang participation, delinquency, and substance use. *Journal of Quantitative Criminology 4*, 329–355.

Burley, H., Barnard-Brak, L., Marbley, A., & Deason, C. (2010). African-American millennials a profile of promise. *Gifted Child Today, 33*(2), 47–54.

Cauffman, E. (2004). A statewide assessment of mental health symptoms among juvenile offenders in detention. *Journal of the American Academy of Child & Adolescent Psychiatry, 43*, 430–439.

Chesney-Lind, M. (2010). Jailing bad girls. In *Fighting for girls*.

Covington, S. (2007). The relational theory of women's psychological development: Implications for the Criminal Justice System. From R. Zaplin (Ed.) *Female Offenders: Critical Perspectives and Effective Interventions* – See NCJ-225923.

Covington, S. & Bloom, B. (2003). Gendered justice: Women in the criminal justice system. In B. Bloom (Ed.), *Gendered justice: Addressing female offenders*. Durham, NC: Carolina Academic Press, pp. 3–23.

Dixon, A., Howie, P., & Starling, J. (2004). Psychopathology in female juvenile offenders. *Journal of Child Psychology and Psychiatry, 45*(6), 1150–1158.

Freire, P. (2000). *Pedagogy of the oppressed* (30th anniversary ed.). (M. Bergman Ramos, Trans). New York: Continuum.

Hannah-Moffat, K. (2010). Sacrosanct or flawed: Risk, accountability and gender-responsive penal politics. *Current Issues in Criminal Justice, 22*(2), 193–215.

Holsinger, K. (2000). Feminist perspectives on female offending: Examining real girls' lives. *Women and Criminal Justice, 12*(1), 23–51.

Hurtes, K. P, & Allen, L. R. (2001). Measuring resiliency in youth: The resiliency attitudes and skills profile. *Therapeutic Recreation Journal, 35*(4), 333–347.

Matthews, B., & Hubbard, D. J. (2008). Moving ahead: Five essential elements for working effectively with girls. *Journal of Criminal Justice, 36*, 494–502.

MS Foundation for Women, Collaborative Fund for Healthy Girls and Women. (2001). *The new girls' movement: Implications for youth programs*. New York: author. Retrieved from: www.cpn.org/topics/families/pdfs/New_Girls_Movement.pdf

Monahan, J., Steadman, H., Silver, E., Appelbaum, P., Robbins, P., Mulvey, E., et al. (2001). *Rethinking violence risk assessment: Mental disorder and the law*. New York: Oxford University Press.

Sharpe, G. (2016). Re-imagining justice for girls: A new agenda for research. *Youth Justice, 16(*1), 3–17.

Suk, E., van Mill, J., Vermeiren, R., Ruchkin, V., Schwab-Stone, M., Doreleijers, T., & Deboutte, D. (2009). Adolescent suicidal ideation: a comparison of incarcerated and school-based samples. *European Child & Adolescent Psychiatry, 18*(6), 377–383. doi:10.1007/s00787-009-0740-1.

Teplin, L., Abram, K., McClelland, G., Dulcan, M., & Mericle, A. (2002). Psychiatric disorders in youth in juvenile detention. *Archives of General Psychiatry, 59*, 1133–1143.

Trulson, C. R., Marquart, J. W., Mullings, J. L., & Caeti, T. J. (2005). In between adolescence and adulthood. *Youth Violence and Juvenile Justice, 3*, 355–387.

Ungar, M., Liebenberg, L., Boothroyd, R., Kwong, W. M., Lee, T. Y., Leblanc, J., Duque, L., & Maknach, A. (2008). The study of youth resilience across cultures: Lessons from a pilot study of measurement development. *Research in Human Development, 5*(3):166–180. doi: 10.1080/15427600802274019.

Veysey, B. (2003). *Adolescent girls with mental health disorders involved with the juvenile justice system*. NY: National Center for Mental Health and Juvenile Justice. Retrieved from www.ncmhjj.com

Watts, R. J., Diemer, M. A., & Voight, A. M. (2011). Critical consciousness: Current status and future directions. In C. A. Flanagan & B. D. Christens (Eds.), Youth civic development: Work at the cutting edge. *New Directions for Child and Adolescent Development, 134*, 43–57.

Chapter 7

She tells us who we are

Empowerment, juvenile hall-style

Dora, 17

I was 13–14 when I first got busted and this is my eighth time here. I basically lived all my teenage life here, pretty much. That first time I had possession of stolen property. I got all the stuff with me that we stole from school. Electronics, like computers, lap tops, cell phones cameras. I wanted the money cause I was on drugs, I was on meth so I wanted to get drugs, and I also wanted the money. But, I was ratted out, but I didn't wanna tell on them so that's why I was arrested. Well, they were investigating me and I was not supposed to go to court, only be expelled and go on probation but they tried to scare me cause I was being a little bad ass. I wasn't talking back, I was being a smart ass, like they were asking me, "Who else was involved?" and I still, like, for my reputation I was like, "Well, you caught everybody so why ask me?" And they were like, "Well do you want to go to juvenile detention?" and I was like, "Yeah I'm curious." So they arrested me and they brought me here but just for one night … and then I got out, I had to go to court and they gave me probation for a year, but I violated it many times. Drugs, stealing, but mostly it was cause I got in a lot of fights … with girls and boys [nervous laughter]. And I've hurt many of them bad. I try not to get mad but when I do, ugh, I get really aggressive, that's why I try not to get mad and to use.

I've changed so many schools. Because we've moved so many places but also cause I get kicked out even from continuation schools. They just don't want me anywhere. I don't show effort and cause I'm really like, when it comes to school … I'm really like, when someone tells me something wrong, I am being a really mean person, I'll say really mean things to them. I just don't like people telling me who I am, or how I am. It wasn't like that when I was younger, like 11–12. I was dorky, I even had a wheel back pack [laughs]. I was in school but then I moved cities, away from my friends and stuff, and I started going on a different school and I guess my friends there were the ones that turned me around … cause they would, like, take my books away and I would like chase them. They were, like, "What are you doing?" I was reading a book and they got me hanging out and I started hanging out with them and they turned me rebellious against my family. Since I moved there my family started being all mean to me so I started being rebellious, like I would take my friends' advice and stuff.

I want to go to military academy, where they help you graduate faster from school. They do training and they're really deep into school and they're kinda strict. I am so used to it being strict here that I think I am gonna handle it. Cause when I got kicked out from school, that's the only place organized like school I can go to, it's every day, I have a schedule, and I'll have work to do in class and it's organized you know … And I'll get out of probation when I get out. I have no hope of finishing school any other way. I'm not the kind of person who goes to school. I don't like school, I am not organized, especially cause, now I'm at continuation once a week only; I'm doing independent study, now, and I have so much free time, I slide. I'm 2 years behind, that's why it's so hard. I can't focus that easy … Cause I get distracted real easy by people or events.

When I was younger, I was being like all depressed all the time, but like, when I moved to a different city I was more on guard, I stood up for myself more. Cause I never really communicated with my mom and dad so it was really hard for me, and my grandma died and I was really close to my grandma. I live at home, but don't go home, I always live with my boyfriend and every time I get arrested I'm arrested with my boyfriend. My parents, I talk to them and they know where I am so it's not like running away. They tell me to come home but I never do. I always used to get in physical fights with my older brother, so I don't wanna go. Usually I'll go to my friends' but if I have a boyfriend I'll go to my boyfriend's. But sometimes I'll hang out with my family. Like, right before I got arrested we went to a bull show, all the family, except for my older brother cause he's out of the picture, cause of me mostly, so my mom would rather have me go cause I am hardly ever around, so she told my brother to stay. I've got two little brothers, and I pretty much raised them cause my parents were never around. My mom used to clean houses all day and my dad worked construction. My brothers, they look up to me but they … my lil brother is depressed when I'm not around, and I feel bad about that. But, they're actually yelling at me for being here [laughs], two little kids yelling at me …

My parents were always arguing … for some reason, they were always irritated with each other … mainly it was money, which maybe that's why I started wanting money. They're still together, though. It's like their forced to be together for some reason. But they fight a lot. When we had barely moved in this new place, I witnessed something, and I guess it caught up to me: my dad got a knife and put it on his chest, cause my mom, she was yelling at him, and I was inside with my little brothers and my little brothers were really all scared and covering up their ears. And then, I guess my dad got really irritated and threw my mom on the ground and hit her in the eye, and he regretted it I guess, cause he got up and he like started screaming, and my mom slapped him and he yelled. "Slap me again!" to take away the pain from hitting her eye, and she got back at him and everybody was crying. I was trying to calm things, all that at 11–12. Cause my dad, they were arguing and my mom starting cussing at him and slapped him like 20 times, and I started crying, and then my dad went to the kitchen and he started saying stuff like, "Oh kill me," and stuff like that and was trying to get my mom to push the knife in his chest and I was really scared so I grabbed my dad – I was really strong – I told my dad: "Stop it!" so as soon as he put the knife down I shoved my dad in the wall, so he could calm down and my dad slapped me and I got mad and then he started slapping himself cause he slapped me then he eventually calmed down, and then my mom went to the other room. That was when we were living with my uncle for a little while cause we didn't have money, and then the social services were involved. Nobody got arrested cause my mom lied and told them it was an accident.

My dad is the kind of guy who shows more toughness than emotion. I never *see* how my dad gets, they tell me … But when I actually *do* see my dad cry or be depressed and stuff, it does hurt me and it makes me want to cry cause he shows so much sadness [voice crack]. He doesn't wanna visit me or call me here, cause he always breaks down and cries, like we can't even talk to him of the times I got caught. To show you what I mean, I was sleeping in the closet, a big walk-in closet, cause we only have two rooms, and we were six. I used to love spending time in my closet, cause it's, like, all quiet and dark, and I could do whatever I wanted and nobody would bother me at all. So, when I was arrested, my mom told me that when I was arrested my dad went inside my closet and he went against the wall with a beer between his legs holding my clothes, crying like a baby. But my mom shows more emotion to me. I messed up to her, cause though she used to be mean to me, she was visiting me and was being nice to me when I was here. So, I regretted putting her through that pain, cause when I was running away I wouldn't tell her where I was always … one time it came to a point she thought I was dead, and so I was crying for that, cause I don't like to see my mom cry. I used to be worse, but little by little … I tell my mom, "You need to give me some time, I'm still bad, in trouble, but you need to give me, not chances, but time," you know?

I actually have thought a lot about what I will do if I have a baby. I will do anything possible to make my kid comfortable with me. Like, I'm not gonna judge my kid; I am gonna listen to what my kid has to say and I'm gonna not talk to them like screaming. If I'm gonna talk to my kid I'll talk to them like I talk to you. I'm gonna listen like when a friend listens or how you listen. I see people in here that talk to me even though they don't know me, like the Bible study people, and I look them in the eye, and I listen and talk to them, and I see that they get emotional and get deep into thoughts. If I can get deep with these people, I can get like this with my kid.

Conflicted, remorseful, and hopeless, Dora had given up on many things: school, friendships with other girls ("Most girls are hypocritical"), romantic relationships ("I had a boyfriend who hurt me so I'm not into guys right now."), and good employment ("It's so hard to find a job outside Jack in the Box."). Whereas she repeated feeling depressed throughout the interview, she rejected therapy, because she did not trust that therapists cared enough: "When I have problems I wanna talk to someone who is close to me." And although she did not want to be told "who I am" or did not respond well to "being judged" by others, she wanted to join military academy, feeling that the structured environment would benefit her. Last, although she wished her parents had been nicer to her, and was planning on being sweet, caring and understanding to her own children one day, she felt that penalties for juvenile delinquents were too soft, and should involve corporal punishment. "I'd be really, really strict even one-on-one, like, I wouldn't allow girls to talk to me at all," she said when I asked her what kind of correctional officer she would make. While her views about human behavior and life in general were ambiguous to say the least, Dora's opinions were crystal-clear about one thing: she was certain that she disliked *Operation Empower [OE]*, the gender-specific reintegration program offered inside the detention institution. She was one of the toughest critics of the program and its counselor, and although she was one of the few girls I interviewed who disliked both, her arguments were compatible with those of all other respondents. Despite my limited access to this program, my interview data regarding it and its counselor are plentiful and highly consistent, whether they came from discussions with girls who liked or girls who did not like the program. In fact, girls cited the same reasons for liking or disliking it. For example, some girls liked the program because the counselor argued very effectively, and "challenges you," while others were frustrated because (again) she argued effectively and "she challenges you."

In this chapter, I will describe the program through the testimonies of those for whom it was allegedly designed, and will contrast their experiences with the program's rhetoric and purposes as they were related to me, before data collection started. I will examine how the program works on the ground, to determine how and whether reintegration and aftercare assistance were realized; and, I will contrast the program's practices and the counselors' attitudes with the philosophy and theory of gender-responsivity and empowerment.

The *OE* program was a product of collaboration among county government, non-profit, community, and private organizations, whose mission focused on gender-specific reintegration assistance through case management, and social, material, and psychological support. That kind of collaboration among different agencies represents a concerted effort that is vital for successful tertiary interventions for youth offenders. Furthermore, *OE* seemed to be the right kind of pre-release intervention as well. It was designed to address gender-specific problems delinquent girls share in abundance (traumas, addiction, mental health issues, relationship dysfunction, family and dating violence, social exclusion, sexism, and multiple marginalization), show sensitivity to cultural and class differences, and build on girls' relational strengths and resilience. Such a program would be not only crucially important given the social status of the female delinquent population served, but also easy to implement inside a correctional environment, where "nothing else happens." Because it involved concerted efforts in and out of detention, and was informed by empirical and theoretical knowledge about women's pathways to crime and delinquency, it was both promising and innovative. Because it emphasized empowerment within a context that was by design disempowering, especially to youth, it was unique and worth examining. Unfortunately, the program was exactly as it sounded: too good to be true. The totalitarian environment of juvenile corrections and once again, the staff's rejection of the goals a gender empowerment program underscores, made its realization very difficult, if not impossible. The program's content and scope were based on a narrow conceptualization of empowerment, focusing on moralization and self-esteem, mirroring normative gender expectations, cowering to hegemonic paradigms of penal control and practice, leaving systemic imbalances of power unchallenged. In the end, the program differed little than other correctional interventions for girls, following the tradition of 19th century juvenile justice reform.

The program counselor: I have a friend in you

Inside detention, *OE* was realized by two weekly group-counseling sessions: the first, was a "big" group, and took place in the common area downstairs. Every resident who was not in room segregation at that moment was welcome to participate, and the discussions were obviously public (since the correctional counselors were close by), dealt with "less serious" matters, such as hygiene or hobbies, and involved "fun" activities such as group games. I was present during two of those sessions, which were run by either one of the two *OE* counselors, Nadia, or Marissa. Per my respondents' descriptions, Nadia was the sweet, friendly, nice counselor who always brought candy. The second group, the "small" one, took place in the privacy of the upstairs room, which I used for the majority of my interviews, and it was exclusively run by Marissa, the more "serious" counselor. This is the session my respondents referenced when I asked them to comment on *OE*.

One of the major weaknesses of *OE* is that it is not a comprehensive, gender-specific reintegration program as it claims to be; rather, it is mostly implemented through these two counseling sessions per week. There is no continuation of the program outside the juvenile hall, except for letters released girls send to Marissa (letters that go unanswered). So, again, when we talk about *OE*, we are talking about these counseling sessions.

As far as my respondents are concerned, one of the counselors, Marissa *embodies OE*. Participant assessments of the program, thus, are largely assessments of Marissa's personal and professional qualities. Some of the qualities she possesses have been cited by research as essential for counselors working with incarcerated girls: Covington and Bloom (2006) propose that staff must "reflect the racial/ethnicity, sexual orientation, and language (bi-lingual)," and that "female role models and mentors reflect the racial/ethnicity and cultural backgrounds" (p. 11) of the clients. Marissa is a Hispanic bilingual woman, who as she tells the girls, "has been there before," because she used to be a juvenile delinquent, has been detained in the past, and has used marijuana.

Marissa's delinquent background seemed to strike a chord with the girls I interviewed. Without exception, all acknowledged it as the thing they liked about her the most. The following quote by Monique, best summarizes most girls' perception of Marissa:

> I feel Marissa's real. Ok, like, Marissa's been through the shit we've been through. Marissa's been drug dependent – I believe. She knows what's up.

> She knows how it is to go through the life most the girls in here have been though – abuse, family, being poor all that stuff, she's been through that. So she knows like, there's a difference in between, like I'm not saying there's anything wrong with people that learn from the book and learn because they're interested but there's a difference. And the other girls here [other counselors], those girls are the girls that I feel are more like pity cases or like, how do I explain it, like they care about us and they do want to help, but I feel like … umm … like it's hard for a lot of girls to relate to them cause they didn't have the hardships or maybe they got teased in school cause they had acne, they didn't have – their parents had the money, they didn't get abused. But Marissa has that. People look at her and respect her, like not in a fearful way but like, man I know this woman needs respect, this woman deserves every respect in this room as possible.

Whether accurate or not, Marissa's alleged disadvantaged background served as an effective platform on which trust and respect, both crucial for successful counseling, were anchored. Marissa's other admirable attributes were being bright and articulate. "The way she speaks," "She knows how to use words," and "She has a way of explaining things to you that makes you agree," were some of the phrases used to describe her undisputed charisma and public speaking skills. And whereas most girls considered those talents commendable, others felt uneasy with the way those skills silenced their not so articulate dissent, exposing what they considered a personal deficit in debate expertise.

> I think she really brainwashes some of these girls … She makes them believe stuff the way she believes stuff you know? I really don't like that … Everyone has their own perspectives and their own opinions and I don't think she respects other people's opinions.
>
> (Dora)

Dora also felt that the other girls in the group were afraid of being honest out of fear that Marissa would shut them down and humiliate them in front of the other girls, cause Marissa "always wins debates."

> Her group is like, she's telling you who you are, what you should do, she's comparing you to others. Girls in the group are not themselves; they try to show off. They don't want to disagree with her.

This interpretation made sense in light of how most girls felt about Marissa. Several of them had in fact grown so fond of her that they viewed her, a person they hardly knew, as the most important individual in their lives, and frequently in their letters they would ask for things she had no ability to provide:

> I have a friend other than God and my mom.

> You are in my emergency list.
>
> Will you still be my mentor when I get out?
>
> Could you bring me my brother here?
>
> Hope that you can visit my baby sisters…

What these exclamations of trust and dependency show is that these girls clinched on to a person they rarely saw, who had now become essential in their life, and whom they are asking to fill in for family, teachers, friends, and other caregivers. Their expectations were not only unrealistic, but weighed heavily on the counselor, who realized that her otherwise minimal role in the program management was stretched way beyond her qualifications and resources. When I had first met her, she solicited my help: "Right now, I'm in desperate need for someone responding to these letters," she said, showing me a large packet of letters she had picked up from the institution.[1] They were addressed to her, but she found little time to write back; her caseload had grown tremendously and given that she counseled at-risk girls outside the justice system too, she was obviously distraught for breaking her promise to children she knew counted on her response. But this despair cut both ways. Marissa was fearful of letting down the girls, and the girls were fearful of letting Marissa down. The fear of disappointing the person they admired and trusted so vigorously, was also very transparent in the letters' content. Brief references to missing drugs, boyfriends, or parties, were typically quickly followed by "But I know I must get over it, move forward," or "But I will not do that, because I need to see the big picture." Even when they discussed more sensitive, family-related problems, some girls added positive spins in the end of their heartbreaking stories as if they were trying to present themselves as strong and unaffected by tragedy.

> I never got to grow up with my mom, so and I don't know if that is a good mom or bad … I take it as if things happen for a reason? Right?

Marissa's strong bond with young women and her authority over their thought process could have been beneficial had she been able to follow through with them. However, most of the higher expectations of the girls she had counseled remained unfulfilled, especially due to the limited *OE* aftercare services, which will be discussed further down. System-involved girls' problems were more complex and enduring for any mentor to combat than just by responding to a letter here and there. This reality might cause girls to feel rejected for not receiving Marissa's full, or even half, expected attention and assistance once they returned home, and to re-experience the trauma of neglect that some of their parents had already put them through. But the most problematic aspect of the program was not just Marissa's limited resources, but the program philosophy and content in and of themselves.

Why do you deserve counseling? (In writing, please)

One – albeit not the only – reason why there is doubt whether this program is able to successfully address the unique needs and strengths of female offenders in this unit is its participant selection process. Many young women who would benefit from any programming and especially from one that claims to be responsive to gender and cultural factors, and that is headed by a positive female role model, were excluded from the pool of participants. There are two principal ways "unwanted" girls are filtered out of *OE*.

First, the decision to allow participation in this (or any other for that matter) program rests on the discretion of the staff. If a girl is on her counselor's bad side, on lock down, on cart, or has received early bed, she may or may *not* be allowed to participate, again, depending on the particular staff, and more so, on how the particular staff feels at the moment, something that was indeed confirmed by the unit supervisor (personal communication). The impact and magnitude of *OE* depends first and foremost on correctional counselors' personal discretion. Consequently, not all girls will have the opportunity to attend, and the ones who are excluded are those labeled "trouble-makers" in the unit, perhaps the girls who are more annoyed with their confinement conditions, and thus the ones who need distraction, intervention, and counseling the most. As pregnant 18-year-old Valentina mentioned, her status in the group was uncertain in the past:

> I'm in the [*OE*] group right now; I was put in there because I was doing good, that's the only reason I was put in there … but then I started messing up a couple days ago, no a week ago, and they didn't let me go…

So, not only are some inmates excluded altogether, but even those who participate in it are prohibited from attending sometimes, when they have been "bad." Girls also miss *OE* because they are transferred before they get a chance to participate or after they have participated a few times. Amy, who has been detained five times already, has rarely attended the program: "I haven't done it too much cause every time I do I am here for one-two sessions and then they send me to camp," she says. Another girl is even more specific:

> Umm, I've never been in here long, like the longest I've been in here is 40 days. So for me to come in the group and lay all my shit out and for her to start working on me, and then all of a sudden I disappear because I've only been here for a couple of weeks, it just doesn't make sense…
>
> (Brenda)

It is definitely not up to the program's managers' authority to determine length of stay in detention. Nevertheless, the program is managed by agencies (including County Probation) that are familiar with the temporary nature of juvenile detention, and one would have expected the managers to designate a continuation plan of care that would keep participants in counseling in or outside secure confinement.

The second filter is the *OE* counselor's own separate selection process. In fact, Marissa's selection criteria mirror, and are possibly influenced by, the subjective and sometimes discriminatory tactics frontline staff use to control the behavior of the young girls in their custody. Her private, intimate group which includes nine to ten girls, mandates and promises confidentiality. As girls told me, a discussion of what was said in the group with "outsiders" is punished with exclusion from the group. But excluded from the group are also girls who, according to the counselor, cannot justify in writing why their participation in this treatment is warranted. Respondents explain:

> You have to write a letter and if it's good, she asks why you deserve to be in the group.
>
> (Monique)

> Well, she told me that we have to write about why we should be in the group. We have to write to her and tell her why we want to be in the group. And, like, what we have to give to her.
>
> (Tanya)

> And then, she has this other group only with the girls she chooses, the girls that feel they want to be there, so you get to write a letter to say what you will bring in the group and what you want to get from the group.
>
> (Yajaira)

None of the girls in my sample complained about this process or found it exclusionary or harsh. Some even justified it by saying that Marissa wanted to have this group be more serious, and she wanted girls in there that would come "for the right reasons." When I asked what reason would be *wrong*, I was told that some girls wanted to be in the group only so that they could get out of their room, or in order to get the candy and other snacks Marissa brings to them.

> Cause some girls wanna be in the group only to get out of their room ... But then there's girls here that want to get something out of it ... But the other girls who just wanna be out of their room they are just here to talk ... you get a snack at the end, and we all eat, little sweets...
>
> (Janice, 15)

Both out-of-room time and tasty food are commodities in the unit, so it is not unreasonable to believe that offering both at the same time increases *OE*'s counseling magnetism. However, Dora suggested that Marissa's purpose for this "application process" was more self-serving: she wanted girls in the group who would be obedient and easier to manipulate into agreeing with her. "They pretend to be someone they are not to please the counselor," she insisted. Other girls made similar interpretations without the negative connotation:

> I think what she means by "what we have to give her" is … listen to her? Listen and pay attention to what she really has to say? I think that's what she means.
>
> (Bertha, 17)

Yet other girls admitted that they understood where Marissa was going with the selection process and they knew how to play their cards right in order to get invited. As Monique reveals: "Well, I know the group cause I've been here so many times, so I know what to write…" Later on, however, the same girl admits that she really does *not* believe she has anything to give to the counselor at all, supporting Dora's claim that girls are encouraged to "play the system" and lie to the counselor in order to receive the counseling:

> I don't think I deserve to be here cause I've nothing to show; I keep coming back, and I will always search for a reason why I or anybody deserves to be in this room … Like there's nobody in here who deserves to be in this room … cause we're all fucked up … What did we prove to her good that we deserve to be here?

This inability of girls to support their case, or to find a reason why they were deserving of counseling, or recreation, or even candy was reflected in many girls' narratives, who had not been able to qualify for the group yet:

> And I don't know what to write … I would [like to participate in the small group], so like I can understand more about like things she talks about.
>
> (Tanya)

> I don't know how to express myself in words.
>
> (Aimee, 15)

> I don't know what I can bring to the group … That is why I haven't written the letter.
>
> (Yajaira)

This might in fact reflect a difficulty in articulating themselves in writing. After all, following from the previous discussion, these girls' education and consequently their grammar and syntax skills, have suffered greatly due to multiple incarcerations. It might, however, also reflect a fear of being considered arrogant and self-indulgent in a space where even the most trivial joys of life, such as stretching out, talking with someone, or watching TV, are withheld from those who are viewed as not good enough to receive them. When I prompted those girls to tell me what the real and most important reason was for wanting to participate, they responded reluctantly that they wanted to understand their situations, and their behavior, but above all, they wanted to talk, and to be listened to. It seems that, perhaps inadvertently, *OE* does the very same thing it is designed to correct: it contributes to silencing system-involved girls' voices.

Counseling topics

Surprisingly, based on the accounts of the young women who participated in the program, discussions rarely delved into serious, complex matters and in the few cases that they did, they were incidental and unintentional. A complex and omnipresent problem in my respondents' lives was victimization due to interpersonal and environmental violence. With the exception of dating abuse, a common topic falling under the "boyfriend" discussion column, *victimization* is hardly ever discussed. That is not only peculiar, given the gendered pathways framework that this program claimed to be founded on, but also disappointing given the program's structure: this was supposed to be the smaller, intimate, private space, where sensitive, sometimes painful topics could be examined and healed through the power of connection and therapy.

In a similar way to the language used by the CU clinical therapists who would see girls diagnosed with mental health issues, Marissa's language when the topic of rape or sexual assault came up revolved around "letting go," "moving on," and "the past does not define you." These quotes may be inspirational, but, they are also untrue. I saw young women whose past had not only defined them, it had defined their image to others, and had severely limited their "re-branding" potential. Directly or indirectly, through substance abuse and justice involvement, their victimizations *had* defined them. That traumatic experiences shape delinquent pathways among girls is not pessimism: it is reality, and it is the theoretical proposition pathways scholarship advances (Daly, 1992). I believe it is also something that all girls I talked to understood intrinsically, yet were systematically encouraged to disregard. That does not mean that their traumas had written their future in stone; changing the future without disregarding, but through critically reflecting upon these past experiences seems like a step toward validation, healing, hope, and empowerment. A truly empowering program would seize this understanding, move it away from the individual, and relate it to a macro-social context of women's victimization as a manifestation of gender oppression in a patriarchal society. Instead of problematizing the individual for being unable or unwilling to "move on" from childhood rape, the group could have problematized men's sexual aggression and the sexualization of female children and placed it in its historical, political, and legal context. Rather than repeating clichés such as "you cannot control others, only your own behavior," the discussion could have examined how women's, especially minority women's behaviors and bodies are defined, surveilled, and controlled by others and that re-claiming control of self could be in part achieved through collective action and women's rights' activism. Yet, none of this happened.

Something else that also did not happen was a critical focus of family disruption. Such issues also arose incidentally, were superficially analyzed, and typically concluded with girls being deemed either too dependent on, or too disrespectful of their legal guardians. Bertha (17), whose drinking and running away came as a reaction to a disordered family environment she had been subjected to at a very young age, explains how Marissa helped her overcome her anger against her mom:

> She made me realize it wasn't my mom's fault, like it wasn't nobody's fault. You know, it's just hard because it's not my mom's fault: why should she have to stay single just because I said so? So, I forgave her and she forgave me.

As discussed previously, this mother's decision to move in with a new partner only a few months after the father's death, had (most likely) inadvertently uprooted then 8-year-old Bertha and her siblings from all things familiar, at a time of incredible crisis resulting from parental death, when children need to hang on to security and comfort. Validating feelings of resentment and pain resulting from this disruption, does not (and should not) pre-requisite faulting the mother for her coping strategies, nor does it uncritically excuse Bertha. Encouraging relationship healing with a parent should not require the absolving of all faults either. Like correctional counselors before, Marissa's expectations targeted the teenager's assumption and showing of responsibility and magnanimity to the adult. This expectation, though framed in gender-empowerment and relational theory-informed pursuits, was no different from the usual blame-based responses to which police, probation, and correctional officers had accustomed adolescent girls. So, although most of the time serious and painful topics were avoided, when they were brought up they were treated by the *OE* counselor in ways that fit the culture and ethos of a penal institution rather than that of a women's rights, feminist organization which Marissa represented.

So far, I have examined the topics (victimization and family disruption) that received minimal attention during the sessions run by Marissa. In contrast, her counseling sessions focused heavily on topics such as drug use, romantic relationships/guys, and self-esteem.

Addiction

Overall, Marissa's power of conviction was employed most forcefully in her attempt to make her clients consent to the following axiom: first, all girls in her group are and forever will be addicted. "Once an addict, always an addict," is a disease-model approach to substance abuse treatment that is compatible with 12-step facilitation. According to this approach, addiction is a terminal, spiritual and medical illness, resulting largely from character flaws such as selfishness. The disease maybe controlled but never cured. In accordance to this model's ethos, challenging this assertion at all, or exhibiting other disease-related behaviors such as fantasizing about drugs or alcohol, playing victim, being dishonest, or making excuses (Hoffman, 2006) was shut down.

> About addiction, she would basically challenge you, and even though I didn't have an addiction she would say, "Well you're still doing it, right? So you're addicted." And I was like, "No, I am not addicted, I do it cause I want to, not because I need it," and she wouldn't believe me…
>
> (Dora, 17)

> She said, "Yeah, I smoked it and it was a stress reliever but I was liking it too much that I stopped cause I didn't want to get addicted." And we're like, "Well, you will not get addicted." Well, some people do, I guess, that's what she said … but I am obviously not addicted to marijuana cause I haven't smoked for a year … Cause I don't want to test dirty and get busted again … but they call it the gateway drug, so maybe I *am* addicted.
>
> (Monique)

> I thought I didn't have an addiction and now, like, she challenges you, like she asks, "What is *addiction* to you guys?" And we get to say what we feel about it, and she challenges us, so, "Is it any different if you smoke weed or doing heroin? NO!" It is still an addiction and it doesn't matter … you are just excusing it…
>
> (Yolanda, 18)

I found that the strategy of convincing young women they were addicted not only got in the way of rapport building with those who denied such assertion, but was also for the most part unnecessary. Most of my respondents had volunteered their addiction to drugs, meth being the most popular one, so they did not need convincing at this point. What they did need, was clear guidance as to how they would be able to overcome that addiction while living among habitual drug users (at home, at school, and in their groups of friends), drug abundance, and many serious personal problems. Marissa's suggestions pointed at desired outcomes to be reached through cognitive and behavioral changes: "stop using excuses," "don't let this little voice in your head control you," "just say no," "cut away from friends and family members who use," were some of them. The process by which these cognitive changes would be facilitated were never detailed. Most importantly, the structural obstacles toward the suggested behavioral changes were similarly unexplored. It is as if these young women were able to choose from several living arrangement options. For most, removing themselves from their homes or their social circles was just not pragmatic: they lacked the financial, but most importantly, the human capital resources to do that on their own. They were too young, and completely unfamiliar, even uncomfortable with so-called "normative" middle-class values; a life in "the hood" as several of them put it, was the only one they had ever known.

Since they were pragmatically unable to change the world around them, the drug-free strategy they exclusively adopted was a cognitive change: if character faults, victim-playing, and self-pity were to blame for their addiction, then adopting a "no excuses" and "switch your bad self off" language and attitude would do it. Hesitant about accepting a fully "rotten" self, many of my respondents found emotional refuge in thinking that they had a split personality. That theory allowed them to both blame themselves for their drug addiction and still feel that they were good enough to deserve some help fixing their problem. Nevertheless, this ambivalence was a great source of frustration and self-defeat. Some girls had trouble figuring out why their "bad" or "weak" personality, was so hard to die, often taking control over the better angel in them. As a result, they would become depressed and angry, and, unable to clearly communicate their feelings with others, they would feel helpless. The following example found in my letters, which describes a disturbing father-daughter phone conversation, was characteristic of this confusion. Dad had forcefully dismissed both the addiction and split personality theory his daughter had advanced to explain her delinquency.

> He made me so mad, I felt like killing him … He didn't believe me when I told him that I have this other personality who takes control and makes me do all these things … He told me, "You don't need no help," and that I was not an addict: "You just need attention!"

In this case, this young woman was presented with a difficult choice: who was she to believe? Her beloved counselor, a woman she felt great admiration for, or her own parent? They both seemed to have pretty strong opinions about who she was, and what she needed, while neither seemed too interested in hearing what she had to say. They both seemed to exercise their respected authority over her in order to define her, but also direct her future actions. The struggle to understand and self-correct was painfully apparent in all letters written to Marissa; as apparent was that system-involved substance abuse girls' options were restricted to these two blame-based alternatives, as if no other reality was possible.

In contrast, Shelley, an 18 year-old among my sample of respondents, was one who had adopted an alternative view of her substance problems that was compatible only with her own lived experiences rather than the hegemonic treatment model pushed by the program. She rejected dichotomous identities, and black-or-white labels, or any labeling done by others at all.

> I guess it's like religion. Even though you believe in God, it doesn't mean that if you're gonna – like if you're Catholic you're not gonna do what

> every Catholic priest tells you to do. I'm looking at alcoholism right now for me, like asthma. Like, I've had asthma since I was young, right? And I had it really bad, like I was having asthma attacks, I was hyperventilating. But then eventually it just started getting better and better and better. And I haven't had an asthma attack for years now. But when I go to the doctor, he's says, "But you still have asthma though." So like, I'm hoping that if I am an alcoholic, I can be a functioning alcoholic.

Guys

Marissa's second most common dictum asserted that all guys lie and cheat, and therefore should not be trusted. In a developmental stage where trust and love are something all girls, especially the ones inside the justice system, crave, such a definitive view of the other sex is a source for additional stress and anxiety for locked-up girls who, already insecure in their relationships, are given an additional reason to worry: infidelity. The theory of male untrustworthiness is therefore a hard one to swallow, for several girls:

> Sometimes I hear things in the group that I don't want to hear ... Like when I had a boyfriend, I didn't want to hear "oh, all guys cheat." I told her, "Not *all* guys," and she said, "Well never count on a guy," so I got mad ... She said basically something like, "OK maybe not *all* guys cheat but most of them do, you can't really trust them." That's why I got mad, cause even though I know all guys lie to get some, you know, I do have the benefit of the doubt for some...
>
> (Dora)

Marissa is not the only OE person to advance the aphorism about the inevitability of male infidelity to participating girls. Joe, the program Director, whose formal role is strictly administrative often engages in programming content. For example, he is the instructor of record for salsa lessons offered inside the unit as part of OE's recreational component.[2] Whereas not a counselor, he occasionally provides informal assistance to clients. His "male perspective" on dating seems to mirror Marissa's motivation to discourage teenage girls from pursuing romantic interests:

> Well, Joe usually tries to tell us how guys think, you know? He tells us that we might like, lets say we go out to go get a nice dress and we spend hours to go get a nice dress and to go to a club and everything; they don't care about the dress and how much we spend on it, they only think, "Oh I'm going to have her tonight," that's how they think. He tells us the club is no place to meet guys. We should look for a hard worker, like a construction worker, or maybe meet someone in church...
>
> (Janice, 15)

Given the correctional system's heteronormative climate and hostility against LGBTQ girls, this anti-male rhetoric leaves girls with only one acceptable option: celibacy. A juvenile justice intervention so preoccupied with controlling girls' sexuality is so 1899,[3] not quite the innovative practice the program claims to be. To wrap this rhetoric with evidence-based and gender empowerment claims is inaccurate to say the least. There is no evidence that such interventions work or could work with adolescents (Kirby, 2008; Steinberg, 2007). It also seems like a hard sell that "ideal woman" standards set by protestant, middle-class morals more than a century ago are what the feminist literature has envisioned in the practice of empowerment. Furthermore, *OE* reinforced a value system that comes to oppose youth culture, but especially these girls' experiences, as most of them (at least all of the ones I interviewed) had been sexually active long before they joined Marissa's group.

It is important to note, though, that unlike with Progressive Reformers in the 1800s, *OE* problematized girls' sexuality, not necessarily with respect to Puritanism, but with the pretext of self-respect and violence protection. Avoiding conservative or religious moralism, the counselor chooses to present abstinence, or delayed sexual activity as an indicator of high-esteem and self-respect:

> We were talking about values … We got a certificate that allowed us to pick two values, like "being in love," "only having sexual intercourse with someone who loves you," "waiting till you're married," "waiting till you're older."
>
> (Yajaira, 18)

> Marissa says, "You guys give it up easily," and she said, "I think you should wait at least 6 months before you do anything" … Cause a lot of girls who are here, only know a guy for a month and they go with them and then they find out he has another girlfriend … And I'm like, "I waited 6 months with my boyfriend, see? My standards *are* high."
>
> (Vienna, 15)

Marissa also makes sure to let young women in her group know that regardless of whether they are sexually active or not, their standards are nevertheless low if they are in love with a boy who is involved with gangs. Given that this institution is located near the epicenter of Hispanic gang activity and thus houses juveniles who live close by, it is reasonable to assume that many incarcerated girls are romantically involved with a gang member, because most of their peers are. In fact, girls are surrounded by gang members, some of whom are their parents, siblings, and cousins. By collectively and authoritatively dismissing all individuals involved with gangs as criminals, abusive, and untrustworthy, Marissa dismisses all male (and some female) models in these girls' lives.

> And then she asked us about our standards, comparing with what the guy we are with is and a lot of people were like, "This guy hits me," and "This guy talks to me down," and I was like, "I have pretty high standards," and then she said, "Well, what is your guy like?" And I said, "He does gang bang, he is an active gang member, but other than that, when he's with me he puts that aside and he doesn't call me names; he doesn't put me down; he never puts his hands on me, and he gives me what other guys don't give these girls, and he gives me my place," you know ... and she said, "They're still low, due to the fact that he's a gang member."
>
> (Vienna, 15)

> She said, "All gang members are the same." And I'm like, "I don't believe that," cause I know people who are gang members and they're not like what she describes, I mean I do know where she's coming from, cause from what she said she has experienced it, but...
>
> (Valentina, 18)

Complex issues such as sexual and physical assault were vaguely and superficially explored, divorced from socio-economic context, and ultimately generating more questions than were answered. For example, the following instruction on how to shield oneself from abusive relationships was a source of stress and confusion for some girls, as the following case reveals:

VICTORIA: Like, at first, at first, like my boyfriend bought me a cell phone. You know that's how those are signs of being controlling?

AT: I didn't know that.

VICTORIA: OK, well, in those classes like, they teach us that, "If he buys you a cell phone, he's trying to control you. He's trying to see who you talk to." So I'm like, "Oh, my God, he bought me a cell phone!" Like, it was crazy and in my head I'm like, "Oh my God!" I told my mom, I'm like "Mom, Vernie is gonna buy me a phone." We call him Vernie. "Vernie's gonna buy me a phone. Isn't that the sign of controlling?" My mother's like, "Well let's see. Get the phone, accept the phone, and we'll see." And he didn't, you know?

Overall, that is about as far these sessions were willing to go into discussing romantic relationships. Of course, most girls are way beyond the "Cosmogirl" type of sex education by the time they get to attend one of these group meetings, and that is why several of them view attending them useless, and more appropriate for younger, more immature girls. The problem is, not that many girls in detention are immature, or inexperienced when it comes to either drugs or intimate relationships. Most, if not all, were required to grow up fast, and these weak interventions appear too careful and consequently too inadequate in reaching the deep-seated issues that torture girls' conscience.

Self-esteem

Self-esteem as a predictor of well-being in general and criminal offending in particular has been the focus of theoretical and empirical examination in several disciplines for decades. Rosenberg's (1979) conceptual definition of self-esteem as "one's self-respect and favorable regard about oneself" (as cited in Oser, 2006, p. 346) is generally accepted in the relevant literature. Whereas research findings on the causal relationship between low self-esteem and externalizing problems such as aggression and delinquency have been inconsistent (Donnellan et al., 2005; Jang & Thornberry, 1998), there is little doubt regarding the relationship between gender and self-esteem. There is a consistent gap between the reported self-esteem levels by adolescent girls and adult women as compared to their male counterparts, and that gap first emerges in puberty, when girls' self-respect and regard drops sharply (American Association of University Women, 1991; Baldwin & Hoffmann, 2002). It is worth noting that the gendered effect on self-esteem is mitigated by race: whereas research on this topic is scarce, there is evidence that black women do not experience a decline in self-esteem during adolescence (AAUW, 1991), especially when they adopt flexible, non-stereotypical gender roles, which black girls often do (Buckley & Carter, 2005). Despite that, a focus on raising self-esteem is not surprising considering the negative impact incarceration has on it (Oser, 2006). And indeed, there is nothing inherently wrong with guiding young women to feel better about themselves and to experience self-worth, even in jail. It is the uncompromising, authoritarian, and at times voice-cancelling strategies the counselor employs that cast doubt at both the intentions as well as the outcomes of the intervention. It is also the subtle, yet persistent push of what Goodkind (2009) calls "commercialized feminism," with its exclusive focus on personal responsibility and self-reliance that promotes a pseudo-empowering, individualistic view of girls' troubles.

Marissa theorizes and firmly announces to her clients that they all have low self-esteem. And what evidence does she offer to support her argument? Rather than assessing each girl individually, Marissa uses circular reasoning to argue that being incarcerated is sufficient proof of low self-esteem. My respondents reported that this issue comes up very frequently in group, and many had bought into the theory, as it pertained to their peers:

> We talk about how most girls in here have low self-esteem ... I do too, cause I envy other people about things, like, oh, her hair ... None of us are really happy with ourselves ... So we try to figure out why are we here, why are we doing the things we do?

> Most girls here have low self-esteem, like you see it in the way they carry themselves ... They carry themselves low.

Sometimes the self-esteem discussion is followed up with a "homework" assignment that helps hone in the message. The assignment is to write a self-reflection paper with the title "Why I have low self-esteem," yet another source of great frustration and identity crisis. "Why do I have low self-esteem?" writes one of the girls and continues: "I am not sure I have low self-esteem," then changes to express herself in a way that does not challenge the purpose or the premise of the exercise: "I think I have low confidence," she clarifies.

At first glance, this conclusion seems self-contradictory. How can a girl lack confidence when she reports a healthy self-esteem? At second thought, it seems like a nuanced assessment, which is both consistent and compatible with the views on this topic that many of my interview respondents expressed. They liked themselves in that they were not the kinds of women who liked to be bossed around, to be put down without resistance. They refused to consign themselves to the submissive role of victim-only. They often fought back, albeit in diverse ways, some of them delinquent – against people and structural disadvantage. They were the Biancas, and the Viennas, and the Doras, and the Moniques, who showed tenacity, resilience, and agency, even in the face of relentless attacks and put-downs. I argue that their low confidence was a consequence, not a cause of their law troubles. It was a result of how others viewed and responded to their actions, and of what these views and responses did to their self-efficacy. Young women liked themselves. What they did *not* like were their odds of success in the form of sobriety, education, and career. They were insecure about what the future would bring for them, because if the past was any indicator, their future would likely involve arrest and detention. They had failed before, not because they felt intellectually and emotionally inferior to others. Sure, many of them had adopted a self-defeatist attitude and constructed a criminal identity of a non-deserving "bad" guy. But this identity was built on the feedback they had received throughout the years. So, it was confidence in welfare, juvenile justice, and family services systems, not on their own talents and strengths that they lacked.

I wish I could say that their lack of confidence in those was unqualified, but I too, did not feel confident that these girls would be offered adequate reintegration assistance. Rather that streamlining delinquent girls down to this one-dimensional caricature, the low-self esteem woman who falls prey to drugs, boys, gangs, and manipulative parents, an empowering mentor could have explored the complexity of these girls' personalities and encouraged them to harness their inner strengths. Instead of building upon these strengths, Marissa rejected them as altogether deviant, alienating some, and suppressing most. In the end, even those girls who resisted the low self-esteem attribute, gave in and accepted that if Marissa says it, it must be true.

> Me, I don't think I have low self-esteem, um, but then again who knows … You know, but I like fixing myself up, I like going places, I like having money. I don't always have to have dirty fun. But Marissa told me I have low self-esteem cause I'm here, so I guess I do.
>
> (Becka, 18)

However, they could not always remember how Marissa phrased her elaborate argument that was powerful enough to convince them, but not reasonable enough to fit their life circumstances, or their actual feelings:

AT: Do you think you have a low self-esteem?
AMY: (reluctant) Uhm, I think I did, but I am much better now.
AT: You felt bad about yourself?
A: Well, I didn't think so, but obviously I did, cause of my actions.
AT: OK, what kinds of actions you think indicated low self-esteem?
A: Drugs … The people I associate with, my relations?

At this point my respondent, Amy (19) pauses, furrows her brows, and looks frustrated.

A: I am trying to remember how she said it … I don't know, just like the decisions I would make … not caring about my future … Which I *did*, but at the time I was living for the moment…

As is the case with most counseling discussed in the previous chapter, Marissa's program also fails to offer any viable, or "hands on" solutions as to how bad choices, or behaviors can be avoided and/or reversed: Marissa seems to exclusively focus on changing young women's sentiments about certain issues, hypothesizing that it is those sentiments that perpetuate their offending behavior. Most girls understood that the counselor's goal was to help them overcome addiction and minimize victimization risks by raising their self-esteem. "OK, so how do you raise your self-esteem?" I asked each time a respondent made that claim. I rarely got a clear answer, or for that matter, any answer at all. I did get a lot of "I don't know" and several answers that sounded like the following:

> Nothing really. Just make sure to surround yourself with positive people … by rewarding yourself, making yourself feel worthy, not putting yourself in situations … Like, not doing drugs, or coming here.
>
> (Becka, 18)

The suggestions about drug abstinence were similar:

> She said to stop putting myself in situations, like hanging out with negative persons and if I get out, not to hang out with users and the other thing was: I can't take responsibility for other people … trying to change them, cause I can't.
>
> (Amy, 19)

Whereas most girls found Marissa's group "fun," and her personality "amazing," "independent," "straight, but not a bitch," the few girls who dared to resist her ideas, theories, and her persuasion tactics claimed that what bothered them the most was the fact that "she's telling you who you are," which was very close to my understanding as well. I wondered if the other girls were willing to give themselves up for interpretation, in exchange for some kind words, group cohesion, and, most importantly, the candy and treats that Marissa would always give them, or if they found these circular and simplistic explanations comforting because they required little self-reflection. When I asked Dora, Marissa's most articulate resister, how she would counsel girls toward a safe, drug-free, and law-abiding path, she gave me an answer that is very close in content with the first part of this chapter:

> I would do like some things, like individual talks, and I wouldn't doubt them like she always does, I wouldn't always tell people … when they would talk to me I would always look at it from their perspective; she doesn't … And then I'd be like, OK, what about this, maybe that, I would not tell them "oh, no it's not like that."

Aftercare support

Counselors inside the facility frequently attempt to promote pro-social attitudes among girls, and advise them to seek positive role models and mentors, at the same time criticizing their bad choices in friends and boyfriends. Marissa, the *OE* counselor, shakes her head with disappointment when she hears that one of the girls is in love with a gang-member. "You guys," she says, "You always go for the easy ones." But neither Marissa, nor any other responsible adult tells them *where* or *how* to find positive role models, family, and friends. Where they come from, options are limited to gang members, abusive fathers, alcoholic mothers, underperforming teachers, and low paying jobs. Most importantly, attempts to provide these girls with the resources they need to overcome this social disadvantage or with links to mentoring, social networking, and other community organizations that would be helpful to their transition efforts, are minimal. Minimal to non existent are also basic aftercare services such as housing, daycare, school, employment, or monetary assistance. As Matthews and Hubbard (2008) report, such provisions would create a sense of security for inmates who are about to be released. Instead, as I was able to perceive from my subjects' narratives and the cries for help that filled up the letters they sent to Marissa, the lack of an aftercare plan, and especially their need for a sober place to live and a job, caused them insecurity and panic.

> I am so scared to get out cause drugs, gangs, and the streets are all I know…
>
> I've been having my doubts that I won't make it on the outs.
>
> It's too hard alone. (I know that sounds childish, but it's true).

> My house is kinda like a trap…
>
> My mom is doing drugs and that's one of the reasons I don't want to go home.

Such was their desperation and lack of information regarding the availability of resources and how to go about taking advantage of them, that several girls would directly ask the *OE* counselor, who did not work for juvenile probation, and whose job was limited to leading group counseling sessions, for instrumental support that she practically was unable to provide:

> Marissa, can you get me a job?
>
> Help me get into a real school. I get sent to access schools in Santa Ana and I keep getting caught up because I know a lot of people in these schools.
>
> Can you send me some envelopes?
>
> I need shampoo.

OE was a self-proclaimed reintegration program providing re-entry preparation and support. The program's Director frequently asserted that case management was the program's number one priority. In support of his assertion, he reassured me that he knew exactly where each of the released girls were and how they were doing. During one of our meetings, he even pointed to his file folders, explaining that program participants were occupying most of the space. My data, however, clearly pointed to the fact that once released from the county facilities (detention or camp) girls were pretty much on their own, and it was up to *them* to make the extra effort to ask for help. In terms of therapeutic (e.g. counseling) or expressive (e.g. emotional) support, girls said that before they left the facility, similar to CU or other drug treatment counselors such as AA or NA, *OE* members would hand them their professional cards.

> You can call them … They tell you to call … they give you their number so you can call them from outside.
>
> (Trish, 18)

It was unclear how a phone call could assist girls in overcoming the multiple obstacles awaiting for them in the real world. "You can call if you feel like messing up again," said Tanya, and that was the only clarification I received. Girls who had participated in *OE* also said that Marissa and Nadia had given them an open invitation to join the groups in the mentoring organization they worked for.

> She told us that if when we're out we can't be at our house or we feel someone uses us and stuff she said don't say you don't have anybody and we can help you, we're out, you can come to the group outside ... Be involved!
>
> (Yajaira, 18)

However, and despite the connection some of the girls felt with Marissa, or their acknowledged need to continue drug treatment outside the facility, none of my respondents had called. One girl said she tried once to call the camp but the line didn't go through so she gave up. Others said they wanted to call but...

> I never gave [Marissa] a chance to help ... She always offered but I never picked up the phone to call...
>
> (Valentina, 18)

> I got tied in to my own, so I don't know...
>
> (Yajaira, 18)

The only time any of the girls got to see one of her counselors, and in particular Marissa, outside detention was because the girl's mother, desperate and scared for her daughter's wellbeing, found the card and called the number on it. The girl was 15-year-old Bianca, who had once again violated curfew and was hanging out in the neighborhood "protecting her street." Bianca's mother, a Mexican immigrant who did not speak any English had called Marissa, a Spanish speaker, and asked her to help her find and bring her daughter home. Marissa, who knew which neighborhood Bianca hung out in (Bianca was very vocal about her street affiliation), indeed drove around, found Bianca, and convinced her to go home. This was the only reported incident in which Marissa, or any other counselor, was active in providing real assistance to one of my respondents. It was an action, however, that reflected Marissa's personal investment in her job, and in no way was it authorized as a formal intervention.

That anecdote also garners support for my personal feeling that Marissa, an outwardly strong, emancipated professional, felt restrained in her role as a girls' empowerment mentor by the strong anti-feminist, paternalistic, and bureaucratic culture of corrections and its anti-relationship building rules. Once the *OE* Director withdrew his support for my research, Marissa refused to talk to me on record. "If Joe wants me to talk, I will." There was no point in my asking Joe, nor did I have any desire to ask his permission to interview an adult woman about her work. Her docile attitude was entirely antithetical to the image she projected on the young women she counseled. Her interactions with juvenile hall staff were relaxed and friendly. She joked around with them and acted in a manner that communicated she was "one of the team." Knowing from having talked to her previously and from my respondents' testimonies that she genuinely cared about detained girls, I had trouble conciliating her politically correct strategy with her confident, feminist, self-reliant persona she was projecting. It was as if she feared challenging the system, and thus concentrated all her efforts into challenging the girls. It seemed to me that rather than becoming an agent of change and altering this culture to fit the gender-responsivity principles her non-profit organization promoted, she instead adulterated these principles to fit the oppressive and punitive ethos of juvenile corrections.

In terms of more practical assistance, the problem was even worse: there was nothing to fill in the gap created by the juvenile justice system's inadequacies. For example, once released, some girls had to wait for about a month before they met with their probation officer and were able to perhaps discuss education, employment, and other plans requiring immediate attention. One month, as Lori said, was too long a time.

> That is normally the grace period when you are more likely to screw up … when I get out of here I'm gonna have a whole month until I get something in the mail that says go report to this person (the PO), so it's kinda like … well now that I'm here (in detention) why don't you just tell me who my PO is and then I meet my PO here and then establish this relationship instead of giving me this grace period where I have to wait a whole month during which you are giving me the chance to screw up…

Indeed, this first month is crucial, especially for girls who are addicted to drugs and are sent back to environments where those are easily available, and sometimes free. In these cases, the absence, or the interruption of therapy for those who were lucky enough to receive some while incarcerated, might be disastrous. As Tanya explains: "It's better for me to get drug classes than going down the street and messing up again." However, even in the cases where counseling for drug addiction *is* suggested, no real effort is made to place the minor in one; again, it is entirely up to the juvenile to make the effort, which is hardly ever made, especially when the juvenile feels that addiction is not a problem for them.

> You could take counseling classes. My PO gave me a list of numbers to call but most places were out, or the numbers were wrong. Either way I didn't want to do counseling. If feel it's not gonna help.
>
> (Nora, 18)

The most common transition concerns, and two that are also interconnected, were housing and employment. As mentioned previously, girls' living arrangements were grossly ignored by their probation officers who, having no alternative residential options to offer, would often advise girls to go back into living in violent or abusive homes. Employment assistance, from vocational training to job search and interviewing skills was unavailable to, albeit highly desirable by girls I interviewed. Dora, for example, who is in desperate need of legitimate income said that she had to find such assistance on her own.

> They do help you here too if you want but … but the only thing they do is turning applications for you and I can do that myself … I already have a resume…

And although Dora was able to find some help with writing her resume independently, she still lacked other job market familiarity that would make her a stronger candidate. She would recruit her friends' advice on how to dress and present herself in interviews:

> My friends, I'll ask them, "Foo do I look gangster?" No, seriously I will ask that, "Or do I look normal?" And they're like, "No foo, even with all the make up you have you still look gangster"

Not surprisingly, Dora complained that nobody would hire her, perhaps due to her "gangster" appearance, her tattoos, or even because of the budget crisis. Either way, although Dora dreamed of one day going to college and then becoming a doctor, a nurse, or a child psychologist (all three among the most popular career aspirations of many other girls I talked to), she is currently just interested in a decent job that pays the bills, in which "decent" excludes fast food joints:

> I was looking like for a job in an ice cream place … not like Burger King … I've done that before and it was hard … So much pressure … I can't deal with pressure … Or I could do brows…

Similar distaste regarding jobs in fast food places, which are often presented to system-involved girls as viable solutions, was expressed very often. As one girl characteristically said:

> I came close to working at KFC, but they found out I was using. I chose drugs over KFC…

In absence of any well-structured plan for their future, and in fear of screwing up yet again once released, several girls were starting to become fond of the prospect of going to military school, or joining the army.

> I want to join the army cause that will help pay my car, anything. And if you die, you are going to have a ceremony … They will respect me. If I die now, who will help my mom get the money to find a place? They can pay for me.

> I want to go to classes for the military. It's by choice … Cause when I got kicked out from school, that's the only place organized like school I can go to, it's every day, I have a schedule, and I'll have work to do in class and it's organized you know … And I'll get out of probation when I get out.

> They are strict, but I'm so used to it here, so I think I'll be able to handle it there…

For some girls, the military seems to be the only option to keep them from recidivating one more time:

> I think that's kind of like a last resort type thing for me … Umm I know that I do well in structure because you know … I just do um better than when I'm doing whatever I want. When I want like if I can't do what I want to be doing and like if everything is like just going downhill or I get caught up in like the same or whatever is going on … If things aren't really going well, that's my last resort.

These interview excerpts reveal my respondents' craving of structure, organization, and clear direction. The *OE* program was supposed to do exactly that. Pull from all the community resources the participating organizations offered, and synthesize a re-entry plan tailored to the needs, strengths, and wishes of each young woman separately. Yes, maybe the program manager was correct to keep track of all released program participants, but that was just one step toward following up. The remaining steps were never taken, and unsurprisingly girls would once again get caught-up in their usual tricks. It made little sense that young women who, stripped of any agency, were not even allowed to turn off the lights in their room inside juvie, were all of a sudden expected to muster self-control and ownership once released, just because someone had told them that is what girls who love themselves do.

Counseling philosophy and style

Marissa's confrontational, "no-nonsense," communication style, her persistence in linking young women's character and reasoning faults to their delinquent status, and her attempts to alter behaviors by changing how her clients perceive themselves and the world around them, are all consistent with a type of cognitive behavioral therapy (CBT) that is based on the principles of Corrective Thinking, or Thinking Errors (Yochelson & Samenow, 1977). This model assumes that individuals behave in certain ways because of the way they think, and a criminal's way of thinking differs than that of a non-criminal in a number of ways. Criminal thinking/reasoning employs self-defeatism, deflection, and blame shifting, while rejecting criticism, empathy, and self-reflection (Yochelson & Samenow, 1977).

An examination of the theory's merits is beyond the scope of the current discussion. Its relevance here is that it provided the theoretical basis on which the *OE* counselor's therapeutic philosophy and methods were seemingly founded. The Thinking Errors approach holds delinquents exclusively responsible for their actions, which are a result of their erroneous way of thinking: they act wrongly, because they think wrongly. During treatment individuals' thinking processes go under heavy attack, in an attempt to alter them, which in turn will alter their consequential (wrongful) behaviors. Because this therapeutic strategy targets an individual's cognition and subsequent behavioral change, it is often classified as Cognitive Behavioral Therapy/Treatment (CBT). CBT programs have fared very well in evidence-based research, which has demonstrated their significant recidivism reduction outcomes (Gendreau & Andrews, 1990; Jewell et al., 2015; Ladenberger & Lipsey, 2005; Sherman et al., 1998; Wilson, Bouffard, & MacKenzie, 2005) and are therefore included in OJJDP's model programs guide. CBT is "a problem-focused approach to help people identify and change dysfunctional beliefs, thoughts, and patterns of behavior that contribute to their problem" (OJJDP, Model Programs Guide).

CBT is a popular model in rehabilitation programs inside adult and juvenile correctional institutions alike. Its use, however, with female offenders requires several adjustments. Whereas this therapeutic model may be effective in some contexts and with some clients, it is nevertheless incongruent with gender-responsive therapy principles, which the program peddled. As Matthews and Hubbard (2008) caution, despite some evidence pointing to the effectiveness of CBT in treating female-specific behavioral problems, such as depression and eating disorders, this method might result in more harm rather than good, unless adjusted for gender differences. The most important modifications need to focus first, on changing the confrontational nature of this style of psychotherapy, and second, on specifying the content of the treatment, to emphasize women's moral and empathic inclinations, and to revolve around maladaptive behaviors that girls are known to commonly use as a response to gender-specific cognitive distortions (Matthews & Hubbard, 2008). Such distortions include girls' excessive concern about disapproval and acceptance by others, and their tendency to internalize blame, which increase their likelihood of developing psychological disorders such as depression and anxiety. Because girls are more likely than boys to use emotional coping, they also are more likely to react to their negative feelings through self-destructive, maladaptive behaviors (Gilligan, 1982; Gilligan, Lyons, & Hanmer, 1990; Miller, 1976). Moreover, Matthews and Hubbard (2008) suggest that the typically highly structured nature of CBT programs is incongruent with girls' need for bonding, and the relational model that gender-responsivity advocates propose for the design of appropriate and effective therapeutic milieus for female clients. Instead, it is suggested that CBT should be carried out less formally, and provide opportunities for relationship, trust, and empathy building among the clients and between them and the counselor (Matthews & Hubbard). In addition to enhancing the content and structure of CBT in ways that acknowledge, but also take advantage of gender-related developmental factors and system-involved girls' subjective experiences, adjustment must also be made to the underlying assumptions, projections, and style of counseling.

Although CBT guidelines today have not only moved beyond confrontation and humiliation, discourage aggressive attacks on clients' thinking patterns

(Carroll, 1998) and some even *invest* on rather than undermining ambivalent feelings, CBT practices, especially within corrections have not adapted to modernity. In fact, they still rely heavily on the assumption that the person must be held fully accountable for their actions, and to better their situation, must first blame themselves for it. That is exactly how *OE* adjusted CBT to make it look like it was gender-specific and empowerment focused. Denying personal agency, treating delinquent girls who have indeed experienced emotional strain and social adversity as passive victims, and generally essentializing the female experience have been criticized as disempowering and counterproductive as well (Goodkind, 2005; Hannah-Moffat, 2010; Pollack, 2000). That is not to say that the only appropriate alternative, however, is treating system-involved girls solely as offenders, and convincing them that their delinquent status is a free choice made in a contextual vacuum. Forcing young women to minimize the impact of structural disadvantage and violent victimization on their delinquent pathways also minimizes their feelings, and implies that their painful experiences should not matter, and when they do, that is because one lacks the inner strength to counter them. Trivializing context and trauma in the "pursuit of normative femininity and gender conformity" (Hannah-Moffat, 2010, p. 201) may result in ideological oppression as well; doing so in the abrasive, forceful manner that youth counselors follow to get through to their clients, might actually be harmful.

Such style might be traumatizing and particularly disempowering when followed in the treatment of female delinquents (Kendall & Pollack, 2003), who often suffer symptoms of PTSD due to past victimizations (Dixon, Howie, & Starling, 2004), and thus may be unable to handle further conflict. Moreover, this type of aggressive criticism against not only the act, abut also the person, might sever adolescent girls' already vulnerable self-image and already endangered sense of safety. Girls are socialized to internalize blame, and take responsibility for their or even the actions of others (Miller, 1976); whereas this view universalizes the woman experience without accounting for race, ethnicity, and culture disparities, it nevertheless accurately describes the respondents' accounts in the current study. Pressuring these young respondents into rationalizing rather than challenging this cognition, while shutting down their search for structural causes of offending as "excusing misbehavior" may contribute to girls' ambivalence regarding the context of their delinquency, and the multiple disadvantages linked to it. Such outcome contradicts the goal of empowerment, as it is conceptualized in the current study, and pushes the same hegemonic ideology of accountability and pathology governing penal institutions, only wrapped in a new progressive and feminist-informed package.

Empowerment: business as usual

OE claimed to be an innovative, reintegration program that was responsive to the unique nature of the problems associated with female delinquency and employed a strengths-based, trauma-informed approach to solving them. As all gender-responsive interventions, it is anchored in feminist pathways theory, links female offending to victimization, and considers both a manifestation of women's inferior status in patriarchal societies. Gender-responsive programming aims at empowering marginalized and oppressed women and girls to overturn the consequences of gender, race, and class disadvantage, of which crime, victimization, and incarceration are consequences.

Empowerment is the theoretical framework my study uses to examine what happens inside this juvenile hall, especially with respect to this specific program. It is conceptualized as a tri-dimensional notion that borrows Simmons and Parsons' (1983) *internality*, Bandura's (1982) *self-efficacy*, and Young's (1994) empowerment definition. Therefore, in evaluating the "empowering" claims of *OE*, I consider a) internal (psychological) empowerment, the process of developing personal qualities such as self-esteem; b) external empowerment, the process of raising confidence in one's ability to achieve set goals by developing skills and enabling access to resources; and c) political empowerment, the process of raising critical consciousness (Freire, 1973; 2000). *OE* aimed solely and, in my opinion, missed at the first (internal) aspect of empowerment, and provided lip service to but very few resources for achieving the second (external). As for political empowerment, *OE* employed rhetoric and methods that not only did not promote, but, instead, discouraged it. Rather than encouraging independent thought and critical reflection, the program rejected the former as deviant, and the latter as "making up excuses." Rather than actively listening to young women's concerns, the program shushed them, and replaced them with alternate concerns that problematized their feelings and moralized their behaviors. Rather than supporting young women to challenge racism, sexism, and injustice, the program ignored the first, reinforced the second, and denied that the third was even relevant. Rather than stressing the multiple sources of their marginality and helping girls link them to thinking and behavioral patterns that perpetuate their disadvantage, the program stressed their low self-esteem. Even if we are to accept that contrary to personal accounts, all these young women suffered low self-esteem, the method employed to boost it risked doing the exact opposite. It's like yelling at someone to calm-down; when has that ever calmed anyone down? Imagine if that someone was calm to begin with, I think that would create the very response it attempted to eliminate.

The most disempowering aspect of the program, however, was the gap between aftercare potential and aftercare delivery. There was no continuation of treatment once the girls transferred to camp or back to their neighborhoods, and assistance for services such as therapy, mentorship, employment, housing, and education were offered on demand. If she called, maybe they would be able to help. I have no way of knowing whether that gap was as wide as described by my respondents. But, does it really matter? While still incarcerated, young women *felt* that the program (or probation) would be of little or no help with real world problems, and that they would be on their own as always. Whether subjective or not, that was their reality, and that reality terrified them. It crushed their confidence, and self-esteem had very little to do with it.

My analysis affirms critiques of women's programming that have been raised by feminist scholarship before (Goodkind & Miller, 2006; Hannah-Moffat, 2010; Young, 1994; Pollack, 2000; Sharpe, 2016). First, empowerment is narrowly conceptualized in these settings, and like all other existing programming, it individualizes women's offending, it denies their agency by asserting a diseased personality (low-self esteem), it trivializes, or/and casts blame for victimization and its long-lasting impact, and it expects blind compliance with rules even when those are designed by systems of oppression. This narrow and ultimately erroneous conceptualization of empowerment is exhausted in teaching delinquents that they are the only ones accountable for "doing bad" and that it is entirely up to them change, and by changing, to magically transcend the factors associated with their failings. While convincing girls that they possess, or should possess the subjective agency to change their life pathways in a way that it is resilient to context, program counselors deny that agency as it relates to girls' views and opinions about themselves. This mixed message leaves young women vulnerable, frustrated, and conflicted. The program fails to alter or at least ameliorate the negative impact of juvenile justice processing and detention. Purposely or inadvertently, the program fits better to the traditional correctional principles of punishment, individualism, moralization, and submission to authority, rather than the gendered justice philosophy. While it calls itself innovative and empowering, it is yet another standard treatment program for juvenile delinquents.

Although depressing, this revelation is not surprising. Whereas I did not initiate this study with the purpose of *critiquing OE*, I was intrigued by it being premised on an ideology that stood in direct contrast to the practice of "penal harm," that dominates corrections in the US and elsewhere. I was hopeful that the management's commitment to gendered justice principles would be enough to pierce through the tradition of domination inside juvenile jail, yet was worried that it would not. Whereas most literature out there ignited my hope with its endorsement of GR expansion in several settings, some scholarship also kept me grounded. Hannah-Moffat (2010) cautioned against uncritically accepting gender-responsive programming as an ideal alternative to existing penal policies, especially given the difficulty with operationalizing abstract GR concepts such as empowerment. Hannah-Moffat (2010) doubted the compatibility of gender-responsivity with the ethos and practice of corrections:

> Cultural and gender *integration* requires examining and responding to issues through different lens. This means, quite bluntly, not doing what we have always done...
>
> (p. 207)

As my observations indicate, the juvenile hall and *OE* were doing what was always done, and for that, they failed at empowering young women. Similar to

Goodkind and Miller's (2006) ethnographic study of a gender-specific art therapy program implemented in a secure juvenile institution, my observations of *OE* revealed a failure to move away from stereotypical, oppressive conceptualizations of gender and femininity, and an endorsement of narrow, cultureless standards of appropriateness and ethics. The culture of corrections, with its almost exclusive focus on security and control, seems to be incongruent with what truly empowering models of treatment entail. This has spilled over to the content of gender-responsive program designs and implementations. Such programs, wrapped with empowerment rhetoric, reinforce disciplinarian goals, and state governance while pretending to advance women's causes and feminist ideals (Hannah-Moffat, 2001).

Notes

1 My role as a volunteer created an expectation that I did something to help out, and although I did, my volunteer help never took the form of my answering letters on behalf of Marissa.

2 Other recreational activities under the *OE* umbrella included cooking, and field trips to the correctional camp for beautification sessions (eyebrow shaping and haircuts), all of which were scarcely offered. For all the months of my data collection, I never witnessed any, so my knowledge of them is indirect (coming from either my interviews or conversations with managers and probation administrators).

3 1899 is the year in which the first juvenile court was established, a significant development that was spearheaded by Progressive era reformers (See Chapter 1).

References

AAUW, American Association of University Women (1991). *Shortchanging Girls, Shortchanging America*. Washington, DC.

Baldwin, S. A., & Hoffmann, J. P. (2002). The dynamics of self-esteem: A growth-curve analysis. *Journal of Youth and Adolescence*, *31*, 101–113.

Bandura, A. (1982). Self-efficacy mechanism in human agency. *American Psychologist, 37*(2): 122–147. doi:10.1037/0003-066X.37.2.122.

Buckley, T., & Carter, T. R. (2005). Black adolescent girls: Do gender role and racial identity impact their self-esteem? *Sex Roles*, *53*, 647–661. doi:10.1007/s11199-005-7731-6.

Carroll K. M. (1998). *A Cognitive-Behavioral Approach: Treating Cocaine Addiction*. Rockville, Md: National Institute on Drug Abuse.

Covington, S., & Bloom, B. (2006). Gender-responsive treatment and services in correctional settings. In E. Leeder (Ed.) *Women and Therapy Journal, 29*(3), pp. 9–33.

Daly, K. (1992). Women's pathways to felony court: Feminist theories of lawbreaking and problems of representation. *Southern California Review of Law and Women's Studies*, *2*(1), 11–52.

Dixon, A., Howie, P., & Starling, J. (2004). Psychopathology in female juvenile offenders. *Journal of Child Psychology and Psychiatry*, *45*(6), 1150–1158.

Donnellan, M., Trzesniewski, K., Robins, R., Moffitt, T., & Caspi, A. (2005). Low self-esteem is related to aggression, antisocial behavior, and delinquency. *Psychological Science, 16*(4), 328–335. https://doi.org/10.1111/j.0956-7976.2005.01535.x

Freire, P. (1973). *Education for critical consciousness.* New York, NY: Seabury.

Freire, P. (2000). *Pedagogy of the oppressed* (30th anniversary ed.). (M. Bergman Ramos, Trans). NewYork: Continuum.

Gendreau, P., & Andrews, D. A. (1990). Tertiary prevention: What the meta-analysis of the offender treatment literature tells us about "what works." *Canadian Journal of Criminology, 32*, 173–184.

Gilligan, C. (1982). *In a different voice*. Cambridge, MA: Harvard University Press.

Gilligan, C., Lyons, N. P., & Hanmer, T. J. (Eds.). (1990). *Making connections.* Cambridge, MA: Harvard University Press.

Goodkind, S. (2009). You can be anything you want, but you have to believe it: Commercialized feminism in gender-specific programs for girls, *Signs, 34*(2), 397–422.

Goodkind, S. (2005). Gender-specific services in the juvenile justice system: A critical examination. *Affilia, 20*(1), 52–70. doi:10.1177/0886109904272061.

Goodkind, S., & Miller, D. L. (2006). A widening of the net of social control? 'Gender Specific' treatment for young women in the U.S. juvenile justice system." *Journal of Progressive Human Services, 17*(1), 45–70.

Hannah-Moffat, K. (2001). *Punishment in Disguise: Penal Governance and Federal Imprisonment of Women in Canada.* Toronto: University of Toronto Press.

Hannah-Moffat, K. (2010). Sacrosanct or flawed: Risk, accountability and gender-responsive penal politics. *Current Issues in Criminal Justice*, *22*(2), 193–215.

Hoffmann, H. C. (2006). Criticism as deviance and social control in Alcoholics Anonymous. *Journal of Contemporary Ethnography*, *35*(6), 669–695. https://doi.org/10.1177/0891241606286998

Jang, S., & Thornberry, T. (1998). Self-esteem, delinquent peers, and delinquency: A test of the self-enhancement thesis. *American Sociological Review, 63*(4), 586–598.

Jewell, J., Malone, M., Rose, P., Sturgeon, D., & Owens, S. (2015). A multiyear follow-up study examining the effectiveness of a cognitive behavioral group therapy program on the recidivism of juveniles on probation. *International Journal of Offender Therapy and Comparative Criminology, 59*(3), 259–272.

Kendall, K., & Pollack, S. (2003). Cognitive behaviouralism in women's prisons: a critical analysis of therapeutic assumptions and practices. In, Bloom, B. (Ed.) *Gendered justice: addressing female offenders.* Durham, USA. Carolina Academic Press, pp. 69–96.

Kirby, D. B. (2008). The impact of abstinence and comprehensive sex and STD/HIV education programs on adolescent sexual behavior. *Sexuality Research and Social Policy*, *5*(18). https://doi.org/10.1525/srsp.2008.5.3.18

Ladenberger, N. A., & Lipsey, M. W. (2005). The positive effects of Cognitive-Behavioral programs for offenders: A meta-analysis of factors associated with effective treatment. *Journal of Experimental Criminology*, *1*(4), 451–476.

Matthews, B., & Hubbard, D. J. (2008). Moving ahead: Five essential elements for working effectively with girls. *Journal of Criminal Justice, 36*, 494–502.

Miller, J. B. (1976). *Toward a new psychology of women.* Boston: Beacon Press.

OJJDP. Model Programs Guide. Available at www.ojjdp.gov/mpg/

Oser, C. B. (2006). The criminal offending – self-esteem nexus: Which version of the self-esteem theory is supported? *The Prison Journal, 86*(3), 344–363.

Pollack, S. (2000). Reconceptualizing Women's agency and empowerment: Challenges to self-esteem discourse and women's lawbreaking. *Women & Criminal Justice, 12*(1), 75.

Rosenberg, M. (1979). Conceiving the self. New York: Basic Books.
Sharpe, G. (2016). Re-imagining justice for girls: A new agenda for research. *Youth Justice, 16*(1), 3–17.
Sherman, L. W., Gottfredson, D. C., MacKenzie, D. L., Eck, J., Reuter, P., & Bushway, S. D. (1998). *Preventing crime: What works, what doesn't, what's promising. research in brief.* National Institute of Justice. No. NCJ-171676.
Simmons, C., H., & Parsons, R., J. (1983). Developing internality and perceived competence: The empowerment of adolescent girls. *Adolescence, 18*(72), 917–922.
Steinberg, Laurence. (2007). Risk taking in adolescence: new perspectives from brain and behavioural science. *Current Directions in Psychological Science, 16*(2), 55–59.
Wilson, D. B., Bouffard, L. A., & Mackenzie, D. L. (2005). A quantitative review of structured, group oriented, cognitive-behavioral programs for offenders. *Criminal Justice and Behavior*, *32*(2), 172–204.
Yochelson, S., & Samenow, S. (1977). *The criminal personality: Vol. 2. The change process*. New York: Jason Aronson.
Young, I. M. (1994). Punishment, treatment, empowerment: Three approaches to policy for pregnant addicts. *Feminist Studies, 20*(1), 32.

Chapter 8

Epilogue

Promises broken

***If You Just Smile* (Poem – Anonymous Detained Girl)**

If you just smile
No one will suspect anything is wrong
If you just smile
I will push you away
Your false happiness sickens me
If you just smile
You will always be alone
No matter how many friends you make
If you just smile
Nothing will ever get fixed
Don't be afraid to say what's on your mind
Because
If you just smile
I may never know you.

This study places system-involved girls' narratives in the forefront of its analysis to raise their voices and reveal the context of their lived realities, especially as those compare to the lived realities inside juvenile detention. Girls' experiences inside the system, are then evaluated against the official rhetoric of rehabilitation and gender empowerment that dominates public discourse with respect to youth corrections. I reveal the many ways through which life inside juvenile jail mirrors system-involved girls' devastating life-stories and reinforces its negative impact on their self-perception, well-being, and prospects, all while juvenile justice officials tout a caring, and feminist approach to youth reform.

Although I aimed to have my respondents' voices rather than my own dominate the discussion, and presented excerpts from all 28 respondents' narratives, I was nevertheless unable to present each girl's entire story verbatim. Instead, I chose to highlight a few that best captured the overarching themes under which the findings were organized. Despite the individuality of each girl's personality, and several differences in the way they viewed the world, their life-stories shared depressing similarities. They shared a collection of family problems such as parental neglect, substance abuse, violence, and crime; absence of or depleted secondary support systems in their immediate communities; sexual harassment and victimization, most of the time inadequately or inappropriately resolved; association with groups or individuals traumatized by similar adversities; self-defeating coping and survival strategies; social marginality; structural disadvantage; institutional neglect; and to top everything off: stigmatization and re-victimization by the justice system and its agents. This comes as no big surprise to those who study female delinquency and crime. My respondents' life-stories parallel past feminist scholarship that delineates the unrelenting personal, structural, cultural, and environmental circumstances shaping young women's pathways toward juvenile jail.

My findings also parallel previous (albeit sparse) literature that exposes the counter-rehabilitative, damaging, and punitive context of youth corrections for girls. Conditions of confinement for incarcerated girls in this study not only ignore, but also are antithetical to the juvenile justice system's foundational purpose, as well as the particular institution's mission statement and commitment to rehabilitation, gender-responsivity, and innovation. Indeed, everything that happens inside the female unit of juvenile hall seems to be designed with the opposite goals in mind: to injure young women's sense of control, confidence, relational strengths, and potential, and to do so in the most gendered of ways.

Female minors inside this institution are routinely subjected to boredom and idleness; room segregation; relationship interruption; privacy and dignity assaults; enforced silence and needless regimentation; vague, poorly articulated, but pervasive rules; anti-supportive, stigmatizing attitudes; and emotional/psychological abuse and neglect. These patterns reflect the counter-rehabilitation view that the institution is designed to deprive, and this, in turn, is based on a dim and pessimistic perception of who these young women are and where they are expected to go in life (Tosouni, 2014). Consequently, the state of condemned isolation that saturates system-involved girls' lives in the outside world is maintained, if not reinforced, inside juvenile hall.

To add insult to injury, intervention programs implemented inside the institution complement rather than combating existing penal strategies, mask girls' lived reality, and silence their voices by pretending to be trauma-informed and empowering. Counselors' superficial attempts to heal, restore, and strengthen young women are almost entirely exhausted in problematizing the individual, decontextualizing offending and victimization, rationalizing punitiveness, and reinforcing heteronormative, white, middle-class, parochial norms. In 2001, feminist criminologist and women's rights advocate Meda Chesney-Lind argued that delinquency programs short-changed girls, and urged juvenile corrections to design "programming as if girls mattered" (Chesney-Lind, 2001, p. 43). That kind of programming would address needs related to girls' traumatic life-stories, would be culturally as well as gender relevant, would provide aftercare assistance, would provide meaningful activities to lift girls out of boredom and idleness, and would follow a strengths-based approach to empower marginalized young girls to advocate for social change. She was of course describing programs that followed the "gendered justice" philosophy and guidelines. But programming inside this juvenile hall followed this model only on paper; in practice it did the exact opposite. It is as if girls' personal histories of traumatic victimizations, the socio-economic context in which these victimizations occur, and the patriarchal arrangements that enable, tolerate, and normalize them do not matter. It is as if girls' own opinions and wishes do not matter. It is as if *girls* do not matter. There is nothing new, innovative, evidence-based, or empowering about that kind of "gendered justice." It is all gendered, to be sure. But justice, not quite.

Promise and delivery: minding the gap?

My findings reveal a gap between speech and practice, as well as a stark contrast between what "ought to be" and what "is" in this juvenile institution. Before discussing why that happens and what implications for policy and research it generates, it is important to place these findings in the context of the professional literature it is part of, and to contemplate whether these findings point to a local, isolated problem or a systemic phenomenon.

Fitting in

My data and, thus, findings are restricted to the female unit of one juvenile hall in Southern California. Their generalizability is therefore, dubious. First, are conditions of confinement and therapeutic programming similar in the boys' units? I have no evidence to suggest, and no good reason to believe that boys are treated much better, though it is possible that they are treated *differently*. Attacks against girls in my study were gendered, targeting areas that teenage girls, especially girls who live with abuse-related traumas, are more vulnerable to. Boys have a gender, too, and I wonder whether attacks against them are also tailored to their unique developmental traits or to hegemonic masculinity constructions. This is far beyond the scope of my study, but I think it is an empirical question worth exploring. I would love to see more researchers go inside youth jails to examine whether and how the speech-practice gap varies by gender.

Second, are conditions of confinement for girls in this juvenile hall similar to those in other detention centers in the country and in countries in other Western systems? I am confident in saying that yes, based on past research, my findings are consistent with those of past literature on which my analysis built. One such account comes from the Human Rights Watch [HRW] and the American Civil Liberties Union [ACLU] (2006) joint report on two state-run juvenile facilities in New York. In-depth interview narratives with 30 formerly incarcerated girls were strikingly similar to those of the current study. System-involved girls in NY were subjected to abuse (including physical and sexual) and neglect inside prison-like facilities that, contrary to their stated purpose, failed to provide their supervised children with appropriate, meaningful, and rehabilitative services. Much like my data suggested, educational, vocational, mental health, treatment and reintegration programs and services were inadequate, haphazard, untailored, or ineffective. Other reported similarities include staff's use of humiliating practices and language, hostility and discrimination against girls who fail to meet socially constructed standards of femininity, blunt favoritism, prohibition of interactions between inmates, forced isolation, idleness, and the use of collective punishment. New York girls complained about being threatened, yelled, screamed, or cursed at by correctional employees. Counselors ignored them, avoided speaking to them, or rejected them. Similar to detainees in my sample, one of the girls in the HRW/ACLU report expressed feelings of being treated like a "dog" or "animal," or not "as human" (p. 85).

My findings are also consistent with those published by Acoca (1998), who also used qualitative observations and structured interviews with incarcerated girls. Reports of emotional, physical, psychological, and sexual harassments were abundant in her interviews. Girls in that sample, like in mine, complained that staff members made them feel worthless, yelled and cursed at them constantly, and used unnecessary restraints, such as handcuffs, which were also used with my sample during transportation from their unit to visitation rooms. It is clear that environmental conditions have not improved at all, as in the 1998 study girls (and researchers) reported that poor quality food, shared clothing, and odd, at times inhumane living arrangements contributed to the degradation of adolescent girls. Limited access to outdoor, or any activities, and isolation in bare rooms contributed to girls' sadness, and depression (Acoca).

Girls' frustration with insulting, humiliating, and offensive treatment by correctional counselors throughout the juvenile justice system, disappointment with their unmet need for love, attention, and individualized treatment, and fear of failing to reintegrate once released were reported in Belknap, Holsinger, and Dunn's (1997) focus group study. Kempf-Leonard and Sample (2000), who also analyzed focus-group discussions, reported that system-involved girls' experiences with the justice system were negative: they entailed perceptions of injustice and disrespect due to gender; overmedication; lack of treatments responsive to experiences of abuse and neglect. And like many girls in my sample, girls in that study expressed their desire for close, caring, stable relationships with well-adjusted adults, to fill the gap of care and family in their lives. In fact, the study cites a quote, which is strikingly similar to one of my respondent, Dianne's dreams of a stable, family-like environment.

> Another girl envisioned, "a foster family but set up more like a group home. It's like a regular house and they have everything from like five-year-olds to like 17- and 18-year-olds there. They all eat dinner at the same table, just like … a normal family."
>
> (Kempf-Leonard & Sample, 2000, p. 113)

Laurie Schaffner's (2006) portrayal of "girls in trouble with the law" captured and contextualized the experience of delinquent girls not only in the juvenile justice system abut also the institutions, formal and informal that surround and interact with it, in similar light. Schaffner voiced girls' negative attitudes toward juvenile detention, which was compared to hell, and further marginalized children who did not conform to traditional and heteronormative conceptions of femininity. She also critiqued youth workers for largely de-politicizing girls violence, and "gender-specific" programming for reinforcing gendered norms, (though she found the idea of such programming promising).

Schliehe's (2014) qualitative interviews with girls who had been previously held in Scottish "closed institutions," including "Secure Care," the equivalent to California's juvenile hall, indicate that conditions of confinement there were not that different than here, and exerted similar damaging effects on inmates' well-being. Locked up girls had little control over their environment, lacked privacy, and viewed their detentions as overly punitive and unfair. Their traumas related to past histories (of family dysfunction, abuse, loss, poverty, and educational neglect) identical to those of my respondents, were augmented with the long-term anxiety, anger, and nightmares in which their confinement resulted. Schliehe argues that system-involved girls are otherized, and their confinement serves to "normalize" them.

> This attempt at re-integration through isolation and exclusion might be seen as contradiction in terms but it reflects common practice and affects increasing numbers of young people in Scotland.
>
> (p. 82)

It is the type of contradiction that is also inherent to the US juvenile justice system. Because as discussed in Chapter 1, contradictions like this have been exposed for almost 200 years, I think what we are looking at here is a systemic failure that must be acknowledged as a social crisis extending further than one particular county in Southern California. The practice of blending care with punishment is botched, because it is premised on two competing principles.

With respect to the current study, this contradiction is all the more evident in the use of gender-specific empowerment programs, such was *OE*, the counseling intervention that I examined through my interviews with participant girls. Which begs a third question. Is *OE* typical of GSP offered in other carceral contexts, or was this particular program an anomaly?

It is uncertain. Qualitative research that looks at such programs through the eyes of those whom they serve is lacking. One study (Gaarder & Hesselton, 2012) found no positive effects, but the examined program blended restorative justice principles with gender-responsivity, and the sample of young women interviewed was very small (4).[1] Goodkind and Miller's (2006) ethnographic study of a gender-specific art therapy program implemented in a secure juvenile institution paralleled my own observations of *OE*. They revealed a failure to move away from stereotypical, oppressive conceptualizations of gender and femininity, and an endorsement of narrow, cultureless standards of morality. Goodkind (2009) also conducted a qualitative review of two GS programs for "troubled" girls, several of whom had been previously confined in youth corrections (one of the programs was implemented in a community group home for girls adjudicated delinquent). The programming rationale and content were founded on ideas of individualism, self-reliance, and personal responsibility, promoting a neo-liberal version of the American Dream, framed in the kind of cautious feminist language that touted empowerment without, however, challenging dominant systems of gender, race, and class structures which facilitate power imbalances. Goodkind argues that commercialized feminism is a vehicle for the ideological oppression penal systems employ to gain women's voluntary compliance and self-regulation. But she also notes that counselors who run these programs *inadvertently* disempower young women, as they sincerely believe that what they do is grounded on feminism and results in helping girls get control of their lives.

In summary, it is uncertain whether GSP with delinquent girls in general is consistent to GSP principles or whether it is just a fad that differs little in substance than other correctional treatments for young women, but so far the little evidence, including the current study, which aimed to bridge this gap in research, points to the latter. It looks like unlike what gender-specific programming asserts, juvenile justice today is no more rehabilitative, or empowering to young women than it was in the 1800s.

Whose fault is it?

This is where I get to theorize how the gap between promise and practice in juvenile corrections emerges. Maybe it's the correctional counselors' fault, is one, I believe obvious argument. Must individuals who work with young offenders, especially girls be vetted and trained better? No doubt. This is a recommendation that is made frequently and rightfully with respect to fixing our justice system. But I am not quite content with individualizing the problem and narrowing it down to a "fix the person" solution – that is exactly what I am critiquing rehabilitation counselors of doing with respect to delinquent girls. I am also not sure that my data reliably lends to that suggestion, at least as far as the juvenile hall unit I studied goes. As previously mentioned, I did not sit down to interview any of the staff working inside the juvenile hall, or the *OE* counselors. My understanding of their behavior is grounded on my respondents' views, and on my own observations, and informal interactions with these adults. There is a lot of interpretation and personal opinion involved in making inferences about their motivations. I do not think acknowledging or having an opinion weakens my findings – to the contrary. There is no place without a view and I am transparent about mine. But some of my views on the subject of frontline staff's motives are colored by emotion, and that warrants some reservation. To be clear, I am very confident about what the staff's intention was: to deprive in order to reform. What I am hesitant to draw definitive conclusions about, is why they thought this was a good idea. With that said, here's what I gathered of individuals working inside juvenile hall.

Regarding managers (probation managers, as well as unit supervisors), I felt they genuinely thought they were putting federal funds to good use in order to help young girls and that they were using evidence-based programming that adhered to GSP guidelines. They naively, or conveniently trusted that their good intentions were translated into good actions, even when they were not around. I also got the impression that Marissa, the *OE* counselor, cared about the girls in her group as well. Whereas I was critical of what she was doing, I tried to put myself in her shoes. In addition to helping others, she had a personal stake in being there, too. She was doing her job. Like me, she knew that her job depended on the good will of staff (and the *OE* Director). She better be nice to them, and she better be following their rules if she wanted to keep that job. She had a lived reality too. She was not there to change they system, and had she tried, she would have failed, anyway. So, instead, she tried to change the girls.

As far as frontline staff are concerned, I am conflicted. I do not think I am in the position to offer a sober assessment. Watching them verbally assault, humiliate, and demean children day in, day out really took a toll on me and it would be unfair to them and dishonest to my readers to argue that I can have an objective opinion about what their inner motives were. But, here's the thing: if this was one of the many, rather than one of the few such research projects to go inside this type of environment and examine its processes on the ground, I *would* have been able to ground my opinions on that research, and form a less subjective account about why practice is so different than the rhetoric. So, if I express a lot of uncertainty about the causes of ongoing human rights violations against girls inside juvenile hall, violations wrapped in a gender-responsive, empowerment, rehabitiative and reintegrative package, with a feminist bow on top, that is not because I am a bad researcher (I hope not.), but a *lone* one. So here is my study's most fervently voiced implication: we need more research raising system-involved girls' voices above the elaborate rhetoric of a system that represses them.

The invisibilization of detained girls

Unfortunately, there is no other published research comparable to mine in the light of which I could discuss my findings on conditions of confinement for incarcerated girls and on the implementation of GS programs inside youth corrections in the US (or abroad). The paucity of qualitative research inside carceral settings in general, whether they confine male or female populations is not necessarily recent, but it is ongoing and increasingly disturbing as the world's prison systems become larger, "browner," and more secretive. In the *Curious*

Eclipse of the Prison Ethnography in the Age of Mass Incarceration Loic Wacquant (2002) decried that after the 1970s, field research in the US abandoned carceral institutions. Wacquant urged social scientists to follow their colleagues' lead from around the world, where prison ethnography is booming. Unfortunately, and despite the extinction of qualitative work in the US, American criminological scholarship "continues to dominate world research" (p. 388), and thus "international" studies are rarely read. This contributes to the silencing and invisibilization of people behind bars. Welcome to feminist criminology's world, I say: system-involved women have been off the radar since forever, "mute" and "invisible" by policy and research, the paucity of which has been extensively examined and protested by feminist scholars (Chesney-Lind & Shelden, 1998) for years. This was always and still is particularly true with respect to adolescent women behind bars, whose pathways as well as prospects have been structured by the marginality caused and perpetuated by the interplay of the multiple disadvantages they have experienced.

What is the reason for this "invisibility" of young women in criminological research? It certainly is not that there is paucity of theoretical understandings of or interest in women's crime and punishment issues, today. Thank you, feminist criminology. Feminist scholarship has contributed tremendously to our understanding of women's pathways to crime, and the connections between female delinquency and women's inferior role in male-dominated cultures. Feminist scholars have successfully pointed to and convinced federal policy makers of the need to acknowledge the distinct impact of gender in maintaining and reinforcing system-involved women's disadvantage; and that, echoing the collective oppression women face in society, women and girls in closed penal institutions, who are predominantly working class persons of color, occupy the most marginalized, stigmatized, and underserved roles. But the powerfulness and receptiveness of this scholarship has not been translated into intense ethnographic accounts from within "the belly of the beast" (Wacquant, 2002, p. 389) that is juvenile jail. Moreover, few such studies adopt an intersectional approach, reducing thus the analysis of a multi-dimensional issue to a single dimension. The few empirical studies that have brought locked up girls out of the beast's shadows, show that the level of raced and gendered maltreatment they receive when arrested, detained, and incarcerated is so perverse that it would not be hyperbolic to assume it reflects a crisis whose dimensions transcend local or even national contexts.

So we have theory, advocacy, and now money to do this, so why do we not? I argue that this kind of research is painful in more than one way, and the experience of pain is not appealing, not even to social scientists, especially when less painful options are available and highly rewarded. The demands of prison ethnography, in combination with a hostile academic culture in a discipline that is content with self-isolation are the sources of such pain. Ethnographic, intense, qualitative work that produces insights grounded exclusively on data, and in particular, data coming from the narratives of the "vulnerable human subjects" themselves, is extremely burdensome to conduct. Some would say it's just not worth it, and before judging them, it is worth considering why they may be right.

Wacquant (2002) attributes the paucity of prison ethnographies to access restrictions. Both Acoca (1998) and HRW/ACLU (1996) mentioned the presence of several obstacles with access and other practical issues during or before the collection of their interview (and observational) data. When researchers from highly respected and internationally recognized organizations such as the National Council on Crime and Delinquency, Human Rights Watch, and the American Civil Liberties Union face obstacles in accessing this population, it is not surprising that graduate students like I was at the time, or junior faculty with little or no status and resources would too. Like the previous researchers, I was confronted with a myriad of obstacles, mostly in the form of bureaucratic delays when trying to gain access to the county facility, which took about a year and a half to go though. A year and a half just to get in. The protocol I had to follow was comprised of 12–15 rigid and precise steps/rules (in a reality game show they would be called "challenges"), which had to be supervised and approved by eight different parties, and that is without counting my school's Institutional Review Board and my faculty adviser. And even when I was finally given the last green light to proceed, I was confronted with yet another, this time larger, obscure, and less reasonable set of rules, posed not by officials, nor by research reviewers concerned with minimizing harm to subjects, but by the frontline staff and supervisors inside the unit where I was conducting my research. Most of these rules were not grounded in my research contract, which was co-signed by the county and my University. Rather, they were arbitrary, unclear, and unevenly enforced; they were, however, rules I had better not violate if I wanted to ever finish my study: that was made perfectly clear to me as soon as I entered the facility. All in all, it took three long and very frustrating years to conduct my observations and interviews with just 28 inmates. Three years for academics is close to a lifetime. It takes longer to graduate, secure a faculty position, work toward journal publications on which job security depends, or toward a balanced personal life on which psychological well-being depends.

All these areas suffered as a result of these three years of intense work, and although I am sure there are strong objections to what I am about to say, my "lived reality" was that this type of work does not weigh as much as sophisticated quantitative analysis. It is seen as less scientific, less objective, less reliable, and less marketable within a discipline, which is about hypothesis testing, program effectiveness, and practice as much as it is about theory and analysis. You can't go very far with qualitative research in criminology, I've been told, because at the end of the day, you need generalizability. I am always reminded of the limitations of ethnographic work, which is viewed with what I perceive as contempt by a large fraction of my peers, and that nothing less but hurts.

"Pain" is I believe an appropriate term to describe this type of ethnography. It is not more *difficult* than other research, but it is more painful. It is painfully long to achieve access; it is painful to collect data (you can read more of this in my self-reflection); it is painful to transcribe, read and reflect on that data over and over again, like reliving a horror movie; it is painful to be constantly suspected for subjectivity, because it's not numbers which "do not lie," but words; and it is painful to know that this work might make not one small difference in the lives of the population that contributed to it the most. It is demoralizing to think that, and I do not know that many of us like being demoralized.

Much like penal societies, our academic societies are closed, introverted, and opaque. Much like juvenile hall girls, criminologists are isolated, and marginalized. We love to read and dissect each other's work in those professional journals our students love to "skim through" and by skim through, I mean quickly read a few pages, then put down. We love to listen to each other talk to us, applaud us, pat us in the back. For those few who want to enter the field as doctoral students, academic conferences where this work is celebrated are fascinating. Hotel lobbies, hallways, restaurants and bars in and around the American Society of Criminology annual meeting vibrate with excitement and vigorous debates about new ideas, tested ideas, critical ones, findings significance at the 95 confidence interval and all that; we are doing great things! We watch with awe top criminologists walk around with poise, owning the space; we are important! But outside that little microcosm, in the real world, where crime, victimization, and incarceration happens on the ground, not in some manuscript, we matter little. Nobody really listens to us, points out Elliot Currie (2007):

> Criminology as a discipline has become increasingly marginal to the larger public discussion of crime and criminal justice, and decreasingly capable of affecting the thrust of social policy.
>
> (p. 176)

If you have doubts about that, consider that as I am writing this very line, a wealthy socialite celebrity is at the White House, meeting with a real-estate mogul-turned reality TV host-turned president and his son in law, a businessman with no public policy experience, to discuss sentencing and prison reform in the US. None of the three has ever studied, worked, or been in prison. Criminologists have no seat on the table and no say in this. They have knowledge, skills and facts, but no voice. Much like my respondents, criminologists are silenced. As ethnographers we have a unique opportunity and responsibility to communicate the realities of the powerless, in my case, incarcerated juvenile women, to the world, and advocate change grounded on these realities. But, we are powerless too; our discipline is crippled. And realizing this, is what hurts the most. But it is not just about me and my feelings.

The worse consequence of this invisibilization is that if we do not reveal the lived experiences of girls in the justice system, we will continue to inform our public attitudes and consequently policy, not only about what ought to happen but about what actually happens, on shady ground. It is also important to expand our understanding of girls' experiences with violence not only as victims but also as offenders. Whereas feminist research has made great strides with response to the former, it has not quite dealt with the latter in a comprehensive way (Carrington, 2013). In-depth interviews with girls who employ physical aggression would inform our understanding of this complex matter, which is now left up to simplistic, dramatic, and anti-feminist explanations found in popular and social media. Leave a gap, criminology, and someone less qualified might just fill it. Right now, Netflix, a popular streaming TV service airs "Girls Incarcerated," and MSNBC, a cable network airs "Locked Up," both documentary-style series profiling juveniles detained in youth corrections (No. I am not sure how difficult it was for them to gain access). I do not think that is inherently problematic – to the contrary. Not only do I not snub pop culture's interest in crime and punishment, I rather see more transparency of juvenile institutions than no transparency at all. These programs, however, tend to focus on the incidental and the sensational with no regard to starting a larger conversation about our penal system, or about the social forces involved in shaping it, and shaping young women's offending and punishment. These shows inform, and affect, but they stay on the description and similar to counseling programs inside juvenile hall, they are unconcerned with raising the public's critical consciousness or pushing for systemic change. Some of them, are down- right harmful. Right before I started my data collection, a local TV news program ran a story on the GS program I examined. I knew this story was going to be on because the program Director had informed me before hand, so I watched. The story offered an unfavorable depiction of both the program and the clients it served. Even the Director was upset about it afterward. The reporter adopted a sarcastic, condescending tone as he was interviewing a young woman working in the kitchen (on cart) while someone was teaching her how to boil potatoes, allegedly as part of her rehabilitation regiment. Then, they showed the Director teaching salsa to a few other girls, and counselors engaging in other "fun" activities, again, in featuring a program geared to address girls' unique needs. This was sad all around. All the more reason for me to go in and write about girls' true needs (potato boiling not being one of them) and all the interesting and substantial things the program emphasized such as gender empowerment, cultural sensitivity, and mutual empathy as part of the therapy. As we saw, I observed none of these things, but even so, a discussion about why they were needed was to be had. This discussion is absent in popular media depictions of life behind bars. But these depictions are dominant in public discourse, and the academic ones are not. That is self-serving academic failure. We are failing our human subjects, but at least we get a PhD, a job, or a promotion as a result. In being content with this end goal of research, we the people who are perhaps qualified to advocate change and social justice, partake in the silencing of these marginalized girls' voices. In a way, we perpetuate the gender bias we condemn.

Here's what would make studies like mine both less painful and worth it: if they meant something beyond the confines of Criminology. So, I ask my academic community to stop talking and praising itself for thinking, and start acting.

First, I suggest that Universities and public research institutes engage in several lines of action that would put pressure on correctional institutions to allow the type of research that offers transparency to researchers like they do to journalists, on how they operate on the ground. Analyzing reports and other documents, interviewing correctional employees, or summarizing inmates' responses in standardized questionnaires provides a snapshot of conditions of confinement for incarcerated youth; it nevertheless cannot provide a clear, undiluted picture of what really goes on behind these walls. It is, I believe, time for universities to stand up for their right to conduct unobstructed research projects inside institutions that are publicly funded. Until then, research studies like the one presented here will remain an unpopular option for researchers and as a consequence the ability of academics to put issues of social justice at the forefront of public discussion will remain undercut. I also agree with Loic Wacquant (2002), that American prison ethnography must engage with the world through comparative analysis, "to internationalize the … discussion … rather than consign it to one or another national tradition" (p. 386), which is particularly relevant here, given that the gender-responsivity and empowerment rhetoric has taken hold in Western penal systems outside the US, and warrants comprehensive assessment. Last, I agree with Currie's (2007) call for opening up our discipline (as well as other disciplines) to less conventional productions and dissemination of knowledge. How is this relevant here, you may ask. Ethnography is not unconventional. It *was* not unconventional, I argue. Today, it goes against many strongly established conventions in higher education, such as for example "the publication imperatives of a few journals" and not only is it not rewarded as much as other methodologies, it is often punished. I hope I do not sound like I am a victim, here. I do not feel personally punished. I enjoy this work and have received my fair (or excessive) share of praise for it. But I want to see more of that. I have had numerous discussions with peers who are stressed out about meeting a certain publication threshold or else. They dream of great projects that they are personally invested in and excited about, but put them aside for a moment to finish up with this secondary data analysis which will get published in that journal, which then will get them tenure. "That's my bread and butter," a friend told me recently, "the real research interest will just have to wait." Universities ought to be a little more flexible with what is considered "tenure-worthy" I believe, if we want the discipline to advance in meaningful rather than superficial ways. Most of us got into this business not to serve some imaginary journal apparatus, but the ideal of social justice. Universities and research organizations ought to assist us in doing exactly that.

Gendered justice overhaul

> I am against the system. I don't think that people shouldn't be locked up for certain reasons. They arrest so many people and they don't have time to

> really take the time out for each person. It's very rushed. You go on court. The person doesn't get looked at as a human being. They get looked at as a convict, a criminal and they don't get any say or get to look at any judge and get respect for what they say. So things get really rushed and people get time whether it's fair or not.
>
> (Shelley, 18)

Along with reforming our research goals and scope to make young women in juvenile detention visible, we must advocate for policy change that takes their lived realities into consideration. The only policy the findings in this research point to, is a complete overhaul of a system that was never designed or designated to deliver the kind of justice that Barbara Bloom and colleagues advocated for in 2003 (Bloom et al., 2003; Bloom, 2003). If this is the justice we want to deliver, and I think it should be, then we must do it somewhere else. Juvenile corrections do not do justice; they punish, and punish excessively at that. Non-profit and community organizations, medical experts, teachers, mentors, or service workers who contract with County Probation to offer therapeutic, restorative, or/and gender-responsive programming inside youth institutions are inadvertently complicit in the abuses, denigration, and humiliation to which detained girls are subjected on a daily basis. They are cooperating with a correctional system that is concerned only with dominating them, reinforces patriarchal gender norms, and re-victimizes them, while pretending to care about their welfare. Legal actors such as judges, public defenders, and prosecutors, government actors, and social science scholars alike, provide a rubber-stamp to these abuses, by assessing intentions rather than performance, individualizing evidence of mistreatment as aberrations rather than as systemic problems, and by requiring micro-level responses to a crystalized culture of cruel (but usual) punishment that is resistant to meaningful change. Even well-intended efforts by well-meaning actors are infested by this culture and eventually become part of it, rather than reforming it. To answer the question I posed in the prologue of this book: rehabilitation, restoration, and empowerment, especially gender empowerment are not only unrealized inside juvenile corrections; they *are unrealizable*.

The juvenile system was never meant to be what it said it was going to be; it was always just another variation of state governance directed at socially marginalized and vulnerable populations. If help is what the system wanted to offer, it would offer it outside courts and corrections. This is exactly what I am proposing. I wholeheartedly agree with Feld's (1997) suggestion to abolish the juvenile court and instead deal with most juvenile offenders through social welfare agencies. That is particularly relevant to female juvenile offenders, who are disproportionately stigmatized and detained for non-criminal acts (ABA & NBA, 2001; Tracy, Kempf-Leonard, & Abramoske-James, 2009), such as incorrigibility and running away.

Although the federal Juvenile Justice and Delinquency Prevention Act in the 1970s prohibited the institutionalization of status offenders, and its reauthorization in 1992 outlawed popular practices, such as "bootstrapping" used by courts to circumvent that rule (Feld, 2009), these types of offenses initiated almost all my respondents' contact with law enforcement. Once under the police radar, girls' system-involvement escalation and subsequent juvenile hall residency became inevitable. Most incarcerated girls are nonviolent, and have committed no serious delinquent acts. Also, most girls, as discussed throughout this study, suffer the effects of childhood trauma, social marginality, poverty, community disorganization, and racial and gender discrimination. In addition, a large number of them have developed substance dependency, and mental disorders such as depression, anxiety, and PTSD. Clearly, the vast majority of these girls need to be helped, not punished; the effects of victimization must be considered and treated; most girls should be diverted to other services, not locked up. Community-based interventions that address the life and environmental conditions that push girls toward trouble and danger are much more appropriate and less stigmatizing.

The possibility that there are juvenile females who do commit serious acts worthy of justice intervention and perhaps closer supervision is of course quite real, as well. Several of my respondents had participated in criminal acts, such as theft. Many admitted to being frequently involved in physical fights, while others engaged in high-risk behaviors such as driving while intoxicated. Abolishing the juvenile justice system does not mean that crimes by juveniles will receive no response. However, there are more efficient ways in which such acts may be addressed, and yes, even punished. The impersonal, rejecting, and ostracizing nature of court processing is not only ineffective, but increases negative outcomes because of its brutalization and stigmatization effects. I argue for more humane, more inclusive, and more democratic procedures that maintain the informality of current juvenile justice procedures but also ensure that the rights of adolescents, their families, and their communities are considered and observed. Restorative justice processing (Braithwaite, 1996; Zehr, Mika, & Umbreit, 1997) encompasses these elements; it is less costly; it gives voice to both offenders and their victims; it encourages active accountability, and it has the potential to resolve conflicts peacefully rather than exacerbating their impact. Restorative practices prerequisite voluntary participation, offender admission, and a willingness to make things right. In my interviews, I heard nothing to suggest that my respondents would not be ideal candidates for such a model of justice. Even the "roughest" girls accepted responsibility for predatory acts, expressed remorse and shame, even empathy for their victims, and a strong desire to repent and to be accepted and respected. Restorative conferences, circles, and victim impact panels are, I believe, more appropriate contexts than juvenile halls, for violent girls to channel these energies. And remember, most, if not all girls I interviewed, especially the fighting girls had been victimized by violence themselves, so restorative interventions would contribute to their own as well as their victims' healing bilaterally.

In search of empowerment

So, a commitment to genuine restoration is one suggestion toward gendered justice; a commitment to true empowerment is the other. Community programming for juvenile women who find themselves trapped in juvenile processing as victims, offenders, or both must focus on empowering them. Gender-responsivity guidelines offer the specific means through which girls' empowerment is possible. My previous critique of GSP was directed at their narrow conceptualization, and implementation within corrections, or other paternalistic institutions, not at their ideological rationale. The idea is good. However, such interventions cannot survive the culture of corrections, with its almost exclusive focus on security, control, and domination. They are also incongruent with therapeutic or educational contexts outside corrections, which tend to decontextualize individual troubles and ignore larger socio-economic and environmental factors reflected in individual choices. In her critique of gender-specific programs and their narrow conceptualization in the literature, Goodkind (2005) cautions against what Carrington (1990) called "deficit discourses," Currie (2004) "therapeutic" Darwinism, and Young (1994) "suspicious therapy." All three concepts reflect the same neo-conservative attitude employed by authoritative institutional agents (counselors, probation officers, teachers, therapists) to construct the deviant person. In this apparatus, the individual is the problem, because she is deficient, or weak, and therefore deserves to be punished, extinguished, or altered. If she does not change, it is not the program's fault, it is hers, and she is viewed as "a lost cause." As Alder (1998) points out, when it comes to treating juvenile girls, the system pathologizes *them* rather than their social context. The same happens in other institutions dealing with "bad girls," such as schools, or treatment programs. That is why effective, truly empowering treatments are not viable in this culture. Alder continues that successful programs for girls can only be designed by taking into account the context of their lives. She proposes that in order to offer policy recommendations, as the current study promised in its introduction, we need to "listen to girls' own accounts of their own life-stories" through ethnographic research (Alder).

The life-stories in this book are stories of victimhood, and abandonment, and pain. But they are also stories of survival, resistance, hope, and resilience. The girls I talked to were beaten down, stomped on, and injured, but they were not fallen. They still imagined a future for themselves; they dreaded the future too, but they still dared to imagine it would be better than their present. The girls I talked to were not very eloquent, but they were wise beyond their age; they were reflective, and observant. They were passionate, and talented. Some of their essays (their letters read like essays) and poems were heartfelt and poignant. I saw so much more in them than the "damaged goods" they were treated as, and I know others did too. There was so much spirit in them to harness and channel toward their own, but also the world's life quality. There is so much spirit in *all* girls to harness and channel toward social change that will lift all marginalized, beaten down women up, because in a world of gender inequality, white male supremacy, and misogyny, all women are beaten down, even if not with the same intensity.

Gender empowerment that targets micro- (internal), meso- (community), and macro- (political) aspects of women's oppression ought to be the overarching goal of any intervention serving the needs of girls, but especially girls that live in the margins. I argued earlier that correctional settings are incongruent with truly empowering programs that raise critical consciousness and challenge dominant systems of inequality, and I still stand by that argument. That is not to say however, that these types of programs are "no brainers" or welcomed in less oppressive settings. Let me offer an anecdotal account to clarify. When I was a faculty member at a college in the American South, two of my colleagues, a sociologist, and a mathematics professor, and I designed a gender-specific math education program to be offered to minority girls attending middle school in the underserved, racially segregated community adjacent to our college. The program was gender-specific because it combined social statistics with gender empowerment instruction. The design was inspired by a large amount of empirical evidence suggesting that the reasons why women lag behind men in science are largely socio-cultural. Effective programming to increase girls' interest in STEM disciplines and thus tackle women's underrepresentation in STEM careers, we argued, must address these socio-cultural forces, namely gender stereotypes, and build on girls' strengths, such as their ability to connect with others and their interest in social causes. To fund this program, we wrote a grant application to be submitted to the American Association of University Women (AAUW) that had funded projects founded in similar rationale in the past. Unfortunately, our grant proposal did not sit well with the University's grant coordinator. In reviewing our work, she took offense at our conceptualization of empowerment, especially the critical consciousness raising part. We clarified our position both in writing and in person, grounding our arguments in the relevant literature, but she remained convinced that this proposal, because of its critical tone would appeal to nobody. We argued back and forth until she finally said: "What are you trying to do here? Get money for an after-school program or create a revolution?" The math professor, a young, passionate black woman in her first year of teaching, ended up dropping out, and decided to design a social statistics after-school program on her own, sans the "revolution" part. We did not blame her, or the grants coordinator. But we did realize how long a way we had to go, when contemporary women working for higher education found critical consciousness too controversial a goal to pursue. If that type of gender empowerment is seen as suspect in that institution, then the road to getting it accepted in less progressive contexts seems to be uphill.

What I am trying to say is that gender empowerment stretching beyond "commercial feminism" and self-esteem, is incongruent not only with correctional culture, but our culture at large. At least that is true about the US culture at this moment – it is not ready to accept or even more, celebrate women who speak up, who rise up, who engage in collective action with other women to protest the unfairness of privileges some also enjoy by virtue of their association with white and wealthy men, and who challenge or bend gender norms. Such women are not "ideal" and are often seen as the problem rather than the solution to the world's problems, and to young girls' troubles in particular. In societies like this one, what happens to girls and women inside closed institutions is not an aberration, but a reflection of what happens to them everywhere. In many ways, the gendered atmosphere, rules, and practices inside juvenile corrections do not deviate, but instead, over-conform to the gendered norms of a patriarchal context. So, if we want gendered justice in our legal system, we must unapologetically and fearlessly pursue gender justice in our social systems and contest all forms of gender violence. Until that happens, all aforementioned policy reforms will remain largely piecemeal and ultimately inconsequential.

Note

1 The same program seemed to have positive effects among girls on probation, however.

References

ABA/NBA. American Bar Association and National Bar Association. (2001). *Justice by gender: The lack of appropriate prevention, diversion and treatment alternatives for girls in the juvenile justice system*. Washington, DC: Author.

Acoca, L. (1998). Outside/inside: The violation of American girls at home, on the streets, and in the juvenile justice system. *Crime and Delinquency*, *44*, 561–589.

Alder, C. M. (1998). "Passionate and wilful" girls: Confronting practices. *Women and Criminal Justice*, *9*(4), 81–101.

Belknap J., Holsinger K., & Dunn M. (1997). Understanding incarcerated girls: The results of a focus group study. *Prison Journal, 77*(4), 381–404.

Bloom, B. (2003). *Gendered justice: Addressing female offenders*. Durham, N.C.: Carolina Academic Press.

Bloom, B., Owen, B., & Covington, S. (2003). *Gender Responsive Strategies: Research, Practice and Guiding Principles for Women Offenders*, National Institute of Corrections, US Department of Justice, Washington DC.

Braithwaite, J. (1996). Restorative justice and a better future. *Dalhousie Law Review, 76*(1), 9–32.

Carrington, K. (2013). Girls, crime and violence: Toward a feminist theory of female violence. *International Journal for Crime*, *2*(2), 63–79.

Carrington, K. (1990). Truancy, schooling and juvenile justice: "She says she hates school." *Australian & New Zealand Journal of Criminology*, *23*(4), 259–268.

Chesney-Lind, M. (2001). What about the girls? Programming as if gender mattered. *Corrections Today*, *63*(1), 38–45.

Chesney-Lind M., & Shelden R. (1998). *Girls, delinquency, and juvenile justice* (2nd ed.). Belmont, CA: Wadsworth.

Currie, E. (2007). Against marginality. *Theoretical Criminology, 11*(2), 175–190.

Currie, E. (2004). *The road to whatever: Middle-class culture and the crisis of adolescence*. New York, NY: Henry Holt and Company, LLC.

Feld, Barry C. (1997). Abolish the juvenile court: Youthfulness, criminal responsibility, and sentencing policy. (Symposium on the Future of the Juvenile Court). *Journal of Criminal Law and Criminology*, *88*(1), 68–136.

Feld, Barry C. (2009). Violent Girls or Relabeled Status Offenders?: An Alternative Interpretation of the Data. *Crime & Delinquency, 55*(2), 241–265.

Gaarder, E., & Hesselton, D. (2012). Connecting restorative justice with gender-responsive programming. *Contemporary Justice Review*, *15*(3), 239–264.

Goodkind, S. (2005). Gender-specific services in the juvenile justice system: A critical examination. *Affilia 20*(1): 52–70.

Goodkind, S., & Miller, D. L. (2006). A widening of the net of social control? "Gender-specific" treatment for young women in the US juvenile justice system. *Journal of Progressive Human Services, 17*(1), 45–70.

Goodkind, S. (2009). You can be anything you want, but you have to believe it: Commercialized feminism in gender-specific programs for girls, *Signs, 34*(2), 397–422.

HRW, Human Rights Watch & American Civil Liberties Union. (2006). Custody and Control: Conditions of Confinement in New York. Human Rights Watch.

Kempf-Leonard, K., & Sample, L. (2000). Disparity based on sex: Is gender-specific treatment warranted? *Justice Quarterly, 17*(1), 89–128.

Schaffner, L. (2006). *Girls in trouble with the law*. Piscataway, NJ: Rutgers University Press.

Schliehe, A. K. (2014). Inside 'the carceral': Girls and young women in the Scottish criminal justice system. *Scottish Geographical Journal*, *13*(2), 71–85, doi: 10.1080/14702541.2013.83863.

Tosouni, A. (2014). We're not supposed to have nothing in here: Life in juvenile jail through the voices of incarcerated girls. *Criminology, Criminal Justice, Law & Society, 15*, 60–79

Tracy, P. E., Kempf-Leonard, K., & Abramoske-James, S. (2009). Gender differences in delinquency and juvenile justice processing: Evidence from national data. *Crime & Delinquency, 55*(2), 171–215.

Wacquant, L. (2002). The curious eclipse of prison ethnography in the age of mass incarceration. *Ethnography*, *3*(4), 371–397.

Young, I. M. (1994). Punishment, treatment, empowerment: Three approaches to policy for pregnant addicts. *Feminist Studies, 20*(1), 32.

Zehr, H., Mika, H., & Umbreit, M. (1997). Restorative justice: The concept. *Corrections Today*, *59*, 68–71.

Appendix A

List of participants

Participant name (race/ethnicity, age, times in detention)

1. Nora (Mexican, 18, fourth time)
2. Jackie (Mexican, 15, third time)
3. Macy (Black American, 17, fourth time)
4. Barbra (White, 15, third time)
5. Janice (Mexican, 15, second time)
6. Isla (Mexican, 15, fifth time)
7. Brenda (Mexican, 18, sixth time)
8. Valentina (Mexican, 18, sixth time, pregnant)
9. Trish (White 18, multiple times)
10. Lori (White, 18, eleventh time)
11. Bertha (Mexican, 17, sixth time)
12. Yajaira (Mexican, 18, third time)
13. Dora (Mexican, 17, eighth time)
14. Joy (Mexican, 18, multiple times)
15. Bianca (Mexican, 15, multiple times)
16. Amy (Mexican, 19, fourth time, pregnant)
17. Tanya (Mexican, 14, third time)
18. Dianne (White, 18, eighth time)
19. Vienna (Mexican, 15, second time)
20. Becka (Mexican, 18, fourth time)
21. Victoria (Mexican, 16, sixth time)

Appendix B

Subject #29 – Anastasia

"OK, so, I'm done. I can't take this anymore. I'm never coming back in here."

That was my last recording. I still vividly remember that Sunday evening, sitting inside my green Echo (that's a car), uttering these words to my little white digital recorder that held my last interview audio file. I had just interviewed Sylvia, a 15-year-old whose story was the last straw that broke me. I had been coming in and out of juvenile hall for a while now (with holiday and summer breaks in between), and not that any of the other times were easy, but they started getting progressively more painful as I was transcribing the audio data, or reviewing what my research assistants had transcribed. Listening to my pre- and post interview notes it is obvious that I was becoming increasingly bitter and unnerved with each visit. There had been times after some interviews, like after Yajaira's, Dianne's, and Tanya's that I felt physically sick and beaten down and had to wait for a few minutes inside my car, my face buried in my hands to calm down and drive back home safely. There had been times when I had paused the interview, turned off the recorder and talked to the girl I was interviewing, human to another human. "Have you talked to anybody about this?" or "I just wanted to say off the record here, because it is not my role, nor do I speak from a place of authority or deep knowledge, I think you are bright and capable and that I am pretty sure you'll be OK." I felt guilty and unprofessional doing that, which is why I didn't want to have a record of it. I was not there to comfort, or to patronize (nor did I intend to), just to do my job and listen. Yet, sometimes listening without commenting just would not do for me.

Sylvia's story, however, was just too much to handle, and furthermore had provided me with no new insight, to be honest, or so I thought: it was the same thing over and over again, different versions of the same exact theme and overarching pattern: "This. Girl. Shouldn't. Be. Here." A few embarrassing pieces of information regarding Sylvia's interview: One, I cut it short. I did. I listened to this interview just a few months ago, for the very first time. I transcribed it then, for the very first time, too. I had chosen not to listen and not to transcribe the interview until I wrote this monograph. How's that for an empowered feminist? So, as I was listening to the recording, just before the end, I heard my own voice making up this silly excuse: "Well, I think they are getting ready for group counseling, are you going to go to that one? I will let you go to your group, I wouldn't want you to miss it." At the moment, I was in denial about what I had just heard from Sylvia's lips; In fact, I thought this was going to be a throw-away interview. But, it wasn't. Once I mustered the courage, a good eight years later to listen to it carefully and with a relatively clear head, I found that I was wrong. It was not a throw-away interview; this was the story of a throw-away girl. Whereas many parts of that story made little sense (for example, she said that while she was running naked in the streets of LA, her mother, whom she had not seen for years, appeared out of nowhere, and like dea ex machina, placed a cover around her estranged daughter, and put her in her car), which had then caused me to think: "This girl is not alright and I do not think there is a point interviewing her." In its totality, the story seemed pretty consistent with my other participants' reality. That reality included mental and psychological distress, physical harm, abandonment, blame, unresolved guilt, and criminalization. She said that she was manic-depressive, meaning she was shifting between opposite poles, but I saw her treatment by the adult caretakers in her life acting bi-polar as well: first they save her from abusive parents, then abandon her because her traumas were so deep that she became difficult to handle, then take her back again, but only for a little while, then blame her for her sister's attempted suicide, send her away again. As one would expect but nobody should accept, having committed no crime, fresh out of rape victimization, she ends up in juvenile hall, because in-patient treatment centers found her too difficult, like her adoptive parents before. Who was bi-polar again? Anyway, my point is, that was the interview that put an end to my data collection.

It had been difficult for a long time, but at that point it became impossible, and as far as I was concerned, futile. I had all the information I needed, and I was confident I had a clear perspective and would get the point across without more data. My adviser was a little hesitant. Let's shoot for 30, he suggested. Why not? My target was 35, truth be told. I explained myself and he understood, as was typical of him. "If you see what I have, you'll agree. I have tons of stuff." I said. But most importantly, "I feel like I am subjecting myself to abuse, and because I know that my 'victimization' is not even one third as bad as the one these girls are subjected to every day, I feel pathetic and ridiculous to even let myself play victim, you know?" It was a cycle of negative feelings reinforced by self-beating. Just even picking up the phone to talk to frontline staff and ask them politely if I could please come in this Saturday, to hear their monolectic answers, like, I'm bothering them and to still go and be polite to them in person, pretending I don't see how abusive they are to minors, or how they snub me going in to talk to them like they are too important or something. They don't really talk to them. They bark at them. They don't even make eye contact with them. They don't even make eye contact with me. They act like they are my boss too. And are they not? For all intents and purposes they are the boss of me. And will be for as long as I continue to collect data. But even after I'm done, I won't be able to call or write to them and ask them to show humanity and empathy and treat these children as their own, no matter how troublesome they are; I cannot remind them that what they are doing goes against international law. First, that will put girls in trouble. "What have you been telling her?" I can imagine them accusing girls I talked to. Second, they are not afraid of me. I'm a nobody to them, a student, a young woman with no real income and what is she gonna do? Write a school paper, or a book? So what? They had no fear of me; they knew I needed them. I depended on these people whose behavior I loathed, and I continued to go back and play nice because I wanted to graduate. And to top everything off, I experienced what is called "survivor's guilt." Even if I was forced to be in there, it was only for a few hours. I got to go back home, go out with my friends, watch TV, have drinks, laugh out loud. They were stuck between juvenile hall and a depressed adolescence. And there was nothing I could do about it.

So, then, I placed all my hopes of helping system-involved girls, and at the same time of delivering some kind of retribution on their behalf and mine, by writing about all this. The thought of this made me feel better. Then, I started writing. First, the dissertation. That was relatively easy but nobody reads that, and thankfully so, because it is not my finest piece of work, "a good dissertation is a finished dissertation" and all that. Then, a journal publication. That was not very easy to get done. A rejection at first, a revise and resubmit, then the published article. Well, that changed nothing in juvenile hall. Ironically, though, reviewers of my work argued that I had to write something about all the reforms taking place in California since the time I collected my data. It had been only three years, but I guess we were going through yet another "we're helping children now" phase. So, I did that, I wrote about the reforms and thought, wow, I really haven't convinced anyone that what happens inside these institutions is not only "unbettered" but also abetted, masked by these rhetorical commitments made in paper. The reality started sinking in that I went through all this and still had not managed to do something to help fix the situation. I had fixed my situation a bit. I changed universities and got the job I really wanted, as my publication helped me prove that I was a good hire. So good for me. But I still felt guilty. I still was haunted by the girl who had asked me sadly, "When are you going to talk to me?" (Never did I; her mother never returned the consent form.) Or the girl that I had interviewed before who wanted to talk to me again because things had gotten much worse since last time I saw her, or the several girls whose eyes sparked when asked: "Really, you are going to write a book about us???" I was haunted by their questions to me: "What do you really think of us? Do you think we're weird?"

Most importantly, I was haunted by what I perceived as an inability to do justice to their stories, which are the stories of silenced voices, victim blaming, multiple marginality, and paternalism, so common inside juvenile corrections and not very uncommon in the "free" world of women. As I was maturing into my teaching career and talking about gender violence with my students, I met dozens of young women, who volunteered life-stories similar to those inside this monograph. Then, I started reflecting on my own and my close friends' experiences that for some reason I had considered completely irrelevant to those of my respondents, until that point. To not be misunderstood, my experiences are nowhere near as devastating as theirs. But when I was asked by one of them, Victoria, a girl who kept repeating that her life had been wonderful, mentioned no abuse, no trauma, nothing, yet somehow her parents had petitioned for her to be locked up in juvie, when I was asked: "What about you? How was your childhood?" I kind of stumbled. That is a good question, I said. Embarrassingly, I couldn't see any differences between mine and her stories, except for the fact that she was arrested, adjudicated, and incarcerated (as I mentioned, she was my only respondent to never reveal abuse other than conflicts with her parents). It was embarrassing, because here I was, a graduate student with her life seemingly in tact, opposite Victoria, locked up, disenfranchised, and school-deprived. "Not that much different," I ended up saying. "My parents were very strict too, but" ... the juvenile justice system where I come from is withheld for minorities and neglected children, of which I was neither, I almost said, but I realized this might sound insensitive to Victoria. It's not as if the American justice system is an equal opportunity type of institution. "I had a really good support system, including many good friends that I was strongly attached to, and I guess I was also very lucky," I said instead. But that question, I came back to often, especially as my students' stories of gendered harm started piling up for reference. How had they ended up in the UC, or other Universities and not in the youth correctional system? How did I? (If you're thinking that my students are all privileged middle-class kids, they're not. I've had many first gen, immigrant, international, minority, single mother, low-income students in my classrooms).

I could never recall a period in my life from age 12 upwards when I had not been a recipient or witness of some form of gender-based degradation. Actually, I have such memories starting at childhood: my brother arguing with me that there is nothing women are better than men at (he was a little kid too, so don't judge), my grandmother, an otherwise strong, opinionated woman recalling with gratitude that grandpa had been a good husband, "He never beat me once," being her reason – it was routine practice for men of her generation to come home after the kafeneio (provincial cafés for older Greek men) and beat the hell out of the wife, just because; my best friend crying after her boyfriend slapped her; my other best friend crying because her boyfriend choked her; my other best friend escaping a sex trafficker; another one recovering from a botched abortion because she was 16 and no adult was advocating for her at the clinic; the experiences of every girl I ever met with sexual harassment in the workplace that ended up with her quitting; and the perpetual street harassment women are forced to sustain like it's nothing to be upset about or protest against. And the big one: the big mouth. I was always called that because of my tendency to verbalize my objections to various such treatments (a trait that obviously remained dormant during my juvenile hall visits). Here, in the US, my voice was dismissed often as a "cultural" difference: "It must be your culture." In my culture, in Greece, I was just a "big mouth." But in both places, what I saw was my deviating from a norm that is universal and wants women to communicate in mild expressions and to avoid casting blame on others for wrongs, because, often they bring the wrongs upon themselves.

I felt tortured by the fact that I would not be able to adequately do justice to my own, my friends,' or my students' stories either. In general, I felt that the stories of my respondents are stories that say a lot about the way we do gender justice inside but also outside the correctional system; that these are stories in which all women's lived realities are somewhat reflected. And I wanted to communicate this argument poignantly and effectively, meaning, I wanted this argument to be heard loudly and to be taken seriously, and to effect some kind of change that would improve actual lives on the ground (not just my own professional life). But I feared that neither my writing skills, nor my academic clout would manage to do that. This is no impostor syndrome, so please do not pin this on me. This is reality. I am not the great writer that the voices I am trying to voice, deserve.

So, I felt demoralized. Then, in January of 2017, a person who is known to regard women as objects of sexual gratification, girls as his future prey, children of color as subhuman, and non-white immigrants as criminals, moved to the most powerful office in the United States. He was not placed there by the majority of voters, or the majority of Americans, but the outcome was all the same in the end: he was there and he was to speak for all of them. The collective angst and outrage that followed his ascent to power were publically released in the Women's March, and its allied marches around the world, where millions of women protested misogyny, racism, heterosexism, and xenophobia. I did not participate in the Women's March that year; I watched the coverage on TV and on Twitter. I had a small child to care for now, and I was fearful that the protests would turn violent, especially against non-natives. So I chickened out, and stayed home, though I was there in spirit. The events surrounding Trump's election strangely invigorated my motivation to write this book. I could not vote (not a citizen), I did not protest (not brave), and I had stopped using social media for politics (don't ask). So, I saw my work as the most appropriate way to raise my voice against injustice, while also lifting up the voices of those that have been mostly harmed by it.

It was very painful to re-listen to the audio and re-read the transcripts, this time multiple times, and re-play them in my head while driving, doing dishes, shopping, or going to sleep. I turned that switch off when I was interacting with my family, especially my child, and sometimes I would purposely delay turning it back on. I emptied my head playing farm games on my Kindle and watching trash TV. But these stories and how to make sense of them kept lurking in. And sometimes switching off was taking longer than usual. After a long day of writing I would snap at my husband for no good reason, because I was still working on the data in my head, and he was talking about normal stuff and how dare he? I found refuge in reading the work of others who had interest in similar causes, which kept me going. It was traumatic to relive my own experiences in juvenile hall or even before that, with trying to get access into the institution. Apparently, I had suppressed these memories that started coming out again with force. I felt sick very often, again. And this time around, there was another girl I also had in mind when writing this book. My daughter. I felt I needed to do justice to her and her generation. I know, you might think I am taking this too seriously or think it is bigger than it really is. I am taking it seriously, and in my head, it is very big.

I still feel that I haven't done justice to these voices. But at least I was straightforward and honest and did not try to adjust my voice to the demands of anything other than what I felt reflected my respondents' narratives most truthfully. One of the most prolific writers in our lifetime (and an under-rated one if you ask me), Stephen King once said: "The most important things are the hardest to say … because words diminish them." I hope my words did not diminish the importance of young women's voiced accounts.

Appendix C

Copy letter of detained girl

May.31. 2007 1:19PM No.1945 P. 2

Hey [redacted]
How are you I hope Good you
I was wondering IF Theres any
places I can Go To When I Get
out. I Want To Do Good But
I Get Removed alot and I Got
mad Today when I Got Removed
and like when They brought
me To my Room. I was Thinking
That Know one care's For me
That im a peace OF Shit
and That I Should Just Kill Myself
I Tried To Kill myself by a
Train Track When I Took my
Grandpa's car I Dont wanna
live no more can you
help me [redacted] please
befor something happen's To
me! please
well Thank you
have a nice Day!

Love

May 31 2007 No. 1945 P 2

Hey [redacted]

How are you I hope good well I was wondering if theres any places I can go to when I get out. I want to do good but I get removed alot and i got mad today when i got removed and like when they brought me to my room. I was thinking that know one cares for me that Im a peace of shit and that i should just kill myself. I tried to kill myself by a train track when I took my Grandpa's car. I don't wanna live no more can you help me [redacted] please before something happen's to me! Please

Well thank you

have a nice day!

Love

[redacted]

Index

CPSIA information can be obtained
at www.ICGtesting.com
Printed in the USA
LVHW082204190820
663695LV00015B/293

9 780815 381518